READINGS IN PUBLIC POLICY

READINGS IN PUBLIC POLICY

Edited by

A. LAWRENCE CHICKERING

ICS PRESS

ICS

Institute for Contemporary Studies
San Francisco, California

Inquiries, book orders, and catalog requests should be addressed to ICS Press, 785 Market Street, Suite 750, San Francisco, California 94103—(415) 543-6213.

Library of Congress Cataloging in Publication Data
Main entry under title:

Readings in public policy.

     1. Policy sciences—Addresses, essays, lectures.
I. Chickering, A. Lawrence.
H97.R43   1984 361.6'1   84—15754
ISBN 0—917616—66—9 (pbk.)

CONTENTS

III

National Security and Foreign Policy

IV
Social Issues

V
Politics and Governance

PREFACE

To commemorate the tenth anniversary of its founding, the Institute for Contemporary Studies has gathered in this volume a selection of the best articles on public policy to have appeared in its books and quarterly journal over the past decade. Included among these essays are some of the finest examples of public policy analysis and writing produced in recent times. Taken together, they tell a fascinating story of the changes that have taken place in thinking about policy—changes, we are proud to say, in which the Institute has played no small role. Virtually every policy issue of major importance, domestic and foreign, is touched upon and illuminated here. It is hoped that this collection will prove of interest not only to concerned citizens, but also to students seeking to write about, and participate in, public administration and governance.

Glenn Dumke
President
Institute for Contemporary Studies

I

Introduction

1

A. LAWRENCE CHICKERING

Introduction

The Institute for Contemporary Studies was founded during a time of great tension and hostility in the American political environment. The year was 1974, less than six months after President Nixon resigned his office. Watergate had aggravated wounds going back to the sixties, and Gerald Ford was trying to manage an uneasy relationship with the Democrats, who controlled Congress.

It was a period, after Vietnam, when America was withdrawing from foreign commitments, and ambitious plans were being made to extend government control over the economy. This happened first in the new "social" regulation of health, safety, and the environment, which appeared in the early seventies; later, with the 1973–74 oil boycott, in economic regulation of energy use and land use; and finally, by 1975, in the general economy.

There were good reasons to be concerned about clean air, clean water, and industrial safety, but policymakers implemented extensive and often wasteful regulations in these areas. In the case of economic regulation, plans being made in Washington drew widespread criticism from economists, who usually tend to be skeptical of claims that government bureaucrats can allocate resources more efficiently than the private market.

In that divisive climate, it is not surprising that most of the Institute's early projects were critiques. Our first publication, *No Time to Confuse* (Armen Alchian, et al., 1975), was a critique of the Ford Foundation Energy Policy Project, which proposed vast government planning for the nation's energy resources. That first ICS book served as a model for subsequent critiques of government credit allocation (1975), land use regulation (1975 and 1976), centralized economic planning (1976), national health insurance (1976), and other initiatives.

Later studies began moving beyond criticism, exploring positive policy reforms. In energy, we followed the Ford critique with a positive program for national policy (*Options for U.S. Energy Policy,* Henry S. Rowen, et al., 1977); and in foreign and defense policy we followed our critique of détente (*Defending America,* James Schlesinger, et al., 1977) with a positive program for restoring U.S. strength (*National Security in the 1980s,* edited by W. Scott Thompson, 1980). Other Institute books focused on domestic subjects such as education, social security, federal tax reform, economic regulation, and the general economy; and on foreign issues including the international economy and the Third World.

By the end of the decade, Institute studies had played an important role in reorienting the policy debate on both foreign/defense and domestic policy issues. By the last two years of the Carter administration, both political parties had become concerned about the rise of government spending. The enthusiasm for regulation was declining as Carter began major initiatives to deregulate the airlines, trucking, banks, and other industries. And concern was growing about the sluggish economy, following a decade of nearly no growth. Talk of central planning disappeared, and the new discussion was about reducing impediments to market efficiencies— especially by restoring incentives to work, save, and invest. Finally, on foreign and defense policy, concern was growing— again, in both parties—about the Soviet military buildup; and President Carter, who had taken office warning about our "inordinate fear of Communism," pledged his administration to real increases in the defense budget.

These "new" ideas were the policy agenda running through all the early Institute studies. Our early critiques of energy planning helped change the policy climate on the value of energy planning, so that the Ford Foundation eventually released a second energy report repudiating the first. Our first study of national health insurance (*New Directions in Public Health Care,* edited by Cotton M. Lindsay in 1975) helped discourage talk about a centralized national health system, and our revised 1980 study revealed how the debate had shifted to exploring ways of using incentives to improve the efficiency of our health care system.

Among other early studies that anticipated future problems were *The Crisis in Social Security,* edited by Michael J. Boskin in 1977 and *Federal Tax Reform,* also edited by Boskin, in 1978. The tax book was one of the first statements of the new generation of economists, who had seen the limits of Keynesian demand management and were devoting their attention to supply-side concerns bearing on incentives to produce wealth. The book was followed two years later in a third Boskin-edited book, *The Economy in the 1980s,* which set forth a comprehensive program for reestablishing the economic growth and stability that had been lost in the seventies.

In 1980, the Institute also sponsored a landmark Black Alternatives Conference. Held in San Francisco shortly after the presidential election, the conference gained national attention for bringing together 150 of the nation's leading black business, professional, and academic leaders, who were disillusioned with government attempts to help low-income groups and minorities. Organized by economist Thomas Sowell, the conference explored new ideas in education, economic development, housing, and other areas. *The Fairmont Papers* (Thomas Sowell, et al., 1981) presented the results of the conference.

As the political debate changed and the ideas argued in early Institute studies gained wider acceptance, our books began emphasizing problems of *implementation.* In the new studies, the concern shifted beyond making the substantive case (on which there was increasing agreement) to consideration of political and institutional impediments to reform. While many of our early studies featured only economists, this changing emphasis was reflected by the increasing participation of political scientists and other policy analysts to supplement the work of economists. These later studies address the policy problems: how can you improve and reform defective policies in the face of institutional and political limitations on action?

This pattern of considering political issues began with our first book on social security, which included an analysis of factors impeding reform. In 1981, *Politics and the Oval Office* (edited by Arnold J. Meltsner) addressed implementation in terms of broad problems of presidential governance. Appearing as President Reagan took office, the study focused on a whole range of institutional problems and audiences the President must deal with, and the book was widely read by people who actually came to occupy key positions in the Reagan White House. Some of the study's conclusions were extremely controversial, particularly as they dealt with audiences that have essentially different agendas than does the President—including Congress, the media, and the bureaucracy.

The emphasis on implementation is also obvious in two studies we published in 1982—*Social Regulation: Strategies for Reform,* co-edited by Eugene Bardach and Robert A. Kagan, and *The Federal Budget: Economics and Politics,* co-edited by Michael Boskin and Aaron Wildavsky—and is a dominant theme in our more recent collection on the issue of industrial policy—*The Industrial Policy Debate,* edited by Chalmers Johnson (1984).

In recent studies, we have done increasing work on international issues—bearing both on U.S. foreign and defense policy and on comparative international economic problems. On foreign and defense problems, in 1983 we published a broad exploration of U.S. foreign policy options after détente (*Beyond Containment,* edited by Aaron Wildavsky). And James Woolsey, in 1984, edited a study of nuclear weapons and strategy (*Nuclear Arms: Ethics, Strategy, Politics*). A forthcoming book on military reform is a single-authored study by Edward Luttwak, entitled *Making the Military Work,* which Simon and Schuster will publish for us early in 1985.

On economics, we have begun trying to "export" our studies of American domestic economic problems to problems facing other countries, both in the industrial and developing countries. Our first effort in this area was *The World Crisis in Social Security,* edited by Jean-Jacques Rosa in 1982 and sponsored jointly with the Fondation Nationale d'Economie Politique, which is based in Paris. The resulting study of the retirement programs of eight industrial countries draws on diverse experiences to explore solutions for this enormous problem facing all industrial countries. The book was published by Bonnel Editions, and has since been translated into Japanese.

A second, even more ambitious study will appear later this year entitled *World Economic Growth,* edited by Arnold C. Harberger. Exploring five industrial countries and seven LDCs on four continents, the book surveys the growth experience in diverse political and cultural settings and sets forth a series of "lessons" for policymakers attempting to improve the growth performances of individual countries. Although written entirely by economists, the contributors have included analysis of the Institute's increasing concern about political and institutional impediments to reform and some of the book's most interesting conclusions focus on problems of trying to implement textbook economics in difficult political conditions.

In some ways, the essays collected in this volume, represent a general comment on the history of American public policy over the last decade. It should be clear the extent to which positions argued here were minority views in the mid-1970s, when the Institute was founded. It should also be clear how these same positions have come to dominate the policy debates and policy agenda of both political parties.

Reviewing the articles themselves, the volume begins appropriately with Armen Alchian's lead contribution to our first book—the critique of the first Ford Energy Project. That book became something of a "classic" among public policy studies, and Alchian's sometimes savage review of a study costing $4 million (in early-1970s' dollars) reflects broad feelings in the economics profession about it. Alchian's paper is also included because we think it presents one of the clearest statements we know of how markets allocate resources to their most valuable uses and how attempts to centrally plan resource allocation disrupt and distort that process.

Michael Boskin's "Taxation and Government" is adapted from the introduction and the conclusion of *Federal Tax Reform,* which he edited. His piece is presented here as a very early statement of "supply-side economics"—a full two years before Ronald Reagan brought that concept to a mass audience in the 1980 Presidential campaign.

William Havender's "Government Regulation: Assessing and Controlling Risks" is the lead chapter in the study of *Social Regulation*—setting forth important arguments on the misuses of social policy. While arguments like these are well known to small numbers of academics and business specialists, they have yet to penetrate to the general public policy debate.

Our final inclusion in the economics section appears in *The Third World: Premises of U.S. Policy*. It was written by the late Wilson Schmidt and is included because we think it is one of the clearest statements we have seen on the role of private capital in the developing countries.

Admiral Elmo Zumwalt's lead chapter in *National Security in the 1980s* presents an impressive overview of the growing U.S.–Soviet military imbalance at the time Ronald Reagan took office. This paper, authored by a former Chairman of the Joint Chiefs of Staff, thus states the substantive background for the current military buildup—explaining why both the Carter and Reagan administrations concluded a major effort was necessary to rearm. Many of the contributors to that volume, in fact, ended up taking high positions in the Reagan administration—implementing important parts of the program set forth in the study.

Wendell John Coats' "The Ideology of Arms Control" is reprinted from the *Journal of Contemporary Studies* and presents an extremely important statement, we think, of limitations imposed by the advent of nuclear weapons on deployment of conventional forces abroad. At a time when American policymakers are increasingly wary of using American troops for active missions outside the United States, this paper states a systemic problem underlying such use. It is a problem that deserves much more attention than it has received in official policymaking circles.

We have included Robert Conquest's splendid contribution to our first foreign policy book for its clear and forceful statement of a problem rarely discussed—namely, the importance of human rights as an indicator of political intentions.

Robert Goldwin's piece from the *Law of the Sea* presents a classic reversal of "conventional wisdom" on this subject. His analysis may well explain why, after all the years of serious attention to this subject, it recently has all but disappeared from public view.

And finally in the foreign/defense section, we include Patrick Glynn's powerful analysis of the moral case for the recent U.S. arms buildup. This article was reprinted in *Commentary* in February 1984. Mr. Glynn, I might mention, has been a Senior Editor at the Institute for Contemporary Studies since 1982, and he has co-edited (with Walter Lammi) the *Journal of Contemporary Studies* for much of that time.

The first article in the section on social issues is the conclusion that Michael Novak wrote for our early book on educational choice: *Parents, Teachers, and Children* (James Coleman, et al., 1976). While his article is focused specifically on education, its message—calling for a "new liberalism"—has important implications for many other areas of social policy.

Thomas Sowell's "A New Agenda on Race" presents his opening statement at the Black Alternatives Conference in November 1980. We include this as an introduction to that historic event, and also to the ideas of growing numbers of blacks and other minorities who are searching for new approaches to minority and low-income problems.

And finally in social policy, Peter Greenwood's "Controlling the Crime Rate through Imprisonment" offers a sample of the work presented in *Crime and Public Policy,* edited by James Q. Wilson in 1983. That book presents views that were very much in the minority even a decade ago but that are increasingly dominating the thinking of policymakers, law-enforcement officials, and academics concerned about crime.

In politics and governance, we begin with Seymour Martin Lipset's conclusion to *Party Coalitions in the 1980s*—which attempted to assess the meaning of Ronald Reagan's victory in the campaign. This book and Professor Lipset's conclusion to it, serve as an interesting background from which to view the current campaign, which is in progress at this writing.

Aaron Wildavsky's "Toward a New Budgetary Order" represents a combined and condensed version of the first two chapters of the book he and Michael Boskin co-edited on *The Federal Budget* (1982). This version appeared in our *Journal,* under the title "The Budget as New Social Contract." This piece serves as an excellent introduction to the contemporary debates on the budget —viewing the problem from economic, political, and philosophical perspectives.

Our last entry, Robert Entman's "The Imperial Media" probably caused the greatest public reaction of anything presented here. His analysis presents highly specific recommendations on how presidents should manage their relations with the mass media. When it appeared, Entman's paper provoked expressions of outrage from the media who queried key White House staff people whether his recommendations would influence White House relations with the media. Despite White House denials, we leave it to the reader to judge—especially in relation to issues bearing on what has come to be known as Reagan's "Teflon Presidency."

It is unfortunate that limitations of space made it impossible to include many other contributions. Among other special contributions, one might mention the unusual uses of political philosophy and historical sociology (by Harvey Mansfield, Jr. and Robert Nisbet respectively) to provide a "solution" for the explosion of public sector union activity in the 1960s (in *Public Employee Unions,* edited by A. Lawrence Chickering in 1976).

There was also Keith B. Leffler and Cotton M. Lindsay's splendid use of econometric modeling in *New Directions in Public Health Care* (1976 and 1980), which estimated the real costs of full national health insurance. They estimated in 1976 that a plan like the Kennedy-Corman bill, which proposed full implementation in the first year, would drive up physician fees some 277 percent in the first year. With price controls, which were widely talked about, physician time would be rationed by queuing, and with full controls the authors estimated the cost of such wasted time would amount to $17 billion in the first year, in 1976 dollars—gradually declining through the rest of the century. Estimates such as these were among the reasons why all talk of national health insurance has disappeared from the policy debates.

The *Journal of Contemporary Studies* has continued the Institute's commitment to publish skeptical, unorthodox political analysis—typically drawing attention to critical issues that, in the heat of political controversy, have been overlooked by both the left and the right. Recent examples include Gary L. McDowell's excellent article "On Meddling with the Constitution" (Fall 1982), which showed the constitutional problems inherent in both the Equal Rights and Balanced Budget amendments; and Mark Greenberg and Rachel Flick's "The New Bipartisan Commissions" (Fall 1983), which contrasted the policy gains achieved by presidential commissions with the troubling implications raised by circumventing the normal institutions of government.

Paul Seabury's "Industrial Policy and National Defense" (Spring 1983), set off a heated debate on the question of whether the debate on industrial policy was not overlooking a prudential concern about the nation's defense industrial base. And Carlisle Ford Runge's "The Fallacy of 'Privatization'" (Winter 1984), also initiated a lively controversy on the merits of the New Resource Economics and the Reagan administration's privatization initiatives.

This volume, then, represents some of the best studies we have published during our first ten years. It provides both an overview of many of the decade's most important public policy issues and a foundation for future debates in the areas of economics, national security and foreign policy, social issues, and politics and governance. Throughout the past ten years the Institute's principal objective was to anticipate next year's issue, to seek out critical issues that others were not addressing, and especially to look for issues and arguments that defied or transcended the familiar left-right formulations which are unsatisfying to growing numbers of people. We look forward to continuing in this same vein over the next ten years.

II

Economics

2

ARMEN A. ALCHIAN

Energy Policy: An Introduction to Confusion

A Time to Choose—better titled *A Time to Confuse*—regrettably confuses energy and environmental issues, enters the Guinness Book of World Records for most errors of economic analysis and fact in one book, is arrogant in assertions of waste and inefficiency, is paternalist in its conception of energy consumption management, is politically naive, and uses demagoguery. That is a shocking indictment of a final Report of a $4 million project financed by the Ford Foundation. Let us see why it is deserved.

Scenarios: Crystal Ball Visions

What problems, according to the Report, call for political control? As a sample: "widening gap between energy consumption and domestic production," "growing dependence on foreign supplies,"

This essay originally appeared as "An Introduction to Confusion" in *No Time to Confuse* (1975).

"energy shortages," "energy budget out of balance," "abrupt withdrawal of foreign supplies," "energy-environment crisis," "inefficient use of energy," "saving energy," "soaring prices," "ensure
adequate supply," "independence of U.S. foreign policy" (pp. 2, 4,
8, 11) —enough? Cutting through the morass, we detected four
events about which it is argued some political action presumably
can or should be taken:

1. Increased imports of foreign energy.

2. Rising costs of energy.

3. Environmental effects not fully counted in market revealed
   costs of energy.

4. Political miscontrol of energy.

The Report proposes three "scenarios" of 1975–2000; one, the
first ("historical growth") assumes continued growth of energy
use at the historical rate; the second ("technical fix") assumes
energy use at about half the past rate, with adjustments in use
responsive to higher price and value of energy with presently
known technologies for substitution of other materials and less
energy-using activity; the third ("zero energy growth") projects a
zero increase in energy use after 1985. All scenarios terminate at
the century's end—a remarkably short horizon. The thesis is that
once "we" understand the implications of these scenarios, "we"
can better choose upon which to embark.

The Report commends the technical fix future, but recommends
a zero energy growth because it is "desirable, technically feasible,
and economical to reduce the rate of energy growth [to] 2 percent
annually," and "provides benefits in every major area of concern,
avoiding shortages, protecting the environment, avoiding problems with other nations, and keeping the real social costs as low as
possible" (p. 325). In fact, it does none of those, as should have
been evident to the authors.

The Report recommends a great debate to determine the future:
"legal maneuvers, lobbying, propaganda and conflict of regional
interests, public referenda, writing to Congressmen, making political contributions, writing letters to newspapers, attending meetings and generally raising their voices" (pp. 9, 11). In a word, as
the authors themselves observe, politics.

The scenarios are, *at best,* worthless for identifying or understanding energy issues. Instead, they present some facts about energy uses and possibilities for adjusting to higher cost energy supplies—issues better understood outside the context of *any* presumed future path. The scenarios are neither predictions of the future nor accurate guidelines for achieving future goals. They are *imagined* future itineraries. In fact, of course, whether we experience faster, lower, or possibly negative energy growth depends upon yet-to-be-revealed costs and values of energy uses.

Economic Analytic Errors

Unfortunately, the Report is inexcusably ignorant of economics — indeed, it is so fatally dosed with economic error, fallacy, and confusion at critical stages as to border on dishonesty.[1]

Needs: singular or plural? A serious, fatal analytic error is the Report's too-frequent refusal to use the fact that the amount of energy demanded can, has been, and will be reduced by a higher price to match the supplies that are available at that price. A famous economic principle of demand is ignored in the Report: the principle that the amount of petroleum demanded depends on the *price* of petroleum. The lower that price, the more we "need," require, or demand. That the Report of a $4 million project would ignore such a well-established, powerful fact of life would be incredible were it not that so many politicians, bureaucrats and even oil industry people also ignore or ignorantly deny it. A similarly powerful, general proposition is that the amount supplied will be larger, the higher the price offered to sellers or producers.

These fundamental, inescapable propositions are shown graphically in the elementary demand diagram in figure 1. As curve D (for *demand*) plainly shows, the amount of a good that is consumed, needed, required, or demanded depends on the price of the good. That "demand" curve slopes from the upper left to the lower right, suggesting a whole *series of alternative* amounts we "need," "require," or "demand," depending on the price. We have needs, requirements, demands—depending on the price. Anyone who ignores these facts of life is irresponsibly playing a dangerous and expensive game. He is increasing society's problems. The way

Figure 1
Needs are Variable Depending on Price

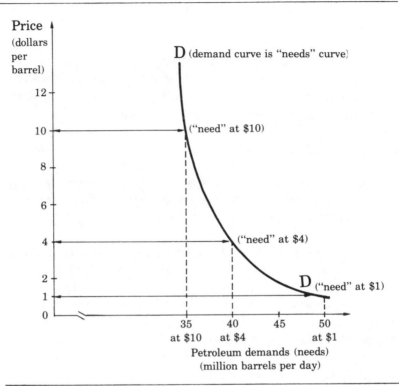

Petroleum demands (needs)
(million barrels per day)

Needs are really a range of petroleum uses not all equally valuable. The lower the price the more petroleum we will put to our lower valued uses. At a higher price, we will deem those lower valued uses not worth achieving. They will no longer be in our "needs." Failure to understand that the variety of petroleum uses have different values leads some people to argue fallaciously that existing supplies will not cover our needs. They are saying all our current uses are of equal importance or value, that we do not regard some uses as more valuable than others; this is a totally incorrect conception, as illustrated by the simplistic fantasy theory graphed in Figure 2.

Figure 2
Naive, but Common, View of Demand and Supply

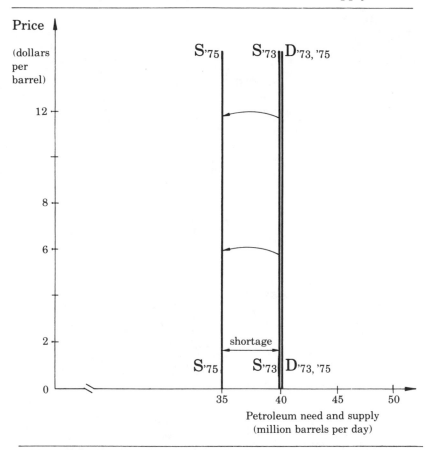

The vertical line of Demand, or Need, portrays the false conception that there is no ranking of alternative uses with some having lower values than others and that regardless of how costly it is to get petroleum we are incapable of deciding that some uses are less valuable than that cost and hence we will not curtail our demand or "need" for so much petroleum. This is the absurd model of human behavior and valuation of petroleum uses employed by people who talk about our "needs," "requirements," and basic necessities and wish us to believe that an increased market price will not bring about a voluntary revision in our uses to match the available supply at the higher equilibrating price, as portrayed in Figure 3.

Figure 3
Price Rations Out Lower Valued Uses

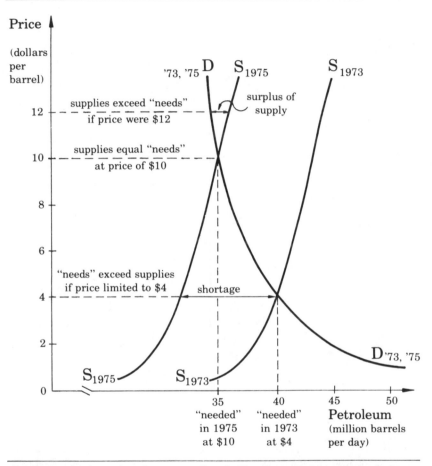

At an open market price, the amount "needed" or demanded is restrained along the demand curve to match available supply. Suppose marketed supplies were reduced—shown by the leftward shifted supply line. If price *within* the U.S. is held below the $10 equilibrating price, shortages occur as people seek to satisfy lower valued uses requiring more petroleum than is available. With a curtailed price, competition by queueing, political and arbitrary allocations, favoritism, and side payments will determine which claims will be denied. If price is allowed to rise to $10, individuals themselves decide which lower valued uses are to be eliminated, so only higher valued uses are satisfied by supplies. (The leftward shift in the supply line only crudely depicts the effect of an oil cartel's output restriction from existing sources by existing producers from existing fields. Also, the effects of higher price on discovery of new fields by other producers should be considered. Therefore, this diagram shows *no* more than the effect of an open market price in changing our "needs" to match whatever supplies are available.)

he conceals those facts of life is to talk of a need or requirement as if it was a natural, unique, given quantity—independent of the cost or price of getting more. Such an intellectually bankrupt—though commonly held—conception is shown in figure 2; "need-requirement-demand" is expressed as a vertical line, with price having no effect. The counterpart to this error is the notion of supply as a fixed amount, regardless of price. Then the difference between the two is, naturally, called a shortage or gap. And anyone who swallows that propaganda probably deserves the consequence: the espousal of political control over the consumer's use of the available supply by allocations, rationing, or political pressures, in order to divert that supply to politically approved "needs."

In fact, the diagnosis is simply wrong, no matter how often it is repeated in the media by political aspirants, bureaucrats, and even some energy industry officials—who of all people should know better. The actual reason, as shown in figure 3, surprisingly, that supply does not approach what people want to consume at the "market price" is that the price is kept too *low*. This is shown in figure 3. If you think the price is too high at $10 a barrel, why did you not think it was too high at $3 a barrel? After all, $1 a barrel or even $.20 a barrel would be better and feasible—*if* there were so much oil that we could put it to such low-valued uses as would be worth only $.20 a barrel.

Today, like it or not, and whatever the reason—embargo, less resources, increased population, you name it—the amount of petroleum available to us is such that, as we progress down to its lower valued uses, we *still* have unsatisfied uses worth on the margin as much as $10 a barrel. That is why the price of available petroleum is now $10 on the world markets. The issue of why we have *only as much* petroleum available as we do is another thing entirely. To fail to separate the two issues—how much oil is available and how much each extra barrel of petroleum is worth to us—is to lead the nation into confusion, not toward rational choice. And it is the demand curve that reflects the use value of extra barrels of petroleum. The less we have, the greater the value of a barrel of petroleum; the more that is supplied, the lower the value of the uses to which the extra oil is put.

Irresponsible talk about an oil or energy shortage leads the nation to confuse (1) the fact of a reduced supply of oil with (2) the fact of people using oil in some low-valued uses while other higher-valued uses are unfulfilled. Thus, the unfulfilled higher-valued uses provoke talk of shortages with regard to *those* uses. Why *do* we use some petroleum in the less valuable ways? The answer is clear and simple. We are told the "price" should be low; therefore, at that price we try to use the petroleum in ways that have use values as low as that artificially low price. In exactly the same way, too-low privately perceived energy costs (that do not include environmental effects) mislead us to abuse the environment—a factor rightly to be deplored.

Those low prices restrained (by domestic price controls) literally mislead us into trying to achieve such low-valued uses of oil, rather than restricting it to our higher valued uses. Each of us is led to think, as if by a malicious devil, that oil is plentiful enough to satisfy those lower-valued uses. None of us is effectively impressed with the fact that the oil we use in those low-valued ways is of greater value to other people in other uses. Prices, as measures and signals that restrain and control the way we use petroleum or energy, are destroyed by such politically imposed price controls.

Seeing the damage wreaked by our attempts to use available petroleum wastefully, politicians complain that the market system of prices and free enterprise won't work—that it must be replaced by political controls. Indeed it must; break the horse's leg and then say it can't gallop. It is no accident that the strongest appeals for political action in the present situation are made by the strongest opponents of free-enterprise activity: those who would prefer to cripple the process of voluntary exchange through market prices, which might otherwise help us reserve petroleum for its highest value uses.

The failure to perceive the fundamental distinction between (1) *schedules* of associated alternative possible amounts demanded or supplied at *alternative* prices, and (2) *a* particular amount demanded and *a* particular amount supplied at some one price leads the Report to other confusions. The word "shortage" is used to mean situations where prices rise because of increased demand *schedules* relative to a supply *schedule*. But it is also used to refer to a very different situation created by political controls on per-

missible price: where the amount *demanded* at that price exceeds
the amount *supplied* at that price, because price is politically fixed
below the open market price. This *undervalued* price *is* the energy
adjustment obstacle. That is a crucial part of our energy problem.

The battle lines are now drawn between politically ambitious
people and those who would rely on a liberal society in which individuals can express, compare, and be guided by their individual
use values relative to those of other people—the condition fulfilled
by market exchange prices! The energy situation is one of the critical battlefields. The issues of the appropriate degree of environmental protection, Arab wealth, and foreign dependence have
been transformed—wittingly or unwittingly—into smokescreens
to hide the real field of battle.

Contrived vs. natural supply change. A reduction in
petroleum availability can result from either a naturally decreasing supply relative to demands or a government cartel, or both.
Each situation commands a different response. Unfortunately,
though the Report discusses both, its recommended responses do
not account for the differences involved. To recommend higher
use taxes to *suppress energy uses,* where prices are rising in
response to natural forces that reduce available supply, is to over-
kill. The higher market price *alone* is sufficient to restrict use and
channel available energy to the highest valued uses. To impose, in
addition, taxes or mandatory controls over uses is to arrogantly
assume that people *over*-value energy uses (as we are prone to
assume they do for smoking, drinking, pornography and gam-
bling) and should be restrained even more than justified by the
true costs of energy. This is the implication of conservation proposals directed to situations in which energy costs are rising
because of decreasing relative supplies.

But if the price rise is caused by a *cartel* of producers who have
banded together to restrict available petroleum, then sale by us to
foreign governments of rights to sell oil in the U.S. market (not
imposition of tariffs) would make more sense in liberal free
society—as a means of taxing the monopoly rents of the cartel
without raising domestic prices. This is a subtle issue, apparently
too subtle for the Report. Indeed, it may be too subtle for political
application, because it is too easily diverted to other objectives.

Nevertheless, the Report should have considered the import quota sale tactic.

Efficiency: technical or social cost? The Report, incorrectly, focuses on technical instead of economic or social cost efficiency. Technical efficiency simply means minimizing the amount of *one* input per unit of output—number of towels used in the washroom per unit of gasoline produced in a refinery, or pounds of steel per automobile produced, or "this" input per unit of "that" output. But total *costs* of *all* inputs are pertinent, not just one component. No engineer or economist worth his salt seeks to minimize gasoline used per mile driven, or electricity or fuel oil per cubic foot of house kept warm—criteria which the Report repeatedly *does* employ in bewailing alleged inefficiency and waste of energy in the past. On the contrary, to use *less* energy in the past would have been wasteful; it would have meant sacrificing more of other useful and desirable things than the energy was worth. This broad, inclusive view of costs and values escaped the attention of the authors of the Report, despite correct statements in Appendix F, "Economic Analysis of Alternative Energy Growth Patterns, 1975–2000."

Ironically, this disastrous failure to acknowledge the totality of inputs and their costs rather than the physical amounts of one input (whose costs can always be reduced by increasing other costs) is cited in the Report as a criticism of *other* people's behavior. The Report *accurately* expressed the well-known fact that not all consequences are contained or reflected in market prices—in particular some (not all!) sacrificed values of the environment. The environment is a resource (air, water, land) and the costs of using it should be known by or imposed on users. Why are they not? Because *no one owns* those resources; no one can control their use, as one can control the use of one's own labor or one's own goods. Otherwise, the abuse would be avoided, as with my labor for which I am paid more by its "abusers" than I would be for any other alternative use. In the same fashion, water or air would be used in some particular way only if that use or abuse were of greater value than the best alternative use. That selectivity is what ownership and marketability of a resource at open market prices induces.

And so it might be with water and air, if only we knew how to enforce property rights in those fleeting, unappropriable assets. But those goods are not yet appropriable as marketable property; everyone uses them as if they were costless. No one has to compensate others for their use and thereby heed the costs that do, in fact, exist. Prices do not reflect *those* costs—abuses of non-owned resources. That is why the environment is abused—exactly as my labor would be abused if I did not have rights to myself, or as my car would be abused if I had no marketable, defined property rights to the car. *That* is the problem of environmental control. Yet, we repeat, it is precisely this *same error of excluding* some components of cost that the Report commits in persistently advocating *technical* efficiency. No useful analysis can be derived by using "technical efficiency" as the criterion.

Present value of costs or present outlays? The Report asserts that buyers of homes and automobiles pay inadequate attention to future expenses that these items entail and are guided only by the current purchase price; therefore, auto producers or house builders have no incentive to economize on energy by using higher initial outlay means of improved mileage or insulation (pp. 54ff). Are these dumb, shortsighted consumers the ones the Report proposes to make a "choice"? And add the frothy topping that capital markets are "imperfect" in not permitting as low a rate of interest in housing as in other markets, so future savings are not capitalized into greater present values. Well, what is the evidence? The Report offers none. Are houses in the cold Northeast built the same as in Florida or California? Are picture windows in California homes used just because the views are better? Are brick two-story houses with storm windows more common in cold areas because bricks are handier and storm windows more fashionable in the East? Are eastern homes more draft-proof than California homes because westerners love fresh air? A realistic interpretation, of course, is that the present costs of avoiding those future costs *exceed* the future costs. It is efficient *not* to overspend for insulation or for low energy use heating equipment that costs much more to produce initially than the value of the energy later saved.

In concluding, the Report makes this profound recommendation: "All possible measures should be taken to encourage the most efficient production and use of energy" (p. 329). If the authors seek technical efficiency in minimizing energy use, the best "possible" route to their objective would be for all of us to commit suicide. But if they are talking about economic efficiency, then those measures are already being taken—in that all of us are interested in reducing costs and balancing more of one use against more of another. The authors appear to think that either developers, builders, and middlemen are insensitive to the sale value of what they produce, or consumer buyers are too ignorant to anticipate future outlays. But they have no evidence to support that charge, and there is much evidence to refute it.

Waste or paternalism? The Report flies in the face of analysis and evidence in alleging energy waste in automobiles or inefficiently insulated buildings. True, many airconditioned buildings have big windows but lose heat and use heating and cooling equipment that uses up lots of energy. Indeed they do, but that was *not* wasteful when the costs of energy use *were* lower than the value of window views and comfortable temperatures. Big cars, with powerful motors, air conditioning, and power steering were *not* inefficient or wasteful. The energy used provided more valuable services than any other use to which that energy could have been put. If that were not true, *no* one would have obtained gasoline for those end services. After all, no one was compelled to buy those cars; those were all options. As prices of energy are bid up, reflecting the higher values of available energy, people use less energy for those particular end results. Those options are still worth as much as before, but are now too costly to indulge in to the same extent. Higher prices induce us to curtail our amounts demanded (needs?) to the amounts available and to use what little is available in ways that give us the highest personal values. With *higher prices* to inform and impress us about the higher value of a gallon of the reduced supply of gasoline, we will foresake the least valuable marginal uses. We will drive smaller cars with greater (not maximum!) mileage per gallon, drive less often, drive slower, all *without* rationing or reduced speed limits or weekend closing of service stations.

Such paternalist, political controls *are wasteful,* because they divert some energy from higher to lower valued uses. If 60¢ a gallon for gasoline permits each user to buy as much as he demands (needs?) *at that price,* he will use it in the ways that are of most value to him. If quick starts and faster trips at 70 mph are worth more to him than more miles slowly, he will get more value from the gasoline through 70 mph speeds than if he, *or anyone else,* used that gasoline or petroleum in some other way. Shouldn't he? Are we to become paternalist life arrangers under the guise of "conserving" energy?

To say that no one could or should value driving 70 mph more than any other use he or anyone else might have for the gasoline, or any other good he could have had if he did not use that gasoline is to say paternalistically that "we" know what is best for everyone else. To advocate a reduced speed limit to conserve energy is to commit an arrogant intellectual error. It does *not* conserve energy. Instead, it *diverts* some of the available supply to less valuable uses. Whatever is made available will be used in one way or another. Petroleum prohibited from use for high-speed driving is diverted in part to fuel oil. The reduced speed limit can hardly be viewed as anything but a political power play to divert petroleum to people with political influence who want fuel oil for their own lower valued uses.

Political controls on our use of energy—whether for outdoor lighting, household heating, or swimming pool heating—means simply that an elite group is undertaking to limit the options of other people. Has the lesson of Nixon's administration been ignored? The Report recommends a higher gasoline tax and mandatory gasoline mileage standards to conserve gasoline—even beyond the amount available at costs that match the price people are willing to pay to get the gasoline (the value they place on it). Such *over*conservation, making the costs of energy use appear higher than they really are, is a kind of masochism.

"Lot's wife" fallacy. Even the hoary sunk cost fallacy is resurrected. "High cash bonus bids for oil lands tend to motivate the lessee to get back his bonus payment through early production. This is, of course, less true when bonuses are low" (p. 290). Of course, except that the rate of extraction is not affected by the bonus. It is affected by the profitability of extracting the oil, regardless of the size of the payment. The authors forget that large bonuses reflect large future profitability of extraction, and so confuse bonus with future productivity as the reason for earlier extraction.

Other related errors are a source of fallacious deductions regarding advisable policy. For example, "Once the resource development rights are sold, the public, as consumer, has an interest in the development of those resources for its use at an early date and at a fair price. Assuming that energy prices are on the rise, if the lessee is allowed to sit on his lease without developing it, it will be costly to the public in two ways. The lessee will have purchased the development rights—with a lower payment to the treasury than at future prices; and by not producing his lease until some future time, he can sell the resource back to the public at a higher price than if he develops it immediately. The legal system is designed to encourage early production of the leased resources and thus discourage private speculation" (p. 289). That is an elementary (and hence inexcusable) error. If prices are on the rise (rising now, or expected—by whom?—to rise in the future) it is desirable to defer use of the resources until they attain higher use value later. Here the conservationist is 180° off course. The role of capital values in preventing abuse and premature use is ignored in the Report.

The authors offer the premise that only political authorities can determine and control the appropriate exploration and exploitation rate. The knowledge and incentive with which these activities will be carried out is left to the presumed "good intentions" of political administrators, despite the Report's own emphasis on their dismal past performance. The Report contends that although past performance was bad, *more* political control will improve, not worsen, the situation. Ever the theme—We'll be better. The future always lies ahead!

Leisure is unemployment. The Report repeatedly calms fears of unemployment with remarkable assurances that reduced use of energy, whether by deliberate policy or natural reduction of available supply, will not create long-term unemployment. Indeed, it would increase employment—it could even bring back the man-drawn plough. If cheaper and more plentiful supplies of energy tend, happily, to reduce voluntary employment by increasing the supply of other goods relative to leisure, then surely less nonhuman energy will induce us to work harder. One cent would be too high a price to pay for the revelation that long-term unemployment could be increased by reducing the supply of *non*human power—let alone $4 million. Yet the Report treats reduced nonhuman power and the consequent inducement to work more (i.e., more employment) as an *advantage* of zero energy growth. Less is more!

Marginal cost pricing, price discrimination, and subsidies. Promotional pricing by utilities is misinterpreted when the Report confuses (1) block pricing with lower prices for large quantities, (2) marginal prices that differ for consumers, and (3) prices below marginal costs. Different *marginal prices* for customers are usually considered to be price discrimination. At worst, they lead to inefficient allocation. At best, they will increase output and avoid the loss of the extra use value (measured by price) over marginal costs. And if marginal prices are equal, then even with lower prices for larger amounts, the effect is to prevent underusage and wasteful failure to produce electricity when price exceeds marginal cost. But the Report thinks promotional pricing means (subsidized) production at marginal costs greater than the value of the extra output, just because some can purchase at a lower price than others, or at lower prices for more goods. That is an error.

Summary. This list does not cover all the economic fallacies and errors in the Report, but it should suffice to illustrate the Report's inadequacy as an instrument for *understanding* and *informed* action. Its main policy recommendations, based on analytic errors, could not achieve the stated objectives: efficiency in energy use, an increase in reliable energy supplies, more accurate reflection of true environmental costs in costs of energy supply and use. What these policies would do is to place more control over consumers in the hands of political energy czars. In this sense, the Report may be viewed as a demagogic appeal for greater political power.

Energy-Related Issues

Throughout the Report, the authors refer to "policy" without defining it, or as though none existed. But the absence of a national political energy policy does not mean the absence of extensive, continuous, private economywide planning of energy uses and production for both present and future. The lack of political management on a national level is not "drift." The Report fails to comprehend economic markets and property rights as controlling and coordinating devices that enable us to anticipate future possibilities and respond promptly to information on current issues.

Foreign supply. The Report provides no careful discussion or exposition of problems possibly caused by reliance on foreign supplies. If foreign *governments* (not private concerns!) can interrupt energy supplies, what do we do? The Report presents a knee-jerk response. Go independent by using less energy, at least to the extent of what would have been imported, and find new domestic sources of energy.[2] To treat the events of Fall 1973 (the so-called Arab boycott) as identical to the cartel policy of restricting output is to generate more confusion. The interruption effects of the Arab actions were not serious enough to change any country's foreign policy toward Arab interests, And *cartel pricing* is not an *interruption* threat. It is a device to increase Arab wealth. To confuse cartel pricing with interruptions is a disservice to economic understanding and efficient response. But the Report is not alone in this error; it is by no means uncommon.

The use of foreign supplies over the long pull (by importing, say, 20 percent of our petroleum) will affect our foreign policy. But *how,* and what will these effects be? And if we are energy independent, but Europe and other western nations depend on imports, are we asked to be so naive as not to revise our foreign actions? The Report would have been of some value had it more carefully analyzed the potential gains from *our* energy independence, instead of naively referring to "independent," "cooperation," "shared interests." The Report suggests "no artificial barriers to ... trade" (p. 175), while proposing to limit our oil imports.

Rising energy costs. Energy prices rise because the demand *schedule* expands more than the supply *schedule* does. That implies that higher prices will be needed to equalize the amount demanded and the amount supplied. As we observed earlier, the Report confuses *an* amount demanded at *a* price with "needs," as if the current demand did not depend on price or costs. This failure to distinguish between (a) "shortages" (resulting from price controls), (b) reduced supply resulting in higher prices, and (c) costs of environmental use not reflected in existing market prices, is pervasive. We adapt to reduced supply (relative to demand) by private actions in response to higher market prices; this process is the economic market in action, doing its job as it always has except when disrupted by government controls on use and price. Unless one understands this operation, one tends to assume that any economic upheaval demands a purposive political response— while in actuality, such intervention works to destroy the effective national energy policy *already* in existence.

After World War II, the government—wisely—refrained from adopting a political policy in response to falling energy costs (due to more plentiful supplies). Market prices and the economic system induced adaptation, exactly as they will today if current higher energy costs continue. No one has to use political power to enforce a pattern of decreed behavior intended to shape the future; the authors of the Report should heed the principles of substitution and pricing described in Appendix F. The market's pricing system *works,* as long as we do not disable it with political controls and allocations (ordered by officials who, unlike private energy providers, are relatively immune to the consequences of such actions).

The Report contends that energy adjustments can be achieved without resorting to government compulsion or force, and then blithely recommends mandatory controls and taxes (p. 68)—not to mention such deceptively authoritarian recommendations as "It is important that Congress debate *and enact* legislation which declares that energy conservation is a matter of *highest* national priority and which establishes energy conservation goals for the nation" (p. 329, italics added).

Appendix F of the Report, "Economic Analysis of Alternative Energy Growth Patterns, 1975–2000" by respected Harvard economists E. A. Hudson and D.W. Jorgensen, predicts substitution of other resources for energy *consequent to higher prices* (reflecting the more valuable uses to which relatively reduced supplies of energy can be put), with an apparently small loss of output consequent to hypothesized lower energy supply. If one believes that Appendix, why fuss about this being a time to choose? One debilitating and disquieting feature of Appendix F's zero economic growth projection is the imposition of a heavy tax on energy use, with the proceeds used by political authority to divert production toward services that use less energy. Compulsory shifts do not correspond to users' valuations. Even if so-called "real" output, with zero energy growth, were to be only 3–4 percent less in 2000 than with historical growth, that is an underestimate because the output conforms less to consumer valuations. Appendix F gives no indication of the magnitude of that bias, nor any test of the sensitivity of the projection to changes in the assumed operative parameters.

Environment. The Report also clouds the problem of environmental use values that are not captured or reflected in market prices. We need an accurate technique for evaluating environmental use, and we must be able to use that measurement to ensure that users will balance environmental considerations against other priorities. Preventing *all* deterioration of environment is not the object, as even the Report (at one point) concedes: " . . . there is a limit to what clean air is worth" (p. 201). Close, but not close enough. It is not a question of *clean* air, but clean*er* or *less* clean; the problem is how to ascertain the values of changes in the environment relative to consequent value changes in other goals and goods. What is the cost (value sacrificed) of more pollution, relative to the value of other benefits thereby attainable? Most of us work—we pollute our leisure and our lives with sweat, tedium, and occupational hazards because we think the gains outweigh the value of our unpolluted leisure. Should any man who is not now working be forbidden to work, to avoid polluting his leisure? Should *any* deterioration in the environment be intolerable, regardless of values thereby achieved?

Reduced energy use does not necessarily improve the environment. On the contrary, greater use of a greater supply of energy could be an effective means of *improving* (not just preserving) our surroundings. While energy production may injure the quality of some natural resources in some areas, cheaper, more plentiful energy permits improvements in other areas (possibly even the energy production locale). Air conditioning improves our environment (in a sense); more gasoline for engines with lower mileage but greater effectiveness in curtailing pollutants would also help; pumping water to arid areas (by means of energy) makes the desert bloom. The correct issue is the optimal degree and type of pollution, the optimal mix of environmental effects, the optimal degree of personal abuse via work or loss of leisure. Despite the Report's seeming bias in favor of energy reduction, nowhere does it actually demonstrate that decreased energy growth or a return to our original environment is the ideal objective.

The Report is not alone in the belief that an all-out rescue plan for the environment is indicated. Some of our laws and judicial decisions prohibit *any* air pollution, regardless of subsequent benefits. But this approach imposes waste on society and requires belated correction after the damages are incurred and revealed. We do not live in an all-or-nothing world, the Report's authors notwithstanding: "Some pollution is unavoidable—either because we don't know how to control it, or because it is inherently uncontrollable" (p. 224). But pollution is inherently *controllable*; the point is, we do not *want* to avoid all of it. The authors oversimplify a complex problem by reducing it to meaningless alternatives: "Ultimately, it comes down to a fundamental value judgement of which is the worse: the risks of nuclear power; or air pollution and the destruction of recreational areas and the fragile coastal environment from oil drilling; or air pollution and disruptive changes in the way of life in the Rocky Mountain region from coal and shale production" (p. 225). As a matter of simple fact and logic, those are *not* the choices facing society. The correct problem is that the optimal degree of pollution is not ascertainable, because we do not yet know how to determine the values of relative amounts of pollution—and persuade the public to heed those values.[3]

Despite its concern for our environment, the Report does not consider how the benefits of reduced pollution might be distributed. For example, how much of the benefit of smog abatement would redound to landowners in central Los Angeles, Chicago, and New York? Would all the benefits accrue to them, while nonland-owners paid higher rents and consumed less of other goods? This issue is not mentioned, yet a report that expresses concern about the distributive impact of higher energy prices should at least hint at the distributive effects of pollution reduction.

There is a role for government action: to help ensure that the cost of resources used in producing and consuming energy are ac-curately and effectively revealed in market prices or user fees. Given that some of those resources are unowned, they cannot be accurately priced, nor can users be effectively charged for them. Yet it appears sensible and desirable that people who use those resources should be made to heed those costs by compensating the owners. Three tasks are involved: (1) assessing the value of the abuse, (2) making that cost impinge on the user, and (3) identify-ing the resource owners. Those *may* be roles for governmental per-sonnel, *if* we believe that gains from government participation would outweigh gains from continued abuse of the resource— which is not a foregone conclusion. Politicians and bureaucrats (as recent legislation controlling any new use of the California coastline suggests) tend to be overly protective. Why assume that *new* uses are less valuable than old ones? What do political con-trollers gain or lose by seeking to under- or over-value alternative uses of a resource? These problems are germane to a discussion of *any* scarce resource—natural or not.

An acknowledgment that the market system has not and will not work in these areas is no more earthshaking than the fact that past political actions have opposed clear, secure, and transferrable property rights that enable us to possess and ex-change goods. The question is, what is the best way to help both open market *and* government fulfill their proper roles—and why have they sometimes performed unsatisfactorily in the past?

Control of energy industry and energy users. Since no government agency overtly controls the energy industry, some po-litical action is needed—in the Report's view—to make private producers responsive and answerable to the public. But the ab-sence of political control by a public *group* does not mean the ab-sence of public control. Consumer decisions on the value of various kinds of energy control the actions of major corporations. General Motors could not make us all buy Cadillacs, or even 1975 models; nor could Ford make us all buy Pintos. Private producers offer, at their risk, the kind of cars they *predict* we will prefer, as evidenced by our willingness to pay the costs. Control is exercised by the people through market-revealed willingness to work at various wages in light of their range of work opportunities, and by their willingness to buy the offered cars in the open market. Producers propose, consumers dispose.

But the authors of the Report, seeing that a few auto company managers are sensitive and responsive to this public control by consumers and workers, confuse response with control and proposers with disposers. Even U.S. senators must consider the wishes of their constituents; in formulating policies, they are trying to forecast what the public will accept. The same holds true for the private sector. But very important differences lie in the speed and accuracy with which true desires are revealed, compared, and enforced and the performers rewarded, punished, or displaced.

If this review seems tart, sample the comments of individual members of the project's Board of Advisory at the end of the Report. Many are in sharp disagreement with its conclusion, particularly industry members (energy users and producers); their observations should be carefully scrutinized, as a balance for the Report's excessive errors. Comments by most of the academic advisors are superficially less critical, though just as devastating in a few instances. (Some of the academics, however, apparently regret that the Report did not err even more extensively on the side of the environment.) Conservationist advisors, predictably, held that environmental preservation should be the dominant factor in determining energy (or any other) policies.

3

MICHAEL J. BOSKIN

Taxation and Government

The enormous growth of government spending is one of the more remarkable features of the advanced economies of the world. Table 1 illustrates the growth of total government expenditure in current dollars, in constant 1958 dollars per person, and as a percentage of gross national product. Even a casual glance at this table reveals a startling growth rate. Just before the outbreak of World War I in 1913, the government was spending less than $100 per capita (in 1958 dollars), and this amounted to less than 8 percent of the GNP. Today, in 1958 dollars, the corresponding figures are almost $1,400 per person, and about 33 percent of GNP.

In fact, these figures actually understate the growth of government economic activity. For, in addition to these direct taxes, the government levies a large number of what might be called quasi taxes. When the government mandates certain safety devices on automobile manufacturers, they are not recorded as the equivalent of taxes, but rather as an increase in that component of GNP

This essay is adapted from the introduction and conclusion of *Federal Tax Reform*, edited by Michael J. Boskin (1978). References to other papers are to chapters in that book.

relating to automobile sales. However—to pick one example—
there is very little difference between the government's requiring
installation of an air bag costing $1,000 and its imposing a tax of
$1,000 which is then used to install the same air bag. Clearly, the
growth of such rules and regulations for both consumers and producers has greatly increased these quasi taxes.

In any event, the total take of the public sector as a percentage
of all economic activity has increased by a factor of 5 since the
turn of the century. While it is instructive to examine the growth
of aggregate government expenditures at all levels, adjusting for
inflation and population growth, the aggregate data also hide a
startling change in the composition of government spending by
function, and dramatic changes in the level of government doing
the spending.

For selected years from 1929 through 1977, table 2 presents figures on total government spending, federal government spending,
and federal government spending as a proportion of the total. As
noted in the table, as late as 1929 only one dollar in four of government spending was done at the federal level. On the eve of World
War II, the corresponding figure was one dollar in two, and today
it exceeds two out of three dollars. While state and local government expenditures have grown very rapidly relative to GNP, as a
proportion of total government spending they have declined substantially. The growth of state and local government spending,
and of the tax systems and intergovernmental fiscal relations
relating to state and local governments, are beyond our present
concern. This book focuses on federal taxes and expenditures, and
especially on issues relevant to federal tax reform.

In examining the composition of federal spending, it is instructive to note the relationship between government spending for
goods and services (mostly public or quasi-public goods), and government spending on transfer payments. In 1952, transfer payments amounted to only $8.5 billion, compared to the almost $50
billion spent on direct purchases of goods and services. Since then
transfers increased markedly as a proportion of total spending,
and by the early 1970s, for the first time in U.S. history, the federal government was spending more on transfer payments than
on direct purchases of goods and services.

In brief summary, then, total government expenditures have

risen very rapidly over the last several decades. During that period, the total composition of government expenditures has shifted toward centralization at the federal level, and in recent times a dramatic rise has occurred in the proportion of total federal spending embodied in transfer payments as opposed to direct purchases of goods and services.

As noted above, the major purposes for which the government raises tax revenue are to provide for public or quasi-public goods, and to support income-maintenance, or transfer, programs. The vehicles used to raise these revenues have changed markedly over time. Focusing just on federal revenues, we note that personal taxes—primarily, the individual income tax—have been the most important revenue devices throughout the post-World War II period. Corporate income taxes and indirect business taxes have also been important revenue devices. The most noticeable development, however, has been the enormous growth of social insurance taxes in the last two and a half decades. As recently as the 1950s and 1960s, social insurance taxes accounted for a very small percentage of total government revenue. Today they are the second largest, and by far the most rapidly growing, source of government revenue. Indeed, as noted by Kotlikoff (Chapter 6), social insurance taxes are scheduled to increase dramatically throughout the 1980s, and this scheduled increase has raised a roar of indignation from the general public.

In addition to raising revenues by taxes, governments have several other alternatives open to them. For example, they can sell some of the output of their enterprises to firms and individuals: e.g., electricity produced at a government electricity plant can be sold to factories. The government may also issue debt. Barro (Chapter 9) notes that issuing debt, as opposed to collecting taxes currently, is equivalent to postponing the taxes to some future date, and one can think of government debt issue as carrying with it a corresponding future tax liability.

Economic Effects of Taxes

Any tax has essentially two major avenues of economic effects. First, taxes, by transferring economic resources from private individuals and firms to government, reduce the after-tax or net in-

come available to the private sector to spend or save. Correspondingly, they increase the revenues available to the government
sector to spend or invest. Second, and in many cases more important, taxes change the relative prices of different commodities and
different factors of production. For example, income taxes or payroll taxes drive a wedge between the gross wage rate paid to workers and the net, or take-home, pay of the worker. A worker earning $5.00 an hour, and working a normal work year of 2,000 hours,
would have annual earnings of $10,000. If this person was in a 20
percent tax bracket, his after-tax wage rate per hour would not be
$5.00, but $4.00. This reduction in the net wage rate itself has two
effects on the work and labor supply decisions of individuals. First,
it makes work in the market less remunerative. By so doing, it
reduces the incentive to work, and this incentive may be reflected
in a lower labor force participation rate, or in fewer hours of work
and less work effort. Second, by reducing the after-tax income of
the individual, it may make work more necessary, thereby creating an incentive to work more in order to recoup the original loss
in income.

A large number of studies have been conducted to ascertain the
effect of taxes on labor supply. It is beyond our scope here to evaluate each of these studies, but some are discussed in the chapters
that follow. As a rough approximation, it appears that the labor
supply of husbands between the ages of 25 and 55 is rather
unresponsive to changes in the net wage rate, but that the labor
supply of wives, elderly workers, and teenagers, often called secondary workers, is quite sensitive to such tax-induced net wage
reductions. Therefore, high rates of income or payroll tax have the
undesirable effect of driving potential workers out of the labor
force and inducing them either to work at home or consume more
leisure.

A second major effect of taxes concerns the consumption/saving
and investment choices. Under an income tax, saving is taxed
twice: since income equals expenditures plus saving, saving is included in the base of the tax. When the saving subsequently earns
a return—for example, in the form of interest—that return is
taxed again. Suppose you put $1,000 into a savings account earn-
ing 6 percent per year; the gross return, ignoring taxes on your
saving, is 6 percent. However, you pay taxes on this interest; if

your marginal tax rate is approximately one-third, the 6 percent is reduced to 4 percent after taxes. Substantial evidence now exists that saving does respond quite substantially to changes in the after-tax rate of return on capital. Our heavy taxes on income from capital, such as the taxes on capital income embodied in the personal income tax and directly in the corporate income tax, substantially reduce the net rate of return to capital and hence private saving, the future size of the capital stock, future labor productivity, wages, and income. These issues will be discussed in more detail by Taubman (Chapter 5) and Mieszkowski (Chapter 2).

Taxes may also affect economic stability and growth. Many economists believe that in the midst of a very deep recession or depression a tax cut can stimulate economic activity, increase employment, and generate an increase in income. Correspondingly, some economists believe that tax increases in the face of a large inflation can help curtail that inflation. Recently, much doubt has been cast on these propositions. While it is not our purpose to review that literature here, in brief summary the argument goes that only unanticipated changes in fiscal or monetary policy will have much impact on the course of the real economy.

When taxes distort relative prices or relative factor returns, as noted above, they induce people to alter their economic activity— for example, to work less or to save less. These distortions cause an *extra* cost to be borne by society for raising taxes. Economists label this extra cost the deadweight loss of the tax. To demonstrate, when the government raises virtually $200 billion by income taxes, the true cost to society of raising that $200 billion may be much more than $200 billion, because in doing so, we have distorted the incentives of the population to work and to save. A variety of studies have attempted to measure the deadweight loss involved in different tax distortions. Most of these studies conclude that the deadweight loss is not trivial, amounting in some cases to many billions of dollars. Once again, the deadweight loss of taxes will be discussed in specific contexts in the chapters which follow. For our purposes, it is only important to note that when considering the costs of running the public sector, of providing government expenditures and transfer payments, these extra, or deadweight, losses must be added to the dollar amount raised by the government. Further, government expenditures are only desirable when, at the margin, the valuation of the government expenditures by households exceeds the total costs, at the margin, of providing the services—the total costs consisting of both the actual taxes raised and the deadweight losses incurred.

It is a fundamental tenet of economic analysis that, as more and more of a good is consumed, its extra, or incremental, value declines. The value of a small amount of food, for example, is enormous; it helps us avoid starvation. Eventually, as we consume increasing amounts of food, the value of this additional food starts to decline and may even become negative. In the case under consideration, it is reasonable to assume that as the ratio of public to private economic activity increases, the extra value of public goods declines relative to the extra value of private goods and services.

Criteria for Evaluating Taxes

The analysis and facts presented above suggest several criteria upon which to judge the desirability of a tax system. The first goal of a tax system is to raise enough revenue to provide the desired amount of public goods and revenues for income redistribution. Public goods have the characteristic that adding an extra consumer to enjoy their use and benefits does not reduce the amount of the good available to other consumers. Hence, for public goods, we must add the marginal valuation of *all* consumers of the public good in order to obtain a measure of the marginal social benefit of the good. This must be compared to its marginal cost, inclusive of the deadweight loss involved in financing the public good.

To raise revenue efficiently, we want to minimize distortions of the major economic decisions, such as the consumption/saving choice, investment and risk-taking choices, labor supply and human capital investment choices, and the like. The only tax which has no distorting effect at all is a so-called lump sum tax, which is levied independently of the activity of any economic agent. Unfortunately, such taxes are impracticable and generally would be considered capricious. Therefore, since we must distort some choices, the task is to find the desirable combination of distortions that is "second best." For example, an income tax distorts both the work/leisure choice and the consumption/saving choice; excise taxes on different commodities distort the pattern of consumption across those commodities. Each of these distortions will be discussed in some detail in the chapters to follow. For our purpose, we merely note that the deadweight loss involved in raising a given tax revenue will be minimized if we place higher tax rates on goods which have the least elastic demands (i.e., for which demand is relatively independent of price), and factors of production—labor and capital—which have the least elastic supplies. That is, we wish to tax most heavily those goods and factors which will respond only slightly, if at all, to the imposition of taxes, and we want to avoid high tax rates on goods and services, or factors of production, whose demand and supply, respectively, are very responsive to taxation. Thus, the first criterion for determining a desirable tax system is that it be *efficient*.

In addition to the economists' notion of efficiency as minimizing the distortions created by the tax system, our tax system should also impose as small an administrative and compliance burden as possible. We do not desire a tax system which is extremely difficult to administer, extremely costly for taxpayers to comprehend and comply with. In short, we should avoid a system that requires a substantial use of resources in order to collect the revenue.

The next important criterion for determining a desirable tax system, again in combination with a desirable pattern of expenditures, is equity. Equity means different things to different people. Some argue quite forcefully for so-called horizontal equity, the equal treatment of equals—which in general has been interpreted to mean that persons with the same income or some other measure of command over resources should pay the same tax rate. In reality, of course, the items we observe to measure ability to pay, whether income, consumption, wealth, or the consumption of specific commodities, are *ex post* outcomes. They are not, that is, *ex ante* possibilities. If we have two people who are perfectly identical—suppose, for example, they are twins—and one undertakes a risky investment and the other undertakes a safe investment, *ex post* they are likely to have very different incomes, even though the difference is due to the fact that one was willing to take the risk of a very high payoff with a low probability, while the other twin was not willing to do so. As a rough approximation, horizontal equity commands much popular appeal, and it is the usual notion of equity employed by lawyers and politicians in discussing tax situations. We often hear of a comparison between Smith and Jones, who otherwise sound equal, but somehow Smith winds up paying much more in taxes than does Jones. Once again, this is sometimes due to voluntary choices made by Smith and Jones, who may have started from equal *ex ante* opportunities.

A second and much more controversial notion of equity is so-called vertical equity, the progressivity or regressivity of the tax system. Most persons find it reasonable and desirable to suggest that the rich should pay more in taxes than the poor. Some will also suggest that they should pay a higher proportion of their income or wealth or consumption in taxes than do the poor. But there is very little consensus on the desirable degree of progressivity. Our current tax system embodies in the personal income tax a nominally progressive tax system. However, as noted in Taubman's chapter, there are many exemptions, deductions, and exclusions which render the effective tax rates very different from the nominal ones. Further, the more progressive the tax system, the higher the marginal tax rate at the top becomes, and the greater are the disincentives to work, save, and invest. That is, progressivity, or increased vertical equity or equality, conflicts to a large extent with efficiency. In the last few years, there has been developed a substantial literature on trading off the twin goals of efficiency and vertical equity in the tax system. While in its pure form this question goes all the way back to the nineteenth-century English classical economists, such as John Stuart Mill and Francis Edgeworth, in recent years the rigorous analysis of this problem has pointed out the substantial conflict between increased progressivity in the tax system and efficiency in the form of eliminating deadweight losses. This will be discussed again below, but let us take a simple example.

Suppose we made tax rates extremely high for the upper-middle and upper income classes. Further suppose that they substantially reduced their labor supplies, savings, and investments. It might then be the case that tax rates became so high that our tax revenues actually declined, leaving us less revenues to provide public goods and to redistribute via transfer programs to poor people. The lesson to be learned is quite simple. The efficiency problems of factor supply—whether labor supply, human investment, savings, or regular investment—may put a strong brake on the optimal degree of progressivity of the tax system. Further, the more progressive the tax system and the higher the tax rate, the more incentive there is to try and accrue income or wealth in nontax forms. This has been a major reason why the tax base in the United States has been continuously eroded. As discussed by Kurz (Chapter 7), and in the chapters by Taubman and Mieszkowski, there is much to be said for a simpler tax system which, perhaps, has a credit and a flat rate, or a few tax rates rather than many, with a broader tax base than currently exists.

Finally, we note the third criterion for determining a desirable tax system: its effects on economic stability and growth. Our progressive tax system has built into it a system of so-called automatic stabilizers. As income goes up, for example, people are pushed into ever higher tax brackets, which thereby act as a brake on the growth of income. Conversely, as income falls—as in a recession—disposable income, income after taxes, falls by less than total income, because taxes fall more than proportionately. Many fiscal experts feel that this is an extremely desirable feature of a tax system, especially when combined with the difficulty of implementing discretionary fiscal policy due to lags and imperfect formation.

However, a major problem exists, because our tax system is not indexed for inflation. While some would applaud the fact that taxes will rise more proportionally when nominal incomes increase due to inflation, thereby perhaps slowing the demand pressure on inflation, there is an insidious side effect of this phenomenon: the extra revenue generated provides politicians with an easy short-run vehicle for financing their pet projects. Instead of having decisions about the size and desirability of the public sector and different public projects made on the basis of real benefits and costs, the inflation component of the tax revenue is a cushion to politicians for spending purposes. Only by continual tax rate reductions—which politicians parade as actual tax reductions when in reality they are only partial compensations for the automatic tax increases that result from inflation—can government spending be checked at all. The question of indexing the tax system and of automatic stabilizers are discussed in the chapters by Taubman and Shoven (Chapter 8).

With this discussion of the U.S. tax system and general analysis of criteria for determining government economic activity and a desirable tax system in mind, let us turn to a discussion of alternative concepts of tax reform.

Three Concepts of Tax Reform

Few issues stir as much controversy as does tax reform. Virtually everyone is for tax reform, but there are almost as many definitions of tax reform as there are supporters of it. Three major types of tax reform appear in popular discussion.

First, tax reform can mean a balanced reduction in taxes and government expenditures. This can mean reductions in the size of the public sector or, in a growing economy, a reduction in the growth rate of government expenditures and taxes—which would reduce the relative size of the public sector in the course of economic growth. This is the sense in which former President Ford discussed tax reform in the last election campaign. It would not be unreasonable to argue that a substantial impetus behind the recent tax revolt—as evidenced by the passage of Proposition 13 in California and the enormous outcry against the 1977 social security tax increases—comes from a feeling that government has gotten too large and too expensive. Indeed, many would argue that government—perhaps, especially, the federal government— is trying to do things now that it cannot do very well, and, in the course of doing so, a substantial fraction of the total resources spent is wasted. Many economists would also argue that leaving a larger share of total economic activity in the private sector would promote competition, efficiency, and stable economic growth.

A second definition of tax reform revolves around changing specific features of various taxes, such as dividend relief, or partial integration of corporate and personal income taxes, or changes in the investment tax credit. President Carter usually uses the term in this sense; i.e., he has stressed limitations on deductions for business lunches, reform of the tax treatment of U.S. investment overseas, and changing a variety of other structural features of current taxes.

Third, tax reform can mean changing the composition of a given tax revenue among different tax bases. Some social security programs could be shifted from payroll tax to general revenue fi-

nance, or we could begin to eliminate savings from the tax base—
that is, switch from income to expenditure as the base of our personal tax system.

The major battlegrounds surrounding tax reform will likely consist of the following types of proposals: first are a variety of tax
policies to stimulate badly needed capital formation in the United
States. The best method for doing so would be to switch from our
current income tax to a consumption or expenditure tax. Partial
proposals include tax-free roll-over of reinvested capital gains,
reduction of capital gains tax rates, and general tax rate reductions.

A second major battleground of tax reform likely to come to the
fore in the years immediately ahead is the possibility of indexing
the tax system for inflation. As noted in the chapter by Shoven,
there is little justification for continuing a tax system based on
nominal, as opposed to inflation-adjusted, values. A dollar in 1978
bears no more relation to a dollar spent in 1965 to purchase an
asset than it does to foreign currencies, yet we are one of the few
advanced economies which have not attempted at least partially
to index their tax system for inflation. This not only results in a
variety of inequities, but, as noted above, it offers the politician the
gravy train of a greater than proportional increase in tax revenues to spend on favorite programs. In the extreme, if we did not
have occasional tax cuts to partially offset this inflationary revenue gain, government economic activity would essentially drive
out all private economic activity as the inflation continued.

A third major potential battleground of tax reformers concerns
the appropriateness of a separate corporate income tax. President
Carter originally proposed, but quickly withdrew, a partial
integration of the corporate and personal income taxes. In the
chapter by Break (Chapter 3), many of these proposals are discussed and analyzed. For our purposes, let us note that a separate
corporate income tax makes very little sense. The income accruing to corporations ultimately accrues to shareholders, and should
be so attributed. Currently, tax-exempt organizations, widows
with very little income, and blue-collar workers whose pensions
are invested in corporate securities, all pay very high corporate income tax rates on their share of corporate earnings. These rates
would be much lower if the corporate tax were integrated with the

personal income tax and their share of corporate income attributed back to them. Worse yet, the corporate income tax probably causes a substantial distortion of economic activity between the corporate and noncorporate form of doing business.

Another major battleground is likely to be the tax treatment of our exports and imports. I do not mean only our tariff policies, although these themselves are important. In the last two decades we have several times witnessed proposals for a value added tax of the type used extensively in the Common Market countries of Western Europe. It was suggested in the 1950s as a substitute for the corporate income tax, and in the early 1970s as a substitute for property taxes. It is often the first new tax mentioned when extra sources of revenue are sought.

A final major battleground concerns welfare reform, and the possibility of the implementation of a negative income tax or some form of guaranteed annual income. Discussed in some detail in the chapter by Kurz, the negative income tax, while intuitively and initially very appealing, runs into some very basic difficulties, the most important of which is the impracticability of transferring a sufficient amount of money or resources to the very poor without also transferring a substantial amount of funds to the nonpoor.

Short of such major tax reforms as a negative income tax, inflation adjustments, substituting a value added tax for the corporate income tax, integration of the corporate and personal income taxes, substituting an expenditure tax for the personal income tax, and the like, there are a variety of partial reform proposals of the type mentioned above as structural changes in existing taxes. As discussed by Taubman, many features of the individual income tax might well be changed. These include the unit and time period of account, the level of exemptions and deductions, and the treatment of a variety of sources of income. Another example would be partial integration of the corporate and personal income taxes, such as the dividend relief originally proposed by President Carter. Included are several structural reforms in social security taxes, such as changes in the rates and base, and changes in the unit of account.

Our tax system has evolved historically through a series of compromises and reforms which have attempted, on the one hand, to achieve some level of efficiency and equity while raising a given revenue and, on the other, have reflected important political forces embodied in special interest groups. But the underlying economic forces which determine the desirability of specific features of our tax laws have changed markedly through time. Who would have predicted many years ago that we would have such a different demographic structure in the United States? It is simply no longer the case that most families have only one worker, a married male, a wife who works solely at home, and children who do not work. We have many more single people, whether never married, divorced, or widowed, than we have had at any time in our history. The age structure of our population is changing rapidly, due to the post-World War II baby boom and the subsequent baby bust of the 1970s. We have had an inflation for the last ten years which has driven prices up to an unprecedented level in the United States. We have an increasingly complex system of international trade which can be strongly affected by taxes, and, by analogy, we have an increasingly complex system of intergovernmental fiscal relations, tax liabilities, and responsibilities for expenditure programs at different levels of government.

Agenda for Tax Reform

The debate over the relative size of the governmental and private sectors of the economy continues to rage unabated. It is clear that the growing size of the public sector, and the large increase in tax rates applying to a growing fraction of the population, have created a variety of perhaps unintended and undesirable outcomes and effects on the private economy. While others in this book may disagree, my own conclusion is that tax rates—especially tax rates on the income from capital—have risen to a point where the combination of inflation and our unindexed tax system seriously retards the process of capital formation. Moreover, current tax rates almost certainly have substantially reduced the labor supply of secondary workers such as the elderly and second earners in a family. The cost to society of these disincentives is very great.

Further, as the relative size of the government sector is expanded, government has attempted to move into areas which are likely to lead to diminishing marginal utility of public sector output. While there are many potentially desirable public and/or private projects, many of those which the government has undertaken have proved to be abysmal failures. Unfortunately, a large number of these retain strong constituencies with effective lobbies which continually pressure Congress to avoid reduction in spending. A book on tax reform is not the place to discuss which expenditure programs are desirable and which are undesirable. At the same time, the serious side effects and unintended adverse incentives created by the growth of the public sector are becoming worse and worse, as the relative size of the public sector continues to expand and marginal tax rates continue to rise. Under the circumstances, it is hard to avoid the conclusion that a substantial case exists for slowing the rate of growth of the public sector relative to the private sector of the economy.

Much more germane to the purpose of this book is the question of how we should go about efficiently and equitably collecting taxes and distributing revenues, given the size of the public sector that we deem desirable. I would like to make the following general suggestions.

First, there is a strong case for gradually switching our base of personal taxation from income to expenditures (consumption). Such a tax, relative to our current tax system, would stimulate badly needed capital formation, remove an enormous inefficiency in the intertemporal allocation of resources across individuals' lifetimes, and increase future productivity, wages, and income.

Second, if a consumption tax is deemed impractical, or is to be implemented only very slowly, there are many important changes that could be made in our current system of income taxation. By far the most important is to index the tax system for inflation. The economic and political harm done by an unindexed tax system, which continually accrues revenues far in excess of real income growth, cannot be overestimated. As Shoven notes, indexing for inflation involves not only appropriately adjusting the bracket rates, but also adjusting the basis of taxation—i.e., the definition of taxable income—to make sure that we are taxing real, rather than nominal, income.

Third, another major income tax revision of extreme importance involves integrating the corporate and personal income taxes. Break points out that this is desirable on a number of efficiency and equity grounds. While it would not be an easy matter to do this partially or gradually from an administrative and implementation point of view, the time is ripe to attempt at least a partial integration of corporate and personal taxes.

Fourth, we should adjust our capital gains taxation to reflect the fact that much of accrued capital gains represents purely inflationary gain. An indexed tax system would accomplish this automatically, of course, and if we switch to an expenditure tax, the need for capital gains taxes would disappear.

Fifth, we must reexamine the basic nature of our social security system, and arrange to separate out the welfare component that provides minimum income support to the elderly from the pure annuity or insurance goal of the system. The former could be financed out of general revenue, and the latter could be financed by some combination of payroll taxes and proof of private insurance for retirement.[1] In brief, separating the transfer and insurance goals, and allowing proof of private insurance for retirement to substitute for social security contributions, would dramatically relieve the immense long-term deficit in social security, and would help to reduce the enormous burden of social security taxes. When combined with income taxes—federal and state—these taxes produce an extremely high marginal tax rate on a very large fraction of the U.S. population.

Sixth, there is much to be said for some form of negative income tax device as a substitute for a wide range of categorical income maintenance programs and subsidies. However, as Kurz notes, there are some immense practical difficulties to be overcome before a reasonable negative income tax proposal is likely to be adopted.

Seventh, we should begin to think of changes in the unit and time period of account for our personal tax system. Whether we keep our individual income tax, or gradually shift to an expenditure tax, the changing demographic pattern of the population, particularly with respect to the formation and dissolution of families, requires us to rethink our basic unit of account for taxation. Currently, it generally pays a husband and wife to file a joint return and split their income; thus they are taxed as if each of them earned half their combined income. Unfortunately, this raises the marginal tax rate on the very first dollar of earnings by the secondary worker in the family to a very high rate. Even in families with very modest incomes, the second worker in a family would face an income tax, under income splitting, of 25 percent to 30 percent. This is extremely inefficient, in view of the sensitivity to after-tax wage rates of the labor supply of secondary workers. It is time for us to consider the possibility of separate rate schedules for the second earner in a family, reflecting lower tax rates than those on the first earner in the family.

Another problem with our individual tax system, whether our current individual income tax or an eventual individual consumption or expenditure tax, revolves around the time period of accounting. Currently we have only very limited procedures for income averaging, and for loss carry-forwards and carry-backs. As capital markets improve, annuity markets develop, and we learn more and more about the typical lifetime pattern of earnings at different ages, we should reconsider proposals to expand the time period of account for taxation. While withholding and annual filing are likely to remain with us for a very long time indeed, we should allow for longer term income averaging and longer term loss carry-forwards and carry-backs than in our current tax system. In short, when we think about the ability to pay—and subject to practical and administrative considerations—we should think about economic well-being over the lifetime as opposed to over an arbitrarily chosen, very short, accounting period.

The Inadequacy of Existing Information on the Effects of Taxes

Every time a tax reform proposal is formulated, a variety of attempts are made to estimate its economic effects. These include estimates of the effect of the reform on the gross national product, economic growth, unemployment, inflation, and tax burdens by income group. The U.S. Treasury traditionally prepares such estimates. Many private nongovernmental sources also produce them. Unfortunately, the available methods of making these estimates are seriously biased. The Treasury model, for example, is simply a cross-tabulation of returns by income and other types of characteristics. That is, there are no behavioral relationships involved in the Treasury model. Therefore, it simply assumes that every firm and every household will continue behaving in exactly the same way before the imposition of the tax reform as they would after the tax change. To take a simple example, suppose we contemplate taxing capital gains in full. The way the Treasury calculates the net impact on tax revenues of such a tax change is as follows: it takes its sample of returns, adds in the extra capital gains which were excluded in the original computation of tax, and then calculates a new tax on that return. In brief, the Treasury would assume that the individuals paying the capital gains tax would go on realizing the same capital gains after the rates had essentially doubled as they did before the tax rate increase! This, of course, is a rather extreme assumption. Suppose that the capital gains rate increased to 100 percent. Who, then, would bother to realize any capital gains at all? Yet the Treasury's method for estimating the revenue gain would assume that people would go on realizing the same amount of capital gains as before the tax increase.

The Treasury is attempting, albeit quite slowly and gradually, to build some behavioral equations into its model. In addition, several private, nongovernmental sources estimate the impact of tax reform proposals. Most of these models are basically designed to serve other purposes. They are almost all Keynesian, short-run, forecasting models which attempt to plot the future course of gross national product and its components over the next several quarters. By their very nature, they are not capable of describing the long-term growth of the U.S. economy. Therefore, they are of very limited applicability in assessing the economic consequences of any tax change which affects capital formation. As an example, if we switch from an income to an expenditure tax, we would gradually increase the capital stock as people saved more and more each year. In the long run, this would lead to a substantial increase in future productivity, income, wages, and tax revenues at constant rates. Unfortunately, the short-run forecasting models are incapable of tracing out such effects.

Therefore, when Congress is presented information about the likely effects of tax policies, the overwhelming bulk of evidence is related to the consequences on revenues this year and next, and on the aggregate performance of the economy over the next several quarters. That is, the deck is stacked against the proposals which temporarily decrease tax revenues but stimulate the long-term growth of the economy. It is perhaps not surprising that poli-

ticians, with a notoriously short time horizon of the period between the present and the next election, focus on such information.
Unfortunately, however, the future course of economic activity
can be substantially affected by such shortsightedness.

A second major device in evaluating tax proposals, which is now
published annually and actually projected over the subsequent
five years, is the so-called Tax Expenditure Budget. This proceeds
from the assumption that any deviation from a certain definition
of taxable income is a tax preference which lowers the tax liability
of certain individuals and firms, and is analogous to direct government expenditure for those purposes. There are several fallacies
in the Tax Expenditure Budget concept. First, before we know
what is being taxed at favorable or unfavorable rates, we need to
know what a desirable tax base is or should be. The Tax Expenditure Budget starts from the assumption that an income tax, or
rather a tax on most market sector income, is the desirable norm.
There is much, analytically and empirically, to suggest that an income tax is not a desirable tax base. For example, saving is taxed
twice by the income tax, which is inferior on both efficiency and
equity grounds to an expenditure tax. Viewed in this light, many
items of so-called tax preferences, such as accelerated depreciation, are really negative tax expenditures, because we are not
allowing depreciation at the same rate as we would under a consumption tax—that is, expensing of capital equipment. Second,
the calculations made of the revenue loss and the size of the subsidy embodied in a particular tax preference in the Tax Expenditure Budget suffer from the same problems as the estimates obtained in the Treasury model—to wit, they assume no economic
behavior.

As noted in the introductory chapter, taxes have two major
effects. They transfer resources from the private sector of the
economy to the government, and they alter the relative prices of
goods and services and factors of production. In so doing, they usually do affect economic behavior—for example, the consump-
tion/saving choice, the riskiness of investment, and the work/lei-
sure choice. Hence the estimates embodied in the Tax Expenditure
Budget are correct *only if all deviations from the allegedly proper
tax base are eliminated simultaneously, and if all supplies of factors
of production are totally unresponsive to tax increases.* It is ex-

tremely unlikely that this is the case. For example, the Tax Expenditure estimate of the nominally preferential treatment given to capital gains amounts to many billions of dollars. If we tax capital gains as ordinary income, however, in this author's opinion there would be far fewer accrued capital gains, a drastic reduction of realized capital gains, and an increase in leisure and income accruing in other nontax forms. Therefore, the Tax Expenditure Budget estimate of the revenue loss to the Treasury because of the lower capital gains tax rate may be a substantial overestimate. The same is true for each of the items which do substantially affect economic behavior.

Towards Improving the Informational Input to Tax Policy

It is clear that there is a very important place to be played by a tax model which takes into account the long-term growth of the economy, capital formation, and labor supply. We need to be interested not just in the effect of a particular tax policy on next year's tax revenues, but on the performance of the economy through time, and on the time pattern of tax revenues. Policies which temporarily increase tax revenues may ultimately decrease them, and vice versa. For example, a large increase in the corporate tax rate might raise more revenue this year, but substantially retard the capital formation process, and hence decrease income and taxes below what they otherwise would have been by a large amount five, ten, or fifteen years down the road. At that time, a new Congress would be faced with the tremendous problem of a much lower tax base than it otherwise would have had, and the necessity of a dramatic increase in tax rates to attempt to raise tax revenues.

In brief, we should attempt to build an analytical and econometric structure which allows us to estimate the future time path of tax revenues over, say, the next ten or twenty years, not just over the next few quarters. Otherwise we will be continuously doomed in any attempt to develop tax policies to stimulate capital formation, because they will continually appear to decrease tax revenues in the short run, with no estimate given of the compensating increase to appear several years down the road as factor supplies expand. Economists have now made enough improvements in their analytical structures, their econometric modeling, and the availability of data, to begin to present reliable information on these matters. This author, for example, together with Professor Martin Feldstein of Harvard University, developed a series of estimates of the likely effect of changes in tax revenues and giving to charity of alternative reforms in the tax treatment of charitable contributions. We estimated a substantial response on the part of charitable donors. The response was large enough that charities would actually lose more than the Treasury would gain, even in the short run, if the deductibility of charitable contributions were eliminated from the individual income or the estate tax.[2] Of course, economists and others may disagree on the precise magnitude of the relevant parameters necessary to analyze each of the tax policy reforms and proposals.

In the chapters above, we saw the importance of certain key parameters. In discussing the switch from an income to a consumption tax, the size of the interest elasticity of saving is crucial. We noted in a discussion of capital gains taxes the importance of a better empirical estimate of the size of the lock-in effect. In the discussion of social security taxes, we noted the importance of estimating the effect of the very high marginal tax rates on the supply of labor. No one would presume that we can yet answer these questions precisely, but much progress has been made in recent years, and our stock of information about these and other magnitudes necessary to assess tax policy has been gradually growing and improving. We desperately need to begin to incorporate this type of information into the tax policymaking process. As noted above, the Treasury is attempting to do so, albeit gradually. The relevant committees of Congress and other interested individuals eagerly await this development. In the meantime, it will be left to individual economists to analyze the effects of tax policies on the supply of the factors of production, in order to enable a prudent legislature to evaluate the long-term consequences of such policies. This requires estimating the impact of tax policies on the growth of the economy, and on the future course of tax revenues.

4

WILLIAM R. HAVENDER

Government Regulation: Assessing and Controlling Risks

The last ten years have witnessed a florescent concern with hazards to our health and with the regulatory measures instituted to deal with them. In fact, it seems almost daily that something else in our food or water or work environment is found to cause cancer (today's newspaper, for example, reports that newspaper ink does so)[1] and these alarms frequently serve as the basis for increased government action to "protect" the public. At the same time, the public is growing weary of this ceaseless crying of "wolf" and impatient with science, which seems able only to raise the alarm but never to solve the problem. This discussion focuses on

This essay originally appeared as "Assessing and Controlling Risks" in *Social Regulation: Strategies for Reform*, edited by Eugene Bardach and Robert A. Kagan (1982).

what science can tell us about these hazards, why science cannot, in truth, presently solve them, and how regulatory agencies handle the problem of decision-making in the context of these uncertainties.

Health risks are commonly divided into acute and chronic. Acute risks are those that result from one or a few exposures, and in which the health effect is apparent immediately or shortly after exposure occurs; poisoning is an instance. Acute hazards do not usually pose intractable problems of public policy because the connection between cause and effect typically is clear, allowing us to assign responsibility for the hazards and to learn relatively quickly how to avoid or minimize them. Chronic hazards, on the other hand, are those where the health effect shows up only after many years of exposure. Examples are lung cancer, which develops only after decades of smoking, and bladder cancer, one main cause of which is thought to be occupational exposure to certain industrial chemicals over a score of years or so. The policy situation with regard to chronic health hazards is very different than with acute hazards since, as we shall see, the area of uncertainty is much, much larger.

Cancer

The chronic hazard of greatest current concern is cancer (although another that is starting to emerge in public discussion is mutagenicity—the long-term harm to generations yet to come). Several factors account for the urgency of this concern and for the difficulty in developing a consensus on cancer policy. First, cancer is a common disease, and is largely incurable. Some 20 to 25 percent of us can expect to develop cancer of one type or another. This is a much higher proportion than used to be the case, although this increase is *not* due to there being a sudden epidemic of cancer attributable to our industrial society. Rather, it is a consequence of the great reduction in mortality from infectious diseases (tuberculosis, diphtheria, pneumonia, smallpox, polio, and others) that public health measures and modern medicine (especially antibiotics and vaccines) have achieved in this century. Almost everyone now expects to reach the age when cancer, which is largely a disease of the elderly, can develop. Cancer incidence figures that have been corrected for the larger numbers of people living into old age (this is called "age-adjusting") show that, with one exception, the overall incidence of cancer has been rather steady or slightly decreasing since 1933, the first year for which all states had to notify the causes of all deaths centrally.[2] The exception has been the large rise in respiratory cancer, for which smoking, not "modern industrial pollution and chemical exposures," is by far the largest cause. Still, the fact that one in four of us will now, in the absence of infectious diseases, get cancer accounts for a large part of the enhanced public concern.

Second, it is now well established that our chances of getting cancer are highly influenced by environmental agents. This proposition is deduced from the fact that the incidences of particular types of cancer vary greatly from place to place around the globe, and also from time to time. Liver cancer, for example, is common in parts of sub-Saharan Africa, but is rare in the United States. Breast cancer is common here but rare in Japan, whereas stomach cancer is common there and uncommon here. That this is not due to a genetic difference is shown by the fact that Japanese immigrants within one generation develop the cancer patterns typical of the United States. Lung cancer, seldom seen at the turn of the century, is now the leading cause of cancer death among men and is rapidly on the rise among women as well, reflecting the historic smoking patterns among the sexes. Persons of Scandinavian and Celtic descent do not have high rates of skin cancer when living in Northern climes, but they do when they move to the tropics where they are exposed to more sun. By a careful comparison of such variations, the World Health Organization concluded in 1964 that "the majority of human cancer" was influenced by "extrinsic factors".[3] This early estimate has been updated and confirmed; currently the best estimate is that 75 or 80 percent of human cancer in the United States is susceptible to environmental factors.[4] This fact raises the hope that cancer, if not curable, might be preventable, and it has led to extremely diligent attempts to identify the causative agents.[5] It has also resulted in a vast expansion of the regulatory apparatus set up to deal with these hazards.

The third distinguishing feature about cancer (and this is where most uncertainties arise in trying to devise reasonable policies) is

that its causes are not usually easy to identify. Despite the
diligence of the effort to find causes, only limited (though extremely important) success has been achieved. Consensus has
been reached on the main cause of lung cancer (namely, smoking)
and on a variety of occupational cancers,[6] but in these cases the
proportional increase caused by single factors has been quite
large, and this does not seem to be the case for many common cancers (e.g., breast and colon cancer). Another difficulty is the
stochastic, or statistical, nature of cancer; that is, among a group
of similarly exposed persons, only some of them—seemingly at
random—will actually develop cancer. Not every smoker of high-
tar cigarettes contracts lung cancer (in fact, only about one in five
does), and not every worker who worked with asbestos comes
down with mesothelioma (a form of cancer associated almost exclusively with asbestos exposure). An even greater problem in con-
necting causes and effects is posed by the long latency of cancer,
where a period of one or more decades passes between the commencement of exposure to a causative agent and the manifesta-
tion of symptoms. This makes it difficult not only to tease out true
causes and hence to assign responsibility, but also to see improvements as a consequence of policy changes. Low-tar cigarettes, for
instance, have been available now for many years, and yet there is
still no proof that they do in fact reduce the occurrence of lung
cancer by a substantial degree. (This is by no means a trivial
point, since we don't know yet whether the right things were
taken out, nor do we know that the flavoring agents added back in
won't themselves prove to be carcinogenic.) Dealing with these
uncertainties can result in enormous costs to society if unbounded
"prudence" is the tactic chosen to deal with them.

There are three main kinds of evidence that are used to try to
establish whether or not a chemical poses a cancer hazard to
humans—namely, epidemiology, animal bioassays, and short-
term tests. Each has advantages and disadvantages.

Epidemiology

Epidemiology is the study in humans of the patterns of occurrence
of disease and of exposure to various suspect agents. This tool has
the great virtue that it directly identifies *human* risk factors, and

once a carcinogenic agent has been identified, there are no further fundamental problems of interpretation as there are with animal bioassays and short-term tests. But it suffers from several inherent defects. It is, for one thing, not a very sensitive technique, which means that it is difficult to establish small effects with statistical confidence ("small," of course, means proportionally; this could still translate into many thousands of cases annually for a sizable population). Partly, this is due to the difficulty of assembling reliable information on large numbers of people, whether by means of interviews or examination of medical records. Partly, it is due to the difficulty of eliminating "confounding variables" from the comparison groups (i.e., eliminating those differences between the groups to be compared that may be spuriously generating or concealing a causal correlation). This can be a problem even when the carcinogenic effect under investigation is large, but when it is at best small (such as the suspected effect of saccharin on bladder cancer or of hair dyes on breast cancer), the problem can be insuperable. Using large numbers of subjects and taking great care in matching up the comparison populations can reduce the problem. Epidemiology's usefulness is also diminished by the difficulty of assembling true zero-dose control groups. If we wanted to test, for example, the hypothesis that caffeine is carcinogenic, it would be hard to find a sizable group of people with *no* exposure at all to caffeine, since it is a constituent in coffee, tea, Coke, and in other common foods as well. One would have to look at groups like the Seventh-Day Adventists, but these would differ from other people on many additional variables, and thus confounding might occur.

Complicating the limited sensitivity of epidemiology is cancer's long latency, which means that to study people who currently have cancer entails asking questions about their personal habits and occupational and medicinal exposures two or three or four decades in the past. People's memories that far back are not usually very accurate—(How many diet pops did *you* drink in 1957? What hair coloring did you use in 1960? Was that dental X-ray in 1962 or 1963? Were you drinking chlorinated water in 1964? Oh, you moved to New Jersey in 1968 and lived near a chemical dump? What, you did *all* of these things?)—and estimates of dose tend, of course, to be even less reliable. Multiple exposure to suspect agents is common (so would it be the saccharin in 1957, the hair dyes of 1960, the X-rays of 1962–1963, the trihalomethanes of 1964, or the dump seepages of 1968 to which the breast cancer of 1981 should be attributed?). The picture can become even more complex because of the possibility of interaction between suspect agents (smoking, for example, greatly increases the already elevated chance that asbestos workers will develop lung cancer, so should we attribute it to the smoking or to the asbestos?).

A final, serious limitation of epidemiology is that it cannot, of course, help us with new chemicals to which humans have never before been exposed. About a thousand new ones are introduced into commerce each year; hence, this is a significant limitation.

Despite these shortcomings, epidemiology can be used—even when it has yielded a negative or marginal result—to set an upper limit on the risk to humans of substances to which they have been exposed for adequately long periods. For there would be certain levels of carcinogenic effect that *could* have been seen in the study with statistical confidence had they been present. Not seeing these levels, then, at least says that the suspect substance is not a "strong" carcinogen; it is at most "weak." The actual meaning to be attached to the words "strong" and "weak" would, of course, depend on the details of the particular study.

Finally, it must be noted to epidemiology's credit that every human carcinogen now known has been identified by means of epidemiology. This tool has established the very phenomenon of human cancers resulting from environmental exposures commencing decades before clinical symptoms were evident.

Animal Bioassays

Because of the ineluctable limits of epidemiology, surrogate means are sought for identifying human hazards, and the predominant surrogate currently in use is animal bioassays. These are studies where the suspect chemical is administered to laboratory animals, usually rats or mice, and the animals then monitored for the growth of tumors. Typically, the chemical is given to the animals in their food or water (or by stomach tube if the substance is unpalatable) for long periods, often for their entire lifetime. The key advantages of bioassays are that rodents live only about two years, reducing the time involved to see a tumorigenic effect from decades to two or three years, and that one can deliberately test any specific chemical of interest—in particular, new chemicals under consideration to be introduced into commerce. The disadvantages of bioassays, however, are substantial. Even these tests, for example, are not inexpensive—$1,000 an animal for a lifetime study is a typical cost—so that a standard-sized test on a single chemical involving an untreated (control) group and low- and high-dose groups with 50 animals of each sex at each dose (300 animals in all) will cost well in excess of $250,000. Yet even such a test would have limited sensitivity; it would probably never pick up a chemical that caused a 1 percent incidence of tumors in high-dose males, and such a chemical might well be declared "safe" even though it would be capable of causing many tens of thousands of cases of cancer a year in humans.

It is to compensate for this limited sensitivity that high doses are commonly employed in animal bioassays. In general, the incidence of cancer will rise as the dose increases, up to the point where the animals are dying off prematurely from simple poisoning. Therefore, to make a bioassay as sensitive as possible, a dose will be included that is the maximum the animals can tolerate over their lifetimes without succumbing early from poisoning. This is the so-called "maximum tolerated dose" (MTD).

But while this procedure undoubtedly maximizes the chance that even a weak carcinogen will be picked up, it introduces other sources of uncertainty, particularly when the only dose yielding tumors is the MTD. Perhaps the physiological events taking place in dose-stressed animals do not occur at all—or at least not in proportion—in normal animals, so that the outcome observed in high-dose animals would not be valid at the much lower body doses common in human exposures.

This reasoning leads us directly to the vexing problem of dose response; specifically, to the question of whether the risk at low dose can be estimated by simple extrapolation downwards along a straight line from the risk observed at high dose. Such a risk/dose relation is called a "linear" dose response. And while this may be a reasonable guess when the extrapolated dose is not very far from the experimentally observed dose, most scientists are very uncom-

fortable with relying on such an estimate when extrapolating to
doses one hundred or one thousand times smaller than the experimental dose, as is often the case. The critical question is whether
one or more inflection points (or a threshold) exist in the dose-
response curve, in which case the true low-dose risk could be much
smaller than under the linear assumption.[7]

In theory, one can readily design experiments to find out what
actually happens to the cancer rate at low doses comparable to
human exposures; but the incidence of tumors would shrink, and
much larger numbers of animals would have to be used in order to
detect these tumors with statistical confidence. This would mean
testing with thousands of animals and with multiple doses ranging
down to the dose of interest, a procedure which would be
prohibitively expensive, not to mention logistically difficult (e.g.,
acquiring thousands of animals of identical genetic background
and age all at more or less the same time, labeling them and maintaining records, and so forth). In any case, the test would pertain
only to the chemical of immediate interest, so it would have to be
repeated for every chemical investigated. This is clearly infeasible
on a regular basis, and so we are reduced for practical purposes to
making extrapolations—i.e., guesses—about the expected risk at
low doses.[8]

Many thousands of words have been devoted to the problem of
estimating low-dose risks from limited high-dose data, and some
highly sophisticated statistical models for extrapolation have been
advanced. The hard fact remains, however, that the verifiable
dose effects are similarly compatible with all of them (not surprising, since the models were developed to fit the available data) and
thus cannot distinguish between them; yet the models differ by
factors of hundreds or thousands in their estimates of the size of
the risk to be seen at very low doses. Of all the various models, the
linear one is not only by far the simplest mathematically, but it
also has the virtue of being the most "prudent"; that is, if its estimates are in error, they are virtually certain to err on the side of
overpredicting the true risk. This means that if a low-dose risk
estimated by means of the linear model is considered to be negligible, then one can feel quite secure in this judgment. For this
reason, the linear model is often adopted as a prudent way of dealing with this profound uncertainty. When, however, the estimate

yielded by the linear assumption is not so negligible (as is the case with saccharin, where the Food and Drug Administration [FDA] estimated an annual incidence of about 1,200 cases of bladder cancer per year in the U.S. population),[9] the procedure leads to dispute.

The other intractable problem with animal bioassays concerns whether rats and mice can be regarded simply as "little men," or whether there can be, in any specific instance, an important physiological difference in the way rodents and higher primates handle a carcinogen. This uncertainty concerns, as does the dose question, both the qualitative outcome (is or is not this chemical a carcinogen in humans?) and the quantitative outcome (can we assess the degree of risk to humans from the degree of risk seen in rodents?). Again, because of the limitations of epidemiology discussed earlier, arguments run on both sides of this question, with science not being able to offer a definitive judgment. The fact that all but one of the proven human carcinogens (the exception is arsenic) have been found also to cause cancer in laboratory animals favors the "little men" argument, at least qualitatively; but the crucial question is, of course, the reverse: can we expect, just because we have found conditions under which a chemical will cause cancer in rodents, that it will pose a true risk in man? There are by now several instances in which epidemiology has been unable to confirm cancer risks to humans suggested by rodent tests (e.g., saccharin, hair dyes, DDT),[10] although because of the limited sensitivity of epidemiology the possibility of small elevations in risk cannot be ruled out. The question becomes even more unsettling when one cogitates upon the peculiarities of the experimental conditions under which carcinogenicity in animals has often been established (e.g., high-dose regimens or, as in the saccharin experiments, *in utero* exposure). Hundreds of chemicals, including table sugar, pepper, eggs, and Vitamin D, have by now been shown to cause cancer in animals under one or another set of experimental conditions.[11] Is it really reasonable to assume on this basis that these substances imperil mankind?

One would feel more confident in making such a prediction if a chemical had been tested in several mammalian species and were carcinogenic in all of them; that is, the qualitative result in any one of them could be used to predict correctly the results in the

others. It is uncommon, however, to have results on the same
substance in more than two species (usually rats and mice), and
even for these two species, discordant results are often seen.[12]

Nevertheless, animal bioassays are the best means we have for
assessing a chemical's carcinogenic hazard in those instances
where we have only poor epidemiologic data or none at all. Some
chemicals are such strong and reproducible animal carcinogens
that there is consensus among scientists about their hazards, but
in general there is a continuity of results grading smoothly down
to situations at the margin of statistical significance, or where
there is reason to believe the MTD has been exceeded, or where
there is dispute among pathologists whether the growths seen
should be classified as tumors or not.

One highly important fact to come out of animal tests, and one
that has yet to be incorporated into routine regulatory decision-
making, is that the relative potencies of different chemicals—defined as the dose needed to produce cancer in half of the test
animals—vary over a millionfold range.[13] In other words, a dose
of aflatoxin (the strongest animal carcinogen yet found) would
cause a million times as many cases of cancer as the same dose of
saccharin (the weakest carcinogen so far detected in animals).
That chemicals' intrinsic carcinogenic hazard can vary over this
enormous scale is a fact of central importance for sensible
policymaking, since it forces one to set priorities and to pay attention to considerations of cost-effectiveness.

Short-Term Tests

In the last few years a new group of human surrogates has been
under development—namely, bacteria and mammalian cells in
tissue culture. These are used in "short-term" tests that examine
the capacity of the test substances to induce mutations or other
genetic damage. These tests have a vast advantage over animal
bioassays in that they take only a few days or weeks to carry out
and they cost only a few thousand dollars per chemical. By far the
best known and best validated of these is the so-called "Ames"
test (named for its inventor, Bruce Ames), which seems to detect
some 90 percent of chemicals that have been shown to cause
cancer in animal bioassays and to have a low incidence of "false

positives" (i.e., the obtaining of positive Ames-test results for a substance that has been adequately tested in animals and found not to be carcinogenic.[14] Still, certain classes of chemicals are missed by the Ames test, such as hormonally active carcinogens like diethylstilbestrol (DES), carcinogens that act by means of chronic physical irritation like asbestos, and some chlorinated hydrocarbons (which category includes many pesticides such as DDT) that are proven carcinogens in animal tests or humans. Dioxin, for instance, which is the highly dangerous contaminant in Agent Orange and the banned herbicide, 2,4,5–T, is an extremely potent carcinogen in rodent tests but is Ames negative. Some short-term tests detect substances missed by others, so that a carefully assembled "battery" may be the best way of utilizing them. But just what the best composition of the battery should be is a matter still under discussion.[15] Currently, the prime utility of short-term tests is in preliminary screening of large numbers of chemicals for exceptionally mutagenic (hence, presumptively carcinogenic) ones, particularly those contained in complex mixtures of chemicals (such as urine, cigarette smoke, drinking water, air pollutants, foods, or cosmetics). Once suspicions have been raised by such a screen, full-scale animal tests can be scheduled.

These are the main sorts of evidence, then, that are used for inferring whether a chemical poses a carcinogenic risk to humans. Currently, short-term tests are in use in thousands of industrial and university laboratories and the National Cancer Institute has a vast testing program under way in rats and mice, with a hundred chemicals placed under test each year. In addition, industry is carrying out a large number of animal tests, as marketing approvals are sought for new drugs and other consumer products. And, of course, a great variety of epidemiology studies are in progress at any given time. Thus, decision-makers are faced with a large and steadily growing volume of information, with only some of it (namely, positive epidemiology findings) capable of establishing human risk unambiguously, and the bulk of it raising questions about the imminence of human hazard but not clearly proving it. This evidence forms a continuum, without clear decision boundaries, ranging from chemicals that show strong carcinogenic activity in several species to disputed results in others, frequently with discordant results between species or sexes or strains, or between animal tests and short-term tests, or between suggestive animal results and decades of safe use in human experience. Science is really at its limits in most of these cases and cannot yield a single, clear verdict concerning human risk. Decision-makers must cope with this reality.

It may be that the best use of scientific evidence will not be for yes/no decisions but will be for *ranking* hazards—that is, one might use uniform assumptions for the dose and species extrapolation problems, assign weights to the various kinds of available evidence, and then rank chemicals in terms of intrinsic hazard. This could then be combined with estimates of current human exposure to get a rough sense of the *relative* human hazard posed by different chemicals. Uncertainties would exist, of course, even for this limited interpretation of the evidence, but one's chances of establishing sensible priorities would probably be higher than if these relative differences were ignored altogether.

A Look at the Regulatory Record

Given these uncertainties, but given also the urgent need to do something prospectively to guard against hazards from the great numbers of new chemicals, what institutional means will work best? The reflex response of the past years has been increased surveillance and rule-making from Washington in the form of various agencies—the FDA, the Occupational Safety and Health Administration (OSHA), the Environmental Protection Agency (EPA), the National Highway Traffic Safety Administration (NHTSA), the Consumer Product Safety Commission (CPSC), and the like. This is not necessarily the only way these problems can be dealt with, although—with the characteristic mix of hubris, naivete, and zeal to do both good and well that is endemic to social planners—this was the general approach that was favored. Identifying a problem (usually precipitated by a crisis) led reflexively to setting up an agency authority to deal with it (clean air, clean water, toxic chemicals, toxic dumps, food additives, new drugs, worker safety, and so forth), but with little thoughtful examination of what spontaneous corrective mechanisms might already be in place or how their effectiveness might be increased by comparatively modest reforms, and also without much thought given to the actual probability that Washington bureaus *could* and *would* solve the problems. Besides, there was also the strategic difficulty of contrasting a known flawed condition (the crisis did, after all, occur) with a hypothetically flawless unknown condition (the new agency). But now we have had a decade's experience (or more) with these bureaus, and there is a fair-sized body of practical fact that we can use to test the hypothetically ideal against the real. As we shall see, these facts feed the growth of doubt and lead to speculation about the possible role of alternative institutions in handling these problems. Could insurance companies become major factors in monitoring and reducing public risks? Could the courts? Could the prospect of being sued so wonderfully "concentrate the mind" as to lead corporate decision-makers to take optimal account of prospective public risks, including chronic ones? These questions will be examined fleetingly here, and in more detail by other contributors to this book.

The last decade's experience with regulatory agencies has made certain features clear about the true nature of regulation:

(1) It is typically slow.

(2) Agencies tend to deal with uncertainty by a "maximin" strategy, i.e., by imagining the worst case that could possibly occur and devising a regulation to minimize the damage from this worst case.

(3) Economic considerations tend to be resisted.

(4) *Increases* in risk that are brought about by delay tend to be ignored, as are increases in risk that result *from* new regulations, particularly when these risks fall outside the authoring agencies' mandated purview.

(5) Agencies tend to ignore information that cannot readily be analytically or scientifically articulated, even when this information may be highly relevant to the issue in question.

(6) Agencies' perspective tends to be central, and hence utilitarian. This can lead to lumping some persons' risks with other persons' benefits, hence obscuring great diversity in individual circumstances, and also to deliberate efforts at redistributing costs and benefits.

(7) Agencies are prone to basing regulations on premature and unconfirmed science.

The first of these points—that regulatory decision-making is characteristically slow—is richly documented. For example, a typical review period for a "New Drug Application" (NDA) at the FDA (a formality required before a new drug can be marketed, and which is submitted after several years of previous research and clinical trials have been completed to support the drug's safety and efficacy in humans) is two to three years, despite a nominal legal limit of 180 days. This is two to three years during which patients are denied the benefits of the new drug, and it is also two to three years during which the patent clock is ticking.[16] And OSHA, in its ten years of existence, has developed standards for only 20 carcinogens, though several hundred suspected carcinogens are in industrial use and many questionable new ones are introduced each year. The process of developing a rule has typically taken three to five years from first announcement to the end of judicial review. And while the Clean Air Act, passed in 1970, required the EPA to list and then regulate all hazardous air pollutants, it has so far regulated only 4 (asbestos, beryllium, mercury, and vinyl chloride) and listed 3 others (benzene, arsenic, and radionuclides). The Toxic Substances Control Act (TOSCA) of 1976 gave the EPA authority to regulate the uses of the 55,000 chemicals currently in industrial and commercial use. But of a priority list of 42 substances selected for EPA review, only 3 have so far been considered by EPA.[17]

Part of the reason for this apparent lethargy is procedural. OSHA, for example, issues regulations by means of a process that is "Byzantine in its complexity," and that is very open and full of points of access and challenge. Having gathered the information to support a rule, OSHA publishes a proposed regulation in the *Federal Register*. Both environmental and inflationary impact statements must be drafted (the latter under executive orders from presidents Ford and Carter). Public hearings are then held at which any interested party may appear, after which there is a period during which "posthearing comments" may be filed. Then OSHA, on the basis of this record, must determine a final regulation to be filed in the *Federal Register*, together with a "statement of reasons" detailing the rationale behind each clause. This final regulation then typically must undergo court review, possibly up to the Supreme Court.[18] Comparable procedures are required of the other regulatory agencies as well.

But another cause of the characteristic delay is the sheer mass of the information that must be transmitted to these agencies and evaluated by them. Much of this information has to do with ascertaining the existing "state" of affairs. OSHA's mandate, for instance, covers *every* firm with at least one employee, from great factories to the corner grocery. Some 4 million establishments are covered[19] and, in theory at least, all of these must be inspected and monitored for hazards and for continuing compliance with regulations. The TOSCA requires the EPA to inventory the 55,000 existing chemicals in use and the 1,000 or so new ones added each year —together with information on their toxicity, carcinogenicity, mutagenicity, and teratogenicity (capacity to cause birth defects) —and to monitor their production, use, and disposal. Under the provisions of the 1970 Clean Air Act and the Federal Water Pollution Control Act of 1972, the EPA must set standards and monitor air and water effluents from tens of thousands of factories across the country. Pesticide use by farmers must be monitored and controlled.

Added to this enormous informational task in simply ascertaining the state of things is the collection and evaluation of all the— typically ambiguous—scientific information concerning each of these chemicals in order to determine tolerable exposure standards. Much of this scientific information has to be generated by requiring experiments to be done, so another reason for delay enters. A typical NDA for the FDA can involve some 200 volumes (and may require several revisions) that must be evaluated before marketing approval can be granted.[20] Clearly, attention can be paid to only a small subset of the submitted information, and even so, delay is usual.[21]

A second feature of regulatory decision-making it that is does not really deal with the true ambiguities of many issues. Instead, a simplifying strategy is used that resolves disputed issues on the side of what is called, to describe it by its hoped-for results, "prudence." That is, the worst possible alternative is assumed on every disputed point and the regulation is framed to palliate this worst case. The problem with this strategy is that instances where the evidence for human hazard is extremely weak but where there is a large range of uncertainty are treated with the attentiveness and determination properly reserved for serious, imminent hazards. A blatant example of this tendency is OSHA's "generic" carcinogen policy that aims to diminish the scientific basis for challenging its rulings by declaring certain recurring, fundamental scientific issues to be "settled" on the side of "prudence." Such general determinations are not challengeable in the course of a specific rule-making, no matter what pertinent evidence might be available in a specific case, and the agency hopes thereby to speed rule-making along. OSHA thus recognizes no such thing as an overdose in animal tests; benign growths are given equal weight with malignant tumors; rats and mice are considered comparable to humans in their response to a carcinogen; "safe doses" for humans are presumed not to exist; a single positive test in any species outweighs any amount of negative evidence in other species or from actual experience in people; and substances that merely "promote" are regulated as though they were as dangerous as totipotent chemicals.[22] The sum of such decisions will, of course, inflate both the number of substances determined to present a hazard and the perceived degree of that hazard (and hence the costs of protecting against it). The EPA has indicated that it will follow OSHA's lead in these matters.

While such an attitude is understandable from the point of view of the agency decision-maker (and indeed it is arguable in the abstract that, given the inherent uncertainties, it is better to err always on the side of prudence), it is by no means clear that ignoring true ambiguities and treating every case as though it were a great hazard will lead to optimal public policy. For one thing, assuming the worst on every disputed point means that substances whose hazards are merely unclear will get lumped with those that *are* serious dangers, thus causing limited regulatory resources to be scattered rather than concentrated on the most urgent needs. For another, the strategy leads to great expense.

Dependence upon maximin thinking in the regulatory process is common. A recent article in *Science* describes the battle over approval of a new artificial sweetener, aspartame, which was finally approved by the FDA in the summer of 1981 after eight years of

effort by its manufacturer, G. D. Searle & Company. This substance is composed of two amino acids, aspartic acid and
phenylalanine, both of which are naturally occurring, ubiquitous
components of the proteins in our diet. Why did it take so long to
gain marketing approval for a substance whose constituents are
already a normal part of our food supply? The reasoning is instructive. There is a rare, inborn ailment called phenylketonuria,
which is an inability to metabolize phenylalanine. Ingestion of
foods containing this amino acid by people with this condition
leads to brain damage and mental retardation, and such persons
must be placed on a phenylalanine-free diet immediately after
birth and throughout life in order to avoid this outcome. About
15,000 people in the United States currently suffer from this dis-
order. Special labeling of products sweetened with aspartame
should be sufficient to warn these people away. But what about an
unborn fetus suffering from the condition, which would normally
be diagnosed only at birth? Could aspartame ingested by its un-
suspecting mother harm the fetus? Well, in most instances a pregnant woman would have to consume huge amounts of aspartame-
sweetened soft drinks, some 28 quarts at a time, to jeopardize her
fetus—an unlikely event. But there are several thousand women
reaching childbearing age each year who suffer from *another* rare
condition where their natural blood level of phenylalanine fluctu-
ates wildly and in whom, should they be carrying a phenyl-
ketonuric fetus, a smaller dose could endanger the fetus. Of
course, such women would already be exposed to other sources of
phenylalanine such as milk or meat and, if no special effort were
exerted to discourage these women from ingesting these foods
while pregnant, it would be hard to make a case for treating aspartame differently. In a few cases, of course, it may indeed be the
aspartame that provides the straw pushing the mother's blood
level past a critical threshold where it might harm her fetus. This
incredible argument, concerning at worst a vanishingly small
fraction of the population, was, according to *Science*, the prime
point in dispute contributing to the eight-year delay in approval.[23]
This is a clear case where the worst imaginable situation was the
determining factor in a regulatory process. (As it happened, no
breakthrough of a scientific nature on these issues finally brought
about approval; rather, a change of administration did so.)

Other instances of maximin thinking are EPA's attempt to devise air pollution standards designed to ease the plight of the most sensitive fraction of the population—namely, asthmatics—and the insistence by federal agencies that even quadriplegics have full access under their own steam to subways, buses, libraries, and all other public facilities.

A third characteristic of regulatory decision-making is the tendency to overlook considerations of cost and economic rationality. Numberless disputes arise between regulators, whose decisions impose costs, and businessmen who, as proxies of the public, have to pay them. Much effort has been expended by scholars of regulation in proselytizing on behalf of cost/benefit analysis, cost-effectiveness considerations, and risk assessment. These ideas seem to be making headway within the agencies, to be sure, but the fact remains that the estimated costs involved in saving a human life vary over a huge range from decision to decision, even within the same agency.[24] This clearly indicates the remaining scope for the implementation of cost-effectiveness techniques since, at least in principle, more lives could be saved with the same limited regulatory resources by "buying" more of the "cheaper" lives and fewer of the "dearer" ones.

Fourth, there is a clear tendency for agencies to ignore risks occasioned by *delay* in decision-making, as well as *increases* in risks resulting from regulations that occur outside the mandated purview of the agency. An astonishing instance of the first is related by Carl Djerassi in his recent fine book about oral contraceptives. Rare side effects among users of "The Pill" began to appear in the 1960s from the doses then in use, but no reduction in dose was allowed until the FDA had completed its review (of efficacy as well as safety) of the new lower-dose formulation. It was not until 1974 that the FDA began approving low-dose contraceptive pills, some five to six years *after* women in Communist China, of all places, had switched to them. In short, millions of American women were needlessly overdosed for half a decade as a direct result of the FDA's dilatoriness. This was not without adverse public health impact, since virtually all the risks associated with oral contraceptives stemmed from the early high-dose pill.[25]

Another instance is the well-documented phenomenon of "drug lag" whereby, as a consequence of the FDA's laborious requirements to win marketing approval, new and effective drugs enter clinical use much more slowly than they do in other countries. In the meantime, of course, patients who might benefit from a new drug must do without it.[26] This zeal had its origin in the worthy desire to avoid a repeat of the thalidomide tragedy. But the opportunity cost of forgone health benefits that is ineluctably bound up with a "go slow" attitude to new drug introduction has largely been ignored by the agency; at least one attempt at estimating these opportunity health costs and comparing them to the health benefits of avoiding future "thalidomides" concluded that the public would benefit on balance from a much speedier process of drug approval.[27]

A similar situation obtains at the EPA; approval is needed, for example, even for plant modifications that *reduce* emissions. In one case, an oil refiner wanted to modernize a sulfur-recovery plant in a way that would decrease emissions of sulfur dioxide, but this modernization was delayed for eighteen months during EPA review of the plans.[28]

DDT illustrates how agencies tend to ignore increases in risks brought about by their decisions when these increases take place outside the scope of their regulatory attention. This pesticide is, as far as acute hazards are concerned, extremely safe for farm workers and consumers to use (indeed, one of its common uses was to kill body lice on humans). Substituting other pesticides for DDT, as became necessary after the EPA banned it, meant that farm workers often must use more acutely toxic substances and apply them more frequently (since one of DDT's virtues, from the point of view of a farmer, is that its effectiveness is long-lasting). So the acute risk to *the workers* goes up. But that is not EPA's concern; it is OSHA's.

Another instance of this tendency is the Delaney clause, which has as an explicit feature that the only health risks it considers are cancer risks from *using* a food additive, not the health risks of *not using* it. Thus it would not matter even if saccharin and nitrites did, indisputably, have unsubstitutable health benefits far outweighing their cancer risk. They would still have to be banned on the showing of cancer causation in animal bioassays, even though this action *raised* the net risk to the public's health.

Yet another instance is the trade-off between fuel economy and

safety. Mandating fuel economy means making cars much smaller
and lighter, but this makes them much less safe in the event of a
crash.[29] The EPA mandates fuel economy, but the exacerbated
safety problems end up in NHTSA's lap.

Fifth, the entire process of gathering information to the center,
and evaluating it in order to make a regulatory decision, puts a
premium on scientifically articulated and documented evidence—
that is, on evidence that can be put into an analytical form that an
expert can understand. Information that does not lend itself to
analytical articulation, however significant, tends to be ignored. A
perfect instance of this is supplied by the saccharin controversy,
where the bioassay information concerning the risks of saccharin,
however slight, was stated in scientific terms but the information
on the benefits was entirely anecdotal and experiential. There was
no controlled study, after all, to prove that the voluntary use of
saccharin-containing foods by consumers actually did yield
measurable health benefits. Instead, there was only a mass of personal testimony; much of it, to be sure, from people who should
know—namely, diabetics and doctors. There was also evidence in
the form of the market actions of consumers after saccharin's
possible cancer risk was publicized (namely, continued demand
for artificially sweetened products and occasional hoarding), and
finally, there was the blizzard of letters opposing a saccharin ban
that buried Congress and the FDA. But none of this really
"counted" with the decision-makers at the FDA who, in the absence of "scientific" proof, in effect assigned a value of zero to the
alleged health benefits of saccharin.

A sixth feature of regulation is this: implicit in a regulator's
Weltanschauung is his perspective from the "center" of things. On
one hand, this can lead to adding someone's costs in with someone
else's benefits, possibly maximizing thereby the sum of public
welfare, but also obscuring the wide diversity in individual
cost/benefit circumstances. On the other hand, this can lead to active efforts to redistribute costs and benefits. The point of view of
individual consumers is very different, and for good reason. One
perennial theme in the saccharin debate, for instance, was how
young children and the fetuses of pregnant women might be
especially at risk. The concern with fetuses arose because of the
necessity for *two-generation* rat studies in order to see any car-

cinogenic effect; *in utero* exposure evidently magnifies this activity. The concern with young children was generated because a child weighs less than an adult, hence the per-pound dose from drinking a diet pop would be much higher than that for an adult doing the same; also, children have a much longer life expectancy ahead of them in which cancer could develop from a childhood exposure. But obviously, neither of these concerns applies to the elderly who are husbanding their weight and who might want to sweeten their morning coffee with saccharin in order to be able to enjoy a cocktail at night without a steady weight gain. Here the calorie reduction would be immediate, while the possible cancer risk would be far beyond their expected time horizon. From their point of view, they could only lose from a saccharin ban, no matter how much the society as a whole, when risks and benefits were centrally summed, might benefit.[30]

In the same way, the FDA faced a dilemma over the drug phenformin, which is an oral antidiabetic drug that has a lifesaving capability for a small number of patients but that also has fatal side effects in some cases. In practice, in addition to the small number of patients for whom the drug was strictly necessary, it was overprescribed to millions of others. In 1978 the FDA withdrew approval of the drug for this reason, despite the clear need for it by certain patients. Once again, the utilitarian calculus of central decision-makers overruled the individualized benefits to particular persons.[31]

And concerning the redistributionist potential of a central viewpoint, OSHA's many attempts to protect workers by imposing costs on industry (bounded only by the consideration of avoiding bankruptcy and hence causing unemployment) often exhibit redistributionist motivations. A clear example is OSHA's resistance to allowing the use of economical personal protective equipment as one means of assuring worker safety; instead, costly "engineering controls" are preferred.[32] No case has been made that personal protective devices cannot be made perfectly effective with the proper incentives for workers (such as a pay supplement) to use them. The main reason for OSHA's preference is simply that it is not as comfortable for workers to use respirators, earmuffs, and so forth.

Another redistributionist instance is the 55 miles per hour

speed limit. This is alleged to save lives, but it does so only at the cost of delay to millions of drivers. Charles Lave calculated that, ignoring the monetary costs and looking only at the costs in terms of man-years of delay to save a life, it "costs" 102 years of extra time riding around in one's automobile to save one life.[33] Since the average age of a saved life would be about 30, with a further life expectancy of some 40 years, this particular safety measure costs more than twice as many life-years as it saves. This is a strikingly perverse result.

A seventh serious problem with regulatory decision-making is that new scientific findings that happen to relate to a current regulatory situation are hastily used to influence decisions before the result has been confirmed by the normal process of replication and peer review. These findings often turn out to be invalid. One instance is the so-called Califano report, which purported to prove that as much as 38 percent of all cancer in the United States could be attributed to occupational exposures. This report was generated within a government agency and offered during testimony to OSHA; but it was never peer reviewed, nor was it published in a scholarly journal, and it had no listed authors (although it had ten listed "contributors," at least seven of whom have since disavowed the claims made therein). The prestigious medical journal, *Lancet*, deplored this report. Sir Richard Doll, one of the world's great experts in epidemiology, called it "scientific nonsense" and, in collaboration with another renowned expert in statistics and epidemiology, Richard Peto, mopped up the floor with this report for its mortally flawed methodological defects in a recent article in the *Journal of the National Cancer Institute*.[34] Yet, like an ever-resurrecting creature from the dead, this report continues to rattle around government agencies, wholly unkillable, influencing regulatory policies.

Another scandalous instance of the use of faulty science to sway policy is the study, released in May 1980, of chromosome defects among the residents of houses near the Love Canal in Buffalo, New York. Apparently due to a management blunder by the EPA, which had hastily commissioned it to develop data for forthcoming litigation, this study overlooked the detail of a matched control group without which it would be impossible to determine whether the observed frequency of chromosomal aberrations really was abnormal and, if so, whether it could be attributed to the toxic seepage from Love Canal. It could, after all, also be due to smoking (tobacco smoke abounds in mutagens), alcohol consumption, medication (including X-rays, which are proven mutagens), or job-related chemical exposures. Despite this fatal defect, the preliminary results were interpreted as possibly suggestive of hazard, and President Carter, four days after this news hit the headlines, decided to evacuate some 700 families to temporary quarters at a cost to the taxpayers estimated by *Time* to be some $30 million. Of more lasting significance is the fact that legislation setting up a "superfund" to deal with the hazards of toxic-waste disposal sites was passed by Congress very shortly thereafter, almost certainly due in part to the publicity generated by this report. Yet an EPA panel set up to review the results of this study, viewing photocopies of the original chromosome slides, disagreed with the preliminary interpretation and concluded that no indication of excessive chromosome abnormalities was present.[35]

A further example concerns nitrites. Two years ago Paul Newberne of the Massachusetts Institute of Technology announced that the incidence of lymphomas (a type of cancer) among rats fed nitrites was twice as high as among controls. This was the first study to implicate nitrites directly in cancer, and then-Commissioner Donald Kennedy of the FDA credulously acclaimed it: "We know more than enough about the Newberne study to be convinced that it is well done and strongly supports the hypothesis that nitrites are carcinogenic *per se*." One year ago, however, the FDA announced that it had reviewed the same data Newberne had used and found his interpretations of pathology to be flawed; the experiment had in fact shown no increase in lymphomas or any other kind of cancer that could be attributed to the nitrite treatment.[36]

Yet another instance is the Canadian epidemiology study announced four years ago that related the use of artificial sweeteners by men to a 60 percent increase in the risk of bladder cancer. While there were serious grounds for doubting this conclusion (such as the fact that *no* other study of this much-investigated chemical, saccharin, had ever shown such an indication), Commissioner Kennedy, already embroiled in the effort to ban saccharin on the basis of suggestive rat studies, hailed the result, saying: "[This study] makes it virtually certain that saccharin is a human carcinogen." Yet this "virtually certain" result has since been decisively refuted by a giant project carried out by the National Cancer Institute, its results reported in December 1979. The NCI research, carried out with vastly larger numbers of subjects, found no elevation in risk among typical users of normal amounts of artificial sweeteners. Two additional studies confirming this result were reported shortly thereafter.[37]

There are other cases in which poor science influenced regulatory policy. The original rat study allegedly showing that cyclamates caused cancer has not been confirmed upon further investigation, and Bernard Oser, who conducted the study, disclaims that result. Yet cyclamates remain banned. And the Alsea II study of the effect of 2,4,5–T spraying on the incidence of miscarriages and birth defects among residents in and around the town of Alsea, Oregon, has been shown to be invalid. But the EPA ban on virtually all uses of 2,4,5–T, for which this study was directly responsible, remains in effect.[38] The frequency of such examples shows that this problem is pervasive and systemic, not anecdotal.

In conclusion, the actualities of regulatory decision-making are a "fer piece" away from what was ideally envisioned in the enabling legislation and the preceding agitation to set up these agencies. Regulatory decisions are often not demonstrably effective, not timely, not in the interest of substantial classes of individuals, not conclusively in the public interest either, and not even predicated on good science. One is led, therefore, to reexamine the question of whether there is a true need for the sort of regulation we have, and to look at other social mechanisms and institutions for ways to secure safety. Could there be existing means, for instance, either in the market or in the liability law, that act in a decentralized, prompt manner to foster good safety practices or that could be encouraged, with a modest amount of tinkering, to do so? One is also led to question the interpretation put upon the classic "impelling events" that have midwifed the birth of the "new" regulation in the first place.

And it doesn't take much in the way of skepticism to discover that many of the celebrated impelling events that led to the setting up of regulatory authorities were *not* due to the negligence or deliberate sloppiness on the part of companies, but were due to genuine ignorance. Others, it turns out, were self-correcting. For example, the thalidomide tragedy, which was instrumental in securing the passage of the 1962 amendments to the Food, Drug and Cosmetics Act of 1938, was wholly caused by the fact that primates have a peculiar sensitivity to the teratogenic effect of this drug. Thalidomide does *not* have this effect on the usual animal test species, i.e., rats and mice. The testing done before it was released was entirely consistent with what was understood to be safe practice at the time. Two points really are pertinent here: first, this drug *was* kept off the American market by *already* existing legislation, so there was no need to pass even more legislation (which imposed more extensive costs and delays in new drug introduction); and second, the many millions of dollars paid by the responsible firms to the victims of this disaster as a result of lawsuits supply a stiff incentive for the management of these and all other drug firms to increase their safety testing in the future.

Likewise, the diethylstilbestrol (DES) calamity—in which, in the years following World War II, this artificial hormone was administered to pregnant women thought to be at high risk of miscarriage (e.g., diabetics)—was at the time recommended by leading medical researchers at Harvard University. That this would lead, two or three decades later, to a low incidence (about 0.1 percent) of a rare cancer in the daughters born to these mothers was something that could not have been foreseen in animal tests. Even to this day there are medical experts still recommending the use of such hormones for particular high-risk pregnancies.[39] It was not negligence, then, that led to this sad outcome, but an absolutely unforeseeable consequence of our best medical science. The companies that manufactured DES are currently being sued under a novel legal doctrine that relieves the plaintiffs of the burden of having to demonstrate that the product of a specific manufacturer resulted in their cancer; i.e., the manufacturers are being held collectively responsible. Such an evolution of the law can be expected to increase the caution with which companies offer products to consumers in the future.

The Love Canal episode is another which did not result from gross negligence on the part of the Hooker Chemical Corporation. The wastes were disposed of in a manner that not only complied with all regulations and good practice at the time but that *did*, in fact, successfully contain them until the barriers were disturbed by the home construction and road building in the area, which included the laying of sewer lines right through the Love Canal.[40] Far from being an instance of crass corporate insensitivity and shortsightedness, and hence a prime example of the pressing need for more regulation by disinterested public agencies, the interpretation is much more complex. Hooker is, not surprisingly, being sued by residents and state and federal government agencies for some $12 billion.[41]

Instead of Regulation

Even this cursory glimpse, then, of impelling incidents shows that they are not at all what they seem, and that they do not lead simply to the interpretations that have traditionally been put upon them. This fact, combined with the defects in actual regulations that we have seen above, leads to the question of whether there are other, less defective, means of securing the safety of the public. These need not be perfect, since we now know that the true comparison should be between imperfect regulatory mechanisms and imperfect market and liability institutions, not between perfect regulation and a be-warted market. Two of the most important of these institutions pertinent to the problem here under review are tort law and liability, and insurance. Both of these will be examined in more detail elsewhere in this volume but, as William F. Buckley might say, "Concerning which, a few observations."

The notable fact about the impelling incidents mentioned above is that the corporations involved did not get off scot-free but were held accountable for their actions by the courts in ordinary damage suits. And the sums involved have been enormous—so enormous that many, many years of routine operations would be needed to generate the profits to pay off these claims. This means that foresighted management will find it worthwhile to spend nearly as much time in avoiding the risk of suits as in ordinary profit-making activities. Several recent quotes from the popular press illuminate the fact that these incentives are having the desired effect:

As doing business has grown more legally perilous, staff lawyers have also come to the aid of their companies by practicing preventive law. Allied Chemical has assigned counsel to follow its products even after they are in the hands of other manufactures. They watch for potentially hazardous uses and, in the process, build a record of responsible action.[42]

There is only one way that you can get societal safety and that's out of liability—making it more expensive to do it in the unsafe way. . . . The Federal Government's efforts in getting a safer society are infinitesimal compared to what we do. It's the difference between a million-dollar verdict and a $500 fine,

says Harry M. Philo, past president of the Association of Trial Lawyers of America, a group whose members, according to the *New York Times*, spend "most of their time suing manufacturers of automobiles, airplanes, collapsing buildings, toxic chemicals and other products described as dangerous and defective in behalf of injured persons".[43]

That statement—"the difference between a million-dollar verdict and a $500 fine"—puts it in a nutshell, since regulatory agencies' sanctions are in fact rather modest. And with the recent growth in litigiousness, and in the sorts of liability claims being entertained by the courts, these incentives are growing ever more formidable. Courts are more and more adopting the rule of strict liability, which means that negligence need no longer be shown in consumer injury cases. This, together with the vast increases in personal awards by juries in recent years, suggests the enormously increased incentive that the liability process has had and will have on decision-making by private business. It is true, to be sure, that the liability process may not work very efficiently or justly in particular instances,[44] but the system as a whole seems to be developing ever more powerful incentives for avoiding situations that cause injury to the public and hence expose corporations to lawsuits.

Nevertheless, certain problems are evident in the use of liability as a general cure-all. One is Workers' Compensation, which strongly limits a worker's right to obtain full damages from his employer for harm he suffers from hazardous working conditions. In particular, he cannot recover for pain and suffering, but only for direct medical costs, lost wages, and impaired future earning capability. This limits the effectiveness of the fear of being sued as an incentive influencing management decisions in the area of worker safety. Another problem is that the proof-of-harm standards that Workers' Compensation tribunals and the courts have developed to deal with ordinary worker-safety issues are not necessarily adequate for dealing with hazards that operate statistically— that is, where only a few out of a group of similarly exposed workers actually develop a disease. As noted, this is the usual case with cancer where, with a type of brain cancer usually found in no more than 1 person among 100,000, a finding of 5 cases in a group of 100 workers would be considered conclusive by an epidemiologist while a jury or judge might wonder why the other 95 workers did not get the cancer. To the extent that courts do not accept epidemiologically persuasive but not traditionally causal evidence, the risk of liability will not be feeding back to influence safety decision–making.

Another difficulty with relying on liability as the full answer to securing justice is the large cost in money, time, and personal commitment required to pursue a lawsuit. This means that the liability system has limited effectiveness where the damages sought are modest. If these weaknesses could be overcome—by reforms that reduce the costs of bringing suit and that establish presumptions or evidentiary rules that would facilitate proof— then liability law could become an efficient inducement indeed.

The other institution that might exercise a substantial role in public safety (especially if the liability system were made smoother and more reliable) is the insurance industry. The essence of the insurance business is to maintain a careful balance between premiums and payouts, with the premiums having to be set at a level that will cover claims but not so high that business is lost to competitors. Risk identification and assessment is therefore something that casualty insurers do every day, and their profits and losses depend on doing it as accurately as possible. More important, such firms can substantially reduce the chances they will have to pay out claims during a term-insurance contract if they provide safety improvement advice to their insurees. Making safety improvements helps everyone in this transaction, since a better safety record will permit lower premiums in the next contract period. Thus there is a joint interest between insurer and insuree to improve safety, rather than the adversarial relation that currently obtains between regulator and regulated party. This structure of incentives favors, at least in principle, the effectiveness of the insurance mechanism as a means of fostering safety consciousness.

Both the insurance and liability institutions would, with reference to the problems of central regulation, share certain advantages. For one, the informational problem would be reduced, since information about the "state" of things would not need to be funneled to a central agency in far-off Washington for decision; local courts, and insurance companies on the spot, would assess the circumstances and make decisions. For another, since the decision-making units would be much smaller, the scope of aggregate, utilitarian thinking, with its obliteration of individually varied risk/benefit situations and redistributionist temptations, would be lessened. Since delay in implementing sensible safety measures would have costs (because of the liability exposure or high premiums during the implementation period), the adoption of safety measures should be speeded. Bad science would be penalized by means of financial losses. Because the incentives guiding decision-making would be to a large degree financial, non-scientifically documented information (such as the experience and opinions of consumers) would be incorporated through consumers' market choices.

Concerning the problem of dealing with scientific uncertainties, a reasonable alternative to the maximin strategy would be to let local decision units differ in their assessments of those uncertainties (and in particular, to allow them to distribute themselves among uncertain alternatives in accordance with local or even individual risk/benefit circumstances), so that when mistakes were made, their harmful effects would be limited to the local area and not spread across the country (for example, banning saccharin could well lead to a public health disaster, if saccharin actually is currently lowering health risks for millions of diabetic and elderly overweight people). And finally, resistance to economic concepts such as cost/benefit analysis, cost-effectiveness, and risk assessment should be lessened, since these techniques are already in wide use by businesses.

There is, then, ample reason for thinking that these institutions, though by no means either perfect or frictionless, could, by

careful reforms, have their effectiveness in the task of risk reduction strengthened. These could complement (and to some extent,
replace) the regulatory structure now in place.

5

WILSON E. SCHMIDT

The Role of Private Capital in Developing the Third World

It is obvious to all that the incomes of the poor people of this world could be increased if they had more capital and know-how with which to work.

It requires only a casual review of the facts to see that the volume of government aid—aid in the sense of gifts and loans at very low interest rates and long maturities—has been stuck at $13 to $14 billion per annum in real terms since the early 1960s. Despite the enormous growth in the real income of the rich countries' governments, they have not been willing to give more. This is a reality.

This essay originally appeared in *The Third World: Premises of U.S. Policy,* edited by W. Scott Thompson (revised 1983). References to other papers are to chapters in that book.

The outlook for stealing is also limited. After their success in forming the OPEC cartel and the less substantial achievements of the International Bauxite Association, the poor countries have few commodities left that are so readily cartelizable. This, too, is a reality.

Faced with these facts, the poor countries have gone to collective bargaining for a New International Economic Order (NIEO), demanding of rich governments in a variety of international forums almost every conceivable dispensation, subsidy, and privilege one could imagine. Their efforts to gain more aid receipts, starting with the United Nations Conference on Trade and Development in 1964, failed; it is doubtful that the new efforts will be more productive, for the myth that it is better to give than to receive has been broken.

The Possibility of Mutual Gain

The problem lies in the fact that there is no mutual gain in aid except in patently political situations. The donor gives up real resources; the poor country gains real resources. It is sometimes thought that by accelerating economic growth abroad through aid, we increase the market for our exports. Higher incomes abroad no doubt do increase our exports. But the absurdity of an argument that aid somehow, therefore, pays for itself is revealed by the fact that private merchants or manufacturers give only samples to their customers; aid to develop their customers is not part of their marketing strategy. The outlook for intergovernmental transfers of resources is grim indeed.

What, then, should the poor do? The answer is for them to give something in return for what they need—something that is tangible, real, and worthwhile, so that the *private* sector of the rich world is co-opted into their progress. The idea of mutual gain is fundamental to energizing the rich to help the poor.

Both the opportunity provided by this prescription, and the poverty of the aid approach, can be demonstrated by a simple numerical example. Suppose the return on capital in a poor country is 20 percent, while the return on capital in a rich country is 10 percent. If the rich country's government gives the poor nation $5 per annum for each of the next twenty years, the rich country is poorer by that amount, while the poor country is equally richer. If the rich country's government loans $25 for twenty years at zero interest, the poor country gains $5 per annum by investing the $25 at 20 percent; the rich country loses $2.50 per annum, because it could have invested the $25 at home at 10 percent. *But* if the rich country were to loan $100 at 15 percent interest for twenty years, the poor country would still gain $5 per annum (investing the $100 at 20 percent, but paying 15 percent interest), *and* the rich country would gain $5 per annum, earning $15 on the loan as compared to $10 at home. Only in the last example is there mutual gain. It hardly takes much understanding of human behavior to see that the transfer of resources is much more likely to materialize when there is mutual gain.

What is required for mutual gain is that the return on capital in the poor countries exceed that of the rich countries, and there is a fair amount of evidence that such is the case. At least, this is what can be deduced from a casual reading of project feasibility reports of the World Bank over the years, and the observation seems to be supported by at least some of the literature surveyed by Nathaniel Leff.[1]

The Burgeoning International Capital Market

There is a great deal of money to be had out there. What does not seem to be fully recognized by the poor countries is that there is an international capital market open to them as well as to the rich, from which they can borrow on terms more cheaply than they can invest at home. In 1977 alone, $74 billion in capital was transferred among countries through international bond issues and Eurocurrency credits. This international capital market has exploded from a mere $8 billion in 1970. The poor countries began to catch on to it in 1968, when the Ivory Coast borrowed $10 million. Use of the market by the poor countries grew from $375 million in 1970 to $16.2 billion in 1977, far faster than that of the rich countries. What is striking, however, is that two countries— Brazil and Mexico—accounted for almost half of the borrowing by the poor countries in 1977 and have, in fact, dominated the figures through much of the last decade. Some countries do not even want to borrow on this market. The Indian government in 1973 limited such borrowing for fear of alienating lenders who offer soft terms—low interest rates and long maturities—which is surely a comment on the donors' policies, if not on the Indians themselves. Clearly, there is money out there for qualified borrowers who desire it.

To qualify, a nation needs to convince the creditor that it can repay the debt and cover the interest in the currency of the lender. If it can do this continually, it need never really repay, because the creditor will be eager to repeat and expand the loan or credit when it comes due.

What makes a country credit-worthy in the eyes of private international lenders is complicated. It includes a variety of measurable features of the borrower, such as the portion of a nation's foreign currency earnings that needs to be set aside to cover the amortization and interest on existing external debt. It also includes a variety of features that are truly immeasurable, such as how good the financial managers of the government are, and how ready their access is to the chief of state.

Cutting through all of the details, the real issue in credit-worthiness is whether the borrowing nation can be expected to come up with the foreign currency to repay the principal and cover the interest. This, in turn, depends on the condition of its balance of payments—the flow of foreign currency in and out of the country.

The two keys to a country's balance of payments are (1) its exchange rate system, and (2) the productive use of externally borrowed funds.

Most of the poor countries maintain fixed exchange rates. They far too often employ exchange controls to limit their citizens' demands for foreign currency and, in doing so, maintain overvalued currencies that in turn restrict their exports because their prices are too high in foreign markets. They seem forever short of foreign exchange. Needless to say, this makes them less credit-worthy.

A costly side effect of the fixed exchange rate system employed by so many poor countries is that these countries waste their own resources. Their central banks hold foreign currency reserves of around $50 billion (this figure excludes members of the OPEC countries). This is partly for the protection of their exchange rates; they can draw upon these reserves when export receipts fall or import requirements rise instead of allowing the exchange rate to depreciate. Such reverse investments to the rich countries probably yield from 6 to 10 percent—there are no figures—which means, in this world of inflation, a zero real return. Were these resources invested at home by the poor, they would, at 20 percent, yield $10 billion per annum, a figure not far from recent aid levels of $13 to $14 billion. (This, of course, is a rough figure open to a number of objections, including the possibility that, if these funds were not held by central banks, private citizens would instead have to hold them. But such an objection is doubtful when one considers that the simultaneous removal of both the fixed rates and exchange controls would bring home capital illicitly kept abroad by residents because of the exchange controls.) No one forces the poor nations to fix their exchange rates. Since April 1978, each country has been free under the rules of the International Monetary Fund to choose its own exchange rate system. Most of the rich countries have wisely chosen to allow their currencies to float, albeit in a managed way.

The second requirement for credit-worthiness is that the borrowed funds be employed productively—either directly or indirectly. This, in fact, is intimately related to repaying the funds in foreign currency and to the exchange rate system. To repay the borrowed funds and the interest, the debtor nation must raise its exports or cut its imports to gain the foreign exchange to repay the debt. This, in turn, means that it must produce more goods and services than it previously used at home in order to create a surplus to be exported. By employing the borrowed funds productively, the national output will be smoothly converted into foreign currency.

The seeming contradiction with an earlier point by Nathaniel Leff (chapter 13) is thus also reconciled. He has argued that the "continuing high rates of output growth . . . require ever-higher levels of imported inputs and hence ever-increasing absolute magnitudes of foreign borrowing" (p. 256). The availability of capital to finance such imports is indeed limited, as he has argued, but with floating exchange rates an adjustment in import levels would be automatic.

A number of the poor countries have unwisely restricted the use of international capital markets to fund projects that would directly yield foreign exchange, either by substituting for imports or by expanding exports. In doing so, they have greatly constrained their borrowing opportunities. Such policies rest on a lack of understanding of how the balance of payments adjusts to exchange rate changes. If the externally borrowed funds are used wisely in projects unrelated to trade, they will yield a return in local currency; when that currency is used to buy foreign exchange to repay debt, the debtor's exchange rate will depreciate, automatically stimulating exports and constricting imports. The export surplus provides the required foreign exchange. There is no requirement that external funds generate foreign currency directly, as long as the authorities are willing to let the exchange rate change.

Multinational Corporations

The other major source of resources that has been less than fully exploited is the multinational corporation. Because they are large and transcend national borders, these corporations have access to enormous amounts of capital. In the early 1970s, such companies in market economies had $165 billion invested abroad. Perhaps a fourth of this was in poor countries. American companies alone had invested $30 billion in the poor nations, out of a total of $137 billion invested abroad by the end of 1976.

The benefits that accrue to the poor countries go well beyond the provision of capital. Multinational corporations provide jobs: a recent estimate put the jobs generated by American multinationals in poor countries at 1.5 million. They provide training to local citizens. They provide scarce entrepreneurial and managerial talent. They provide production know-how, market information, and sales organizations. They provide markets for local suppliers. Because they are multinational, they connect the poor with the world, widening their horizons and increasing their opportunities. And they even provide a conduit for tax funds from the rich nations; e.g., under U.S. law, a multinational corporation's tax liability to the Internal Revenue Service (IRS) is reduced, within limits, to the extent that it pays income taxes abroad.

Despite these benefits, the normal rhetoric of the day has the multinational corporation as the villain of the piece. The catalog of charges: stifling local entrepreneurs, employing too little labor per unit of capital by virtue of transferring excessively advanced technology; evading taxes; producing products that the poor buy but ought not to be allowed to have; charging excessively for know-how; absorbing poor countries' savings through local borrowing; using bribery; charging extreme prices behind tariff protection; depending on head-office decisions that can adversely affect the jobs, foreign exchange receipts, and real income of the host nation, etc.

It is difficult to feel sorry for a corporation—after all, it is not a natural person. But sometimes it is subject to absolutely ludicrous complaints.

Some of the charges appear to be flat wrong. Some are right, but only if one grants certain assumptions about the good society, assumptions that are arguable. Some are right, but miss the culprit. Some are, in fact, backhanded compliments, for they amount only to the argument that the host country is not getting as much as it should from the multinational, rather than that the multinational is doing harm.

The charge that the multinationals use more capital-intensive techniques of production, implying fewer jobs in the host countries, appears to be wrong. A number of studies confirm this conclusion. A particularly interesting one reports that multinationals from both the West and the East exhibited lower capital/labor ratios than their domestic counterparts in over two hundred manufacturing firms in Thailand.[2]

The charge that the multinationals produce goods that people ought not to have—e.g., Coca Cola—somehow misses the misery of the poor, the relief that such simple pleasures provide from grinding poverty. I doubt that those who make such charges would wish to dictate or even comment on the religious choices of the poor; why should they dictate or comment on their other consumption patterns?

Tax evasion is said to arise through transfer pricing. For example, if a foreign affiliate of an American parent corporation produces a product that becomes a component of another product produced by the parent in the United States, the price charged for the component determines where the profit is. Opportunities for profit shifting, and thus tax evasion, occur as long as these are not arm's-length transactions. But research in the area fails to point in any particular direction. In any event, since it is clear from the data that the host countries receive substantial revenue from the subsidiaries of multinationals, this is the backhanded compliment that the host countries do not get enough.

The complaint that multinationals charge excessive prices behind protection from imports misses the culprit. Added to this complaint is the argument that the excessive profits are then taken out of the country. This at first appears to be correct, because we have shown that the external funds must be used productively if they are to provide the extra goods and services required to increase exports in order to pay the earnings transferred abroad. The proper answer to the charge is that if, in fact, the protection reduces the real income of the country, it should not have been afforded to the product in the first place by the host government. Furthermore, the fact that the income may be taken out of the country is irrelevant; if local investors instead of foreign investors provide the resources, the country's real income is still reduced, because the local investors' investible funds are wasted in projects with artificially inflated returns.

Bribery obviously does exist. The odd element in the picture is that it is the multinationals, and not their critics, who should complain. Unfortunately, in many poor countries corruption in government is the norm. To get action, a bribe must be paid. Because this raises the costs to the multinational, the necessity to bribe is a deterrent to investment. It is indeed unfortunate that the laws, regulations, and procedures of many poor countries put officials in a position to demand bribes. The thief is the one who accepts the bribe, or the government that gives such people positions of power.

There are a variety of methods by which the poor countries deter the inflow of capital and know-how through multinational corporations. One is plain, if perhaps unintended, harassment. For example, a number of years ago I had a casual conversation with an American middle manager in a very poor country. He told me that he had just solved a very serious problem—namely, getting a work permit for a highly skilled welder to come into the country for a brief period of time. He had solved his problem by bribing the clerk at an airline company to inform him when a certain high official of the government would next be flying out of the country. When he got that information, he further bribed another clerk to reserve a seat next to the official. In the course of the flight, he raised the problem of the work permit, the official invited him to visit his office when he returned from the trip, and after that meeting the work permit was issued. It struck me as a hard way to do business.

Another deterrent is the threat of expropriation. During 1946–1973, no less than $2 to $3 billion of U.S. investment in poor countries was expropriated (not including the nationalization of Middle East petroleum producers). Presumably, the risk of appropriation deters some investments altogether. In other cases, it causes the multinational to commit less capital to the host country while still achieving the scale of operations it desires. It can do this, for example, by borrowing capital in the host country for some of the investment in plant and equipment, thus reducing the amount of the parent's assets at risk. Alternatively, it can sell equipment to a host country leasing corporation, which leases the equipment to the parent's subsidiary. Both techniques reduce the net transfer of capital to the poor country. By borrowing locally, it does not put its money into the country in the first place. By leasing, it gets its money for the equipment immediately by selling it to the local leasing company.

Obviously, multinationals do not like to have their assets expropriated. But if they are, they would then like fair compensation for them, as is thought to be the rule of international law. This, however, has been a serious problem. One estimate puts uncompensated losses at $6 billion in the postwar period. As one United Nations study recently put it:

Although compensation in the event of nationalization is usually guaranteed under investment laws, legislation tends to be vague concerning the criteria for the assessment of compensation and the modalities of compensation payments. Consequently, disagreements over the amount of compensation due to a nationalized enterprise have become a frequent source of investment disputes.[3]

Another deterrent to multinational investment is the frequent requirement in the poor countries of some minimum amount of local control and ownership (sometimes majority) —by either the host government or local nationals—of foreign-owned subsidiaries. Clearly, all other things being equal, a parent corporation would prefer to own 100 percent of its foreign subsidiary, if for no other reason than that it makes the operation simpler. The adverse effect of Colombia's requirement, along with other restrictions under the Andean Common Market, that foreign corporations divest their majority ownership, is shown by the fact that in the four years after the decision (in December 1970), registration of new foreign investments in Colombia averaged $31.4 million per year, compared with $114.7 million per year in the preceding four years. The sad part of this is that the host country puts up cash that it needs badly for other purposes, and puts it in the place of funds that otherwise would be available from abroad. For example, there was one government in a poor country that insisted on owning half of a small refinery that the foreign investor was willing to carry 100 percent. The government's presence surely would not have made it more efficient, and thus added nothing to the national welfare. What the government wanted was the income, when projects elsewhere in the economy cried out for financing. One would have thought that, in its own national interest, the government would have at least insisted that the foreign investor put the relinquished funds somewhere else in the economy.

Still another deterrent is the limitation imposed by some governments of poor countries on the transfer of profits of foreign subsidiaries to their parent corporations, and thus to their stockholders. Some impose limits on payments of royalties for patents and know-how. Some restrict the payments of externally owned debt. And some place limits on the repatriation of capital originally invested.

Obviously, all of these controls limit the freedom of action of the multinationals and, therefore, make foreign investment less attractive to them. More specifically, the delays in the repatriation of profits have dramatic effects on the rate of return from foreign investment, because compound interest takes its toll. Thus, an American parent corporation able to invest at home at 15 percent will find that its yield on foreign investment whose income is blocked for five years will fall by 25 percent, as compared to the situation in which it can repatriate the foreign income annually. Future managers of multinational corporations are now being tutored in the concept of the terminal rate of return—the return they obtain after the profits are unblocked. As foreign investment decisions are most often based on rates of return, such restrictions markedly reduce the incentive to invest.

As explained above, what is so senseless about restrictions on the repatriation of profits is that profitable foreign investment produces a rise in the national output that, if the exchange rate is allowed to move, automatically transfers the profits at no net cost to the nation. The multinationals are often charged with taking more money out of the country than they bring in. Even if such were the case, this argument shows that it is costless as long as the original capital investment is employed productively.

Finally, many of the poor countries prohibit foreign investment in selected areas. Some of these may make sense, such as national defense industries. But others, like banking and insurance, do not. The capital and money markets of many of the poor countries are sorely underdeveloped; the presence of more bank and nonbank financial institutions would help to relieve the glaring defects in the mechanisms for allocating scarce capital within those countries. Particularly objectionable are the restrictions—such as those imposed in India and in the Andean Common Market countries—on foreign investment in industries already "adequately serviced" by existing enterprises. By dulling the threat of competition, the performance of the existing countries clearly is worsened.

Having mentioned the wide variety of restrictions on foreign investment imposed by poor countries, one should note the incentives that many of those same countries provide to foreign investors. These often take the form of exemptions from various import duties on raw materials and components, as well as income tax holidays. As anyone familiar with the notion of gains from trade knows, the exemptions from import duties are, with or without foreign investment, a step in the right direction from the standpoint of the poor country. The income tax holidays are, however, a useless incentive, as we shall see below.

The Problem of Subsidies and Mutual Gain

We began by emphasizing the importance of mutual gain if the private sector of the rich countries is to be co-opted into the progress of the poor. When looked at from the standpoint of the rich countries, the extent of mutual gain is suspect by reason of the policies of their governments.

The United States government has for years provided insurance to American foreign investors against losses due to wars, civil disorders, expropriation, and currency inconvertibility. In 1974, Congress mandated that the Overseas Private Investment Corporation (OPIC) increase private participation in these activities and ultimately withdraw completely from direct underwriting of these risks by 1979–1980. Subsequent to the mandate, OPIC made major efforts to gain the participation of private insurance companies in its portfolio, but this has largely failed, presumably because the risks are too great given the premiums. The Carter administration recommended that OPIC be continued without the mandate for privatization. In 1981 the Congress, with Reagan administration support, lengthened the list of OPIC insurable risks to include civil strife and extended the agency's underwriting authority to late 1985.

Failure to attract private insurers suggests that there is no true mutuality of interest. In effect, OPIC is a subsidy. The rate of return to the United States, given the risks, does not exceed the rate of return on investments at home. If it did, OPIC would not be necessary. In such circumstances, *if some public purpose* is served by providing help to the poor countries where investors will not go without such guarantees, the optimal policy is no investment at all. Instead of subsidizing private investment by continuing OPIC, the Reagan administration should replace it. It is cheaper to simply apply a straight grant to the poor, as a simple numerical example will show.

Reversing the constellation of yields on investment assumed earlier, imagine that the return on capital in the poor country is 10 percent, while in the rich country the return is 20 percent. Clearly, there is no loan or investment that will benefit both the rich and the poor country simultaneously, inasmuch as the lender (investor) would require 20 percent or more, whereas the poor country would gain only if the charge for the capital were less than 10 percent. If the rich country's government were to subsidize the loan (investment) to the extent of 11 percent, both the *private* lender (investor) and the poor country would gain. For example, the lender (investor) could charge 9.5 percent on a loan of

$100; the poor country would gain $0.50 per annum by investing the funds at 10 percent, and the private lender (investor) would gain $0.50 with a 9.5 percent return, plus the 11 percent subsidy included, compared with a 20 percent return at home. But the true cost to the rich *nation* is $10.50 per annum, because it obtains a return of 9.5 percent from abroad but foregoes a return of 20 percent at home on the $100 loan or investment. It would, in fact, be far cheaper simply to give the poor country $0.50 per annum. There is no loan on any terms that would benefit the poor country and also cost the rich country less than $0.50. Subsidized loans or investments are not the economical option when the yield on capital in the poor country falls short of that in the rich country. Hence, even if some public purpose is served, OPIC is not the answer.

The other reason why the notion of mutual gain is suspect stems from the U.S. tax code. As suggested earlier, the multinational corporation provides the poor with a conduit to the U.S. Treasury. Within certain limits, the Internal Revenue Service permits American investors to take a credit against their U.S. income tax liability for income taxes levied by foreign governments on the income they earn abroad. The consequences of this for mutual gain can also be seen from another numerical example.

The United States actually loses real income on some of our investments, because multinationals choose between foreign and domestic projects on the basis of their comparative returns after taxes. For example, suppose a multinational had a choice between a domestic and a foreign project, both of which yielded $100 before taxes, and both of which required the same investment. If the foreign corporate tax rate were 40 percent, while the U.S. corporate tax rate were 50 percent, the domestic project would yield $50 to the company (with the other $50 going to the IRS), while the foreign project would yield $50 (with $40 going to the foreign government and, because of credit, only $10 going to the IRS). Here we see that the U.S. credit would decline if the host country provided an income tax holiday, so that the $40 foreign tax would fall and the after-tax profit on the foreign project would remain unchanged, making the tax holiday ineffective.

Since the after-tax return would be the same, the multinational would be indifferent between the two projects. But if the company flipped a coin and the foreign project won, America would lose. The reason is that the United States gets only $60 of foreign currency with which to buy foreign goods and services from the earnings of the foreign project, whereas it gets $100 of additional goods and services from the domestic project. The total amount of goods and services available to Americans as a whole is $40 lower than it could be. In effect, foreigners take $40 of the output in one case, and none in the other. If the investment were made at home, our taxes could be $40 lower.

This situation would be rectified if the U.S. tax code were amended to reduce the U.S. corporate tax rate on income from domestic investments to offset the effect of the credit. The same result could be achieved if the code allowed the American corporation to deduct as costs (rather than credit) foreign taxes in computing its tax liability to the IRS. In that event, the investment committee would be choosing between a foreign project that yielded only $30 after all taxes ($100 gross income minus $40 foreign taxes equals $60 net income before U.S. taxes; $60 less the U.S. corporate income tax rate of 50 percent equals $30) and a domestic project that yielded $50 after all taxes. It thus would prefer the domestic project; therefore, the United States' real income, measured in terms of goods and services available to it, would be higher than it otherwise would be.

One estimate, clearly rough, suggests that annual American investment in the poor countries would decline by half if the deduction were substituted for the credit. That still leaves a substantial flow of capital to help the poor, a flow that would be enhanced if the poor would reduce their restrictions on private foreign investment. After adjusting the U.S. tax laws and rescinding OPIC, there would be a mutuality of gain.

Development Strategies and Obstacles

Benjamin Franklin may have been a great diplomat, a fine editor of the Declaration of Independence, and perhaps a superb flier of kites, but he was a lousy economist: "He that goes aborrowing goes asorrowing." "A man may, if he knows not how to save as he gets, keep his nose to the grindstone." Franklin obviously did not perceive the value of capital markets. He did not see that, by borrowing the savings of others, the grindstone and the nose are soon parted.

As long as the rate of return on capital in the poor countries is higher than in the rich countries, a fact for which there is fairly persuasive evidence, there is a possibility of mutual gain by the transfer of capital from the rich to the poor countries. By offering a tangible return to the rich, the poor can co-opt the private sectors of the rich countries into their progress, gaining the benefits of their capital and know-how. With aid levels roughly constant in real terms since the early 1960s, and with the outlook for further stealing limited, capital transfers that provide mutual gain are the most viable option to enhance the economic well-being of the poor.

Unfortunately, the poor countries have not taken full advantage of the international capital market, which has grown rapidly in the 1970s. Because they employ fixed exchange rate systems in so many cases, their ability to repay debts is weakened and their credit-worthiness impaired, making them less attractive to lenders than they otherwise would be.

Furthermore, the poor countries have imposed a variety of obstacles to investment by multinational corporations, institutions that have great access to capital and knowledge that could be put to work in the poor nations to the benefit of both. Complaints about the performance of the multinationals are flat wrong, miss the culprit, or are really backhanded compliments amounting to the charge that they do not do enough for the poor.

To insure mutual gains to the rich countries, some adjustment in their tax systems is required, along with the cessation of such subsidies as insurance against various losses.

III

National Security
and
Foreign Policy

6

ELMO R. ZUMWALT, JR.

Heritage of Weakness: An Assessment of the 1970s

The central consensus of U.S. security policy is that national security and prosperity are tightly linked to the security and prosperity of Western Europe and Japan. After World War II the United States built a strategic nuclear deterrent, formed the North Atlantic Treaty Organization (NATO), allied itself with Japan and other western Pacific allies, and rebuilt Europe's and Japan's war-devastated economies. These policies were an immense success. Our strategic superiority and conventional capabilities to reinforce allies guaranteed the security of Western Europe and Japan, with the consequence that the world would soon witness the "economic miracles" of their recovery.

In the Third World, America's vast military, technological, and economic superiority was apparent. Deployed U.S. forces inhibited

This essay originally appeared in *National Security in the 1980s: From Weakness to Strength*, edited by W. Scott Thompson (1980).

Soviet adventurism, promoted stability, and prevented the West's isolation. Economic cooperation with Western Europe and Japan helped to promote the smooth flow of trade and capital. An economically open world ensured mutual prosperity and linked the Third World to the West.

But by the 1970s these strengths had given way to weakness. The United States failed to match the Soviet Union's investments in military power. The Soviets achieved an exploitable nuclear superiority. Growing Soviet conventional and tactical nuclear forces now have the capability to overrun NATO and to cut sea lines of communication critical to the free world. The buildup of the Soviet Pacific Ocean fleet and the fortification of the Kurile Islands threaten Japan's security.

The Soviets' emerging capacity to project power on a global scale (including the skillful use of proxy forces) has made it much more difficult and costly for the United States to maintain stability in the Third World. Since Vietnam, the nation has been less willing to make the attempt to preserve stability. Yet the West remains dependent on imports of oil and other mineral resources. Instability in the Third World, then, is a clear and present threat to Western prosperity.

In short, both the security and prosperity of the industrialized democracies are hostage to the Soviet military buildup and to increased Soviet activism in the Third World. This chapter compares that buildup with what has happened to U.S. military power and then assesses the economic and political implications of the "balance" for the enduring competition with the Soviet Union.

Assessment of the U.S.—USSR Military Balance

We must begin with a harsh truth: In the 1970s Soviet defense outlays steadily increased while those of the United States declined. It is difficult to estimate Soviet defense expenditures precisely, but serious estimates agree. The dollar value of Soviet military expenditures now exceeds U.S. military spending by 25 to 50 percent (see figure 1).

Between 1970 and 1978 the Soviet Union increased real defense expenditures by at least 4 percent a year. Real U.S. defense expenditures declined steadily from 1970 to 1977. In the 1970s Soviet

Figure 1

**U.S. and Soviet Defense:
A Comparison of U.S. Outlays with Estimated
Dollar Costs of Soviet Activities**

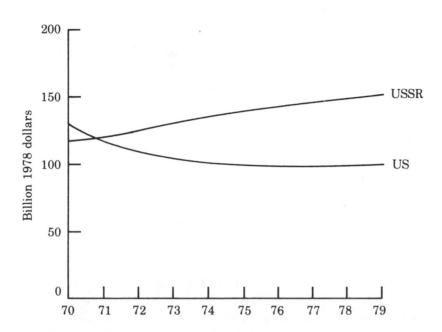

military expenditures totaled nearly 30 percent more than ours. Soviet procurement of strategic forces was more than two and one-half times that of the United States. Soviet general purpose force acquisitions exceeded ours by 50 percent. These diverging trends in military spending have a predictably adverse impact when our military strength is compared to that of the Soviet Union.[1]

Strategic balance. The results are especially apparent in the strategic nuclear balance. The Soviets drew abreast the United States in the number of strategic launchers in 1971—a simple measure of the strategic balance. They now surpass us, 2,582 against 2,141 (figure 2).[2]

If SALT II (Strategic Arms Limitation Talks II) is ratified, the Soviet Union by 1985 will have, in comparison to the United States, twice the area destruction capability, twice the throw

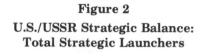

Figure 2
U.S./USSR Strategic Balance:
Total Strategic Launchers

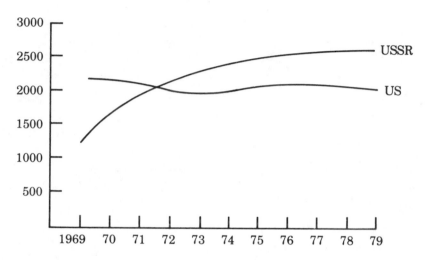

weight, thrice the megatonnage, and quintuple the ICBM/SLBM (intercontinental ballistic missile/sea-launched ballistic missile) hard target kill capability, plus at least equal accuracy. The United States may have an advantage in independently targeted warheads. But the Soviets are rapidly adding warheads and, according to the latest intelligence, they may have as many or more than the United States by 1985.

To the extent that our obsolescent B–52s can get off their bases and arrive close enough to launch their cruise missiles, to the extent those cruise missiles can penetrate to their targets through unconstrained Soviet air defenses, and to the extent no allowance is necessary for the offsetting capabilities of their Backfire bombers, we will have a continuing—in fact, growing—superiority in what is called delayed countermilitary potential. But this will not be sufficient to offset the other factors.

The United States has phased out most of its continental air defense capabilities. The Congress has forced the virtual deactivation of the U.S. antiballistic missile (ABM) defenses permitted under the ABM treaty. The U.S. Navy has never been permitted to ask for equipment, men, or funds for the purpose of developing antisubmarine warfare (ASW) capabilities designed to attack Soviet SLBMs.

The USSR has persistently put more emphasis on active defensive capabilities than has the United States. The Soviet Union has devoted a truly enormous effort to air defenses. It has deployed 12,000 surface-to-air missiles (SAMs) and approximately 2,700 interceptor fighters. It has deployed thousands of inter-netted air defense radars and ground-control-interceptor centers. It is deploying a new high capability mobile phased-array radar/missile system called the SAX–10. It has recently been reported that the SAX–10 is being deployed on surface ships, thus affording the Soviets the beginnings of a capability to deploy a forward barrier defense against our bomber aircraft.

The Soviet Union has maintained and somewhat improved those ABM capabilities it had earlier deployed in the Moscow area. It is significantly increasing the capabilities of its phased-array ABM "early warning" radars around the periphery of the USSR. This is permitted under the ABM treaty on the assumption that such a network, being close to the periphery, could be destroyed with limited effort in the event of war. It is also assumed that even more powerful radars in the Moscow area could, with greater effort, be destroyed. However, the large Soviet phased-array radar deployments, when coupled with the development of a transportable phased-array ABM radar and high-acceleration interceptor combination, could give the USSR a reasonably rapid breakout toward an important "damage limiting" ABM capability, particularly against U.S. SLBM reentry vehicles (RVs).

Even more important are the civil defense aspects of the problem. Many who have carefully studied the situation concur that a well-executed civil defense program—to evacuate most of the population of Moscow and Leningrad would take several days— can reduce fatalities by a factor of five to ten and can also substantially reduce industrial damage and the time necessary for economic recovery. There is now little doubt that the Soviet Union is working on civil defense much harder than was realized as recently as two years ago.

It was reported in 1979 that the executive branch would request an expansion of the U.S. civil defense program to include work to enable more rapid evaluation of our urban population in the event of a crisis. Approval of such a program could have been of major importance. Later, however, the president reversed his position. It should be noted, however, that our program, had it been approved, would have cost about one-tenth of what the executive branch estimates the Soviets are spending on civil defense.[3]

When one takes all factors into account, including the fact that the initiative is apt to be theirs—that their command, control, and wartime intelligence facilities are substantially harder and more diverse; that they have more and harder hard targets; that their active defenses and their civil defense preparations are substantially greater than ours—it is quite evident that strategic parity is slipping away from us and that the Soviets can be expected to achieve meaningful strategic superiority, probably by 1982 and most certainly by 1985, unless we take the most urgent steps to reverse current trends.

More complex measures of the strategic balance thus give us the same picture as figure 2. The Soviets have been ahead since the early or mid-1970s and are getting further ahead.[4]

The higher megatonnage and increasing accuracy of Soviet warheads give the Soviets a significant counterforce against our land-based missiles. With this they will have the capability to launch a first strike capable of disarming America's land-based missile force, a reality that no strategic arms agreement will change.[5] The Soviets will achieve this capability in the early 1980s.

It is argued, of course, that despite the annihilation of our land-based missile force our deterrent would remain effective; that we would strike against Soviet cities by sea-based missiles and long-range bombers. But we must remember that Soviet strategy envisages warfighting. The Soviet leaders would be emboldened in confrontations with the United States by their calculation that the low average yield of our remaining weapons would render damage levels "acceptable." They believe that an effective civil defense plan (city evacuation, dispersal of industry, etc.) would limit casualties to 3 or 4 percent of their population. Though this figure is probably a bit low, the Soviets seem to believe it. The loss of our land-based missile force, the low average yield of our sea-based missile force, and a potentially low level of fallout (resulting from the U.S. decision in the 1960s to reduce the "continuing radiation" potential in exploded U.S. warheads) might well hold down Soviet casualties.

But the story with U.S. cities is much different. They would be exposed to a second strike by the Soviets' remaining land, sea, and air-launched strategic forces against which we have little or no defense. The higher megatonnage of the Soviet weapons (and their failure to reduce the "continuing radiation" levels of their exploded warheads) would guarantee horrendous American casualties. Thus, in a future crisis, a U.S. president may be faced with a stark alternative: strike first—to avoid loss of the land-based missiles but in a strike which would be incapable of destroying more than 65 percent of Soviet ICBMs and incapable of gaining poststrike strategic nuclear advantage—or yield without a fight.

How did we come to such a pass in such a vital military capability? There were faulty perceptions of the Soviet Union and its strategic doctrine. We long failed to recognize that the Soviets aimed at an ability to fight and survive a war with strategic nuclear weapons. U.S. reliance on deterrence by an assumed "mutual assured destruction" also contributed, as did the mistaken notion that Soviet programs were mere reactions to ours. With these views, our leaders not unnaturally limited the size of our forces and slowed the development of new weapons. These mistakes were compounded by an unwillingness to devote sufficient resources to defense when other national problems demanded attention and while the Vietnam war and Watergate crises generated a public antipathy toward adequate defense budgets. Finally, the American arms control community sees strategic arms limits as an end; the Soviets see arms limits as a means of achieving nuclear superiority.

Tactical nuclear balance. This balance is particularly important in Europe. Tactical nuclear weapons are generally embedded in conventional forces, making it difficult to compare U.S. and Soviet tactical nuclear forces. Nevertheless, in 1979 the USSR, in comparison to NATO tactical nuclear weapons, had two to three times the number of theater nuclear systems, six times the area destructive potential, ten times the throw weight, and twenty-five times the megatonnage.[6] This balance, too, has been shifting against the United States.

Table 1
U.S. and Soviet Theater Nuclear Systems in Europe

	USSR/Pact	U.S./NATO	Ratio: Pact to NATO
Delivery vehicles			
Missiles	1,213	326	3.72
Aircraft	4,151	1,679	2.47
Total	5,364	2,005	2.68
Tactical nuclear warheads			
Missiles	978	232	4.22
Aircraft	1,266	1,179	1.07
Total	2,244	2,411	1.59

Source: International Institute for Strategic Studies, *The Military Balance, 1979–1980* (London: International Institute for Strategic Studies, 1979), pp. 118–19. Figures exclude U.S. Navy Poseidon missiles, not a tactical system, which had to be taken off Soviet strategic targets in the early 1979s and directed against Warsaw Pact targets to partially relieve NATO's tactical nuclear defensive.

Table 1 demonstrates the two- to three-fold advantage that the Warsaw Pact enjoys over NATO in the numbers of nuclear capable systems that could be employed in a European war. Table 1 also shows that the Warsaw Pact enjoys a more than 50 percent edge in the number of warheads available. These advantages are likely to grow if the Soviets continue to introduce rapidly the SS–20, a mobile intermediate range ballistic missile (IRBM) that can hit targets in Europe from the Soviet Union.

The December 1979 NATO decision to deploy 572 Pershing II and cruise missiles to Western Europe constitutes a minor political plus for NATO but does not redress NATO's tactical nuclear disadvantages.

Conventional force balance. Our inferior strategic and tactical nuclear forces are particularly worrisome in view of the increasing strength of Soviet conventional forces.

Striking the balance of conventional forces is difficult; nevertheless, the trends of the 1970s are clear—the Soviets have achieved conventional military superiority. During the 1970s the

Figure 3
U.S./USSR Military Manpower 1964–1979

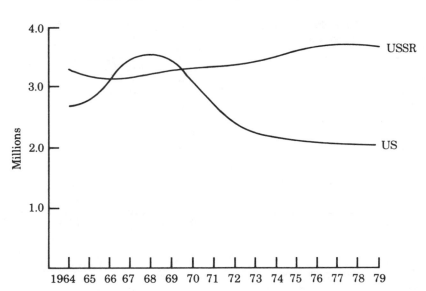

size of U.S. conventional forces declined steadily and our qualitative *advantages,* despite many technological developments on our
side, declined as well. Meanwhile, most Soviet forces were growing
impressively in size and capability.

The number of men in the armed forces is one measure that indicates overall conventional force capability. As figure 3 shows,
Soviet military manpower has grown steadily since the mid-1960s.
Manpower strength in the United States exceeded that of the
Soviets while we were engaged in Southeast Asia, but is now
nearly 25 percent below the 1964 level. In 1979 Soviet forces num-
bered 1.6 million men more than ours—80 percent larger. This
confers immense potential advantages. (The enormous military
manpower of the People's Republic of China [PRC] is often cited as
an offset to Soviet manpower advantages over NATO. But Moscow
has added to its Warsaw Pact forces while compensating for PRC
manpower along the Siberian border.)

To mold manpower into effective fighting forces requires
deployable units, armed with appropriate weapons and provided

Figure 4
Trends in U.S. and USSR General Purpose Forces

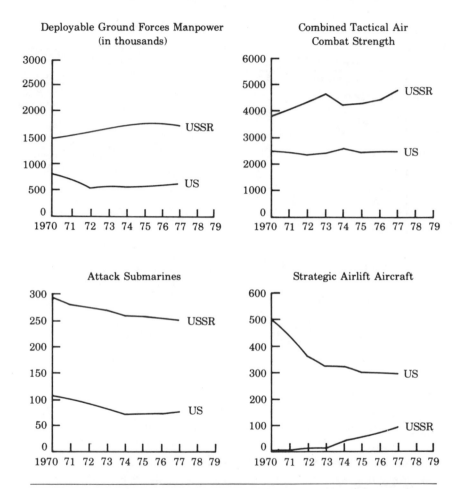

Source: John M. Collins, *American and Soviet Military Trends* (Washington, D.C.:
Center for Strategic and International Studies, 1978).

with the necessary training, support, and leadership. These
dimensions make the comparison of conventional forces difficult.
But the charts of figure 4 indicate the trends in the balance of
general purpose force capabilities.[7]

In each of the main force categories—land forces, tactical air,
and naval forces—the Soviets have some important advantages.

Their deployable ground force is three times the size of ours. Similar comparisons of the equipment for ground forces such as tanks and artillery show large and growing Soviet advantages. Tactical air combat strengths favor the Soviets by a two-to-one edge; only in sea-based tactical air does the United States have an advantage. Naval forces are even more difficult to compare. Submarine forces are shown in figure 4 because of their importance in Soviet general purpose naval forces. They pose the most severe threat to our sea lines of communication. It is true that the United States has an overwhelming advantage in aircraft carriers and sea-based aviation, but the Soviets have an overwhelming advantage in long-range land-based aviation with antiship cruise missiles— backed up with increasingly global access to client states' airfields. This advantage is further enhanced by the asymmetries of geography, which place most critical theaters (the Persian Gulf, in particular) close by Russia and far from the United States. And in their surface forces the Soviets outnumber us in warships and embarked cruise missiles. In my judgment, *the Soviet naval and air forces are clearly capable of gaining control of the Western Pacific and the Eastern Mediterranean in a fight with the United States.* U.S. control of the North Atlantic in a major war would be doubtful.

Note that the United States is still ahead in strategic airlift, reflecting a long-recognized need to be ready to support our allies overseas. Not shown is our clear advantage in amphibious and marine troops assault capability. But in another important component of mobility, merchant shipping, the United States is falling further and further behind the Soviets with each passing year.

These comparisons have stressed numbers of forces. Numbers do not tell the whole story, but they tell a vital one. They affect perceptions of U.S. strength and of commitment by political leaders and their constituencies around the world. And the perceptions relate to real advantages that larger forces provide. They can fight in several places at once. They can attack without lengthy and visible concentration of forces. They can saturate defenses. They can absorb losses and fight longer. Outcomes of war games, fleet exercises, and analytical calculations confirm that a conventional war at sea with the USSR would probably lead to our defeat.

Europe. On a smaller but more pertinent scale, the erosion of U.S. military strength is evident when comparing the East-West balance in Europe. In 1962 the total number of U.S. forces in Europe was 434,000; the number is now about 300,000. On the other hand, the Soviet Union has increased the number of divisions in Eastern Europe from 26 in 1967 to 31 today, while adding some 25 divisions to the Chinese front. The Soviet divisions in Eastern Europe are also larger now than in 1967. Indeed, Warsaw Pact forces today enjoy a significant edge over NATO forces in men, tanks, and tactical aircraft. While NATO has been improving the quality of its forces, the Warsaw Pact has done more. Although NATO forces retain the edge in some areas like tactical aircraft, Soviet weapons in such other areas as surface-to-air missiles, some armored vehicles, and artillery are superior. However, the introduction of new weapons like precision-guided missiles and antitank and air-defense missiles may cut down the Warsaw Pact's advantage in tanks and planes. But these weapons alone are not NATO's salvation. Without adequate numbers, without adequate maneuver capability, without the ability to counterattack, with scandalously inadequate logistic support, NATO remains inferior. The balance in Europe has shifted against the West.

What practical options do these advantages in tactical nuclear and conventional forces in Europe open to the Soviets?

The first, most obvious, and most dangerous is a disarming first strike with theater nuclear weapons against Western Europe. Given the number, accuracy, and yield of those weapons they now possess, Soviet leaders might feel confident of achieving success while suffering only small losses themselves. They might calculate that they could destroy a very substantial portion of NATO's nuclear storage and delivery systems (including French and British weapons) along with most of NATO's reserve and conventional munitions. This result could be achieved with a sudden surprise attack. The experience of the Czech invasion in 1968 suggests that final Soviet preparations could be concealed from NATO even during a period of building international tensions. They could also attack NATO command and control centers, leaving Western Europe's cities more or less intact as hostages against an answering nuclear blow from NATO.

In this situation Soviet leaders could reasonably hope that the political will of NATO's European members would disintegrate. After all, NATO's options would be stark indeed: their nuclear counterforce capabilities would be devastated, their capacity to fight for long at the conventional level would be sharply reduced, and to mount countervalue nuclear strikes against the USSR would seem to invite suicide.

And what of the political will of the United States in the face of these Soviet actions? The Soviets would almost certainly assure the United States that their war objectives were confined to the European theater and back up that claim with an explicit threat to launch an all-out nuclear attack on the United States if we interfered. After all, they would explain, U.S. casualties in Europe had been purposely held to a minimum and the remaining Americans there were at their mercy. More fundamentally, the Soviets would explain that Europe was in the Soviet sphere and not that of the United States. "A nuclear war would be pointless; the United States would gain nothing and could lose everything," they would tell us.

These are not very attractive prospects for NATO, but they are one potential consequence of being on the short side of the military balance in Europe. The scenario can be varied, of course, and no doubt will be Soviet conventional superiority continues to grow.

A second likelier option is a nonnuclear attack against NATO. The Soviets realize that a more desirable course would be to defeat NATO with a conventional force blitzkrieg *before* NATO political authorities could fire the alliance's nuclear arsenal. Recent changes in the structure of the Soviet forces in Europe are designed to achieve that objective while also improving the capacity of those forces to fight in a nuclear environment.

The third and likeliest option is the use of the threat (of their capabilities to carry out the first two options) to achieve, without fighting, the dissolution of NATO and Finlandization of Western Europe.

Asia. In the Pacific, naval forces weigh more heavily in the overall conventional force balance. The general picture of the naval balance is reflected in naval deployments to the Pacific: ours decline as theirs grow.

The Soviets have added at least one new major surface ship and one submarine to their Pacific force every year over the last decade. Their fleet now has 70 major combatants, 75 submarines (3 nuclear-powered), and more than 350 naval aircraft. With the addition of vertical takeoff lift (VTOL) aircraft carriers, the Soviets have added a whole new dimension to their naval warfare capabilities in the Pacific.

The U.S. Seventh Fleet, on the other hand, has declined by a third since 1970. Three years ago a carrier task group was withdrawn, leaving the fleet with about 45 ships: 2 carriers, 3 cruisers, 15 destroyers and frigates, 10 amphibious ships, 15 auxiliary ships, and about 4 submarines. Because of its responsibilities in both the western Pacific and the Indian Ocean, the fleet is stretched very thin. Today the United States could not meet simultaneous contingencies against Soviet-supported forces in the Persian Gulf and the Korean peninsula, for example. In the event of war in Europe, the need to transfer some U.S. ships from the Pacific to the Atlantic means that we would be unable to keep open the sea lanes to Japan.

Since naval forces provide our visible presence in Asia, the Soviet naval preponderance there raises serious questions. Japan may see itself potentially cut off from both the sources for its raw materials and the markets for its finished products. The enormity of the economic consequences of such a predicament could induce the Japanese to seek a separate accommodation with the Soviets.

Soviet naval superiority in Southeast Asia as a result of access to Vietnam's bases has flanked and weakened the PRC.

Third World. The Soviet Union began to project conventional military force in the Third World in the late 1960s employing growing airlift, naval, and sealift forces, military advisors, advanced logistic depots, and proxy forces. The Soviet Union clearly created an important new threat to Western interests during the 1970s — a capability to project military power into areas far from the Soviet Union to help accomplish Soviet foreign policy goals.

Medium-range and long-range transport aircraft have given the Soviets the ability to airlift arms, munitions, and personnel to distant parts of the globe. A new aircraft, the Il–76, substantially increases their airlift capability. The Soviets have also created three new airborne divisions, presumably for use in the Third World. The introduction of a new armored vehicle which can be dropped by parachute enhances the effectiveness of these airborne forces.

Soviet long-range naval aviation and worldwide client state bases have given Moscow a capability to cut sea lanes and to project power. The introduction of *Kiev*-class aircraft carriers has now added a capability to project sea-based air power. The size of the Soviet naval infantry has doubled in the past decade. The Soviets' newest amphibious ship is a large, fully capable, amphibious warfare unit. Further, the Soviets continue to add new roll on/roll off ships to their merchant fleet. These ships, now numbering over twenty, can deliver military equipment quickly and efficiently to underdeveloped ports or even over the beach. All Soviet merchant ships contribute to naval capabilities. In addition, the Soviets have been able to employ Cuba's armed forces as proxies.

In some areas of the globe, i.e., the eastern Mediterranean and northeast Asia, Soviet projection capabilities are now clearly superior to ours. In other areas their projection capabilities are still inferior to ours—if we have the will to employ them. If we examine the balance several hundred miles from the USSR: our marine corps far outnumbers the Soviet naval infantry; the transport capacity of the U.S. amphibious fleet is three times that of the Soviets; our thirteen large aircraft carriers outclass the Soviets' smaller VTOL versions; the U.S. Navy has a much greater capacity for sustaining combat at sea than the Soviet Navy; Soviet air transports have a shorter range and lift capability and cannot be refueled in flight; in terms of ton miles per day, Soviet airlift capacity is only half that of the United States.

If we were called upon to intervene in an area where Soviet land lines to the area are available—say, in the Persian Gulf—it would be a difficult matter. The secretary of defense has declared: "The United States would defend its oil interests in the Middle East if necessary."[8] However, there is no NATO plan to react to an interruption of the oil flow. Nor is NATO participation likely. So we would probably have to act alone. Our forces would have to move quickly and in sufficient numbers to overcome the Soviet Union's advantages in manpower and in geographical proximity. Given our limited force levels, we could not call on armored forces; they could not deploy quickly, and if they could their use would weaken our European force.

The proposed quick reaction force (still unfunded) of 100,000 men—if it comes into being at all—is likely to be composed of airborne troops and marines with tactical air support. A division's personnel could be airlifted to the Persian Gulf area in about a week. Unless their equipment is prepositioned at sea, it could take the marines as long as a month to arrive by sea.[9] Offsetting this future U.S. reliance on airlifted forces is the Soviet capability, flying from USSR and Afghani airfields, to destroy all pro-U.S. facilities within a 600-mile radius of Dhahran on the first day. Most important, there is good reason to doubt whether U.S. "light" forces would be effective (even without Soviet force opposition) against heavily armed proxies in the Mideast (Iraq, Syria), a region where war has been dominated by armored units; some recent studies show Iraq conquering Kuwait and Saudi Arabia without Soviet assistance—before the U.S. Marines could be anywhere near the oil fields.

Summary. Clearly, the U.S. military capabilities declined during the 1970s. Just as clearly, Soviet power grew. Soviet force-building efforts have been long underway and now have an impressive momentum. The shift of the strategic balance to Soviet superiority could be disastrous; dominance at the ultimate level of violence gives them freedom to act politically. Their current European tactical nuclear forces and their growing conventional forces there and in other regions allow them to support friends and coerce enemies.

Political Impact of Soviet Military Advantages

If the military balance continues to shift against us in the 1980s, the political effects will be dire indeed. Who can seriously question that the Soviet Union's increasing weight in the military balance now threatens the cohesion of our alliances with Western Europe and Japan? If current trends are not reversed, is not America's implicit alliance with China likely to be short-lived? Wouldn't Soviet activities in the Third World become even more intense? One doesn't need any special insight to answer these questions. The evidence is all around us and new reports appear daily.

Europe. Some in Europe, like the eminent and thoughtful Frenchman Raymond Aron, described the Soviet Union as having the "most powerful army on the planet." The result, according to Aron,[10] is that Europeans no longer put their trust

in NATO, in conventional forces, or in the American nuclear umbrella. They, rather, trust the prudence of the Bolsheviks, sensitive to the incalculable perils of massive attack against Western Europe, and to the importance of economic aid they receive from the West.

The Soviets have hardly been reluctant to exploit this attitude for their benefit. Brezhnev recently tried to intimidate the Western Europeans into dropping plans for modernizing NATO's theater-nuclear forces.

Brezhnev threatened NATO with warnings of unspecified "consequences" if such plans were implemented. To mask the threatening nature of the warnings, he announced a meaningless withdrawal to the Soviet Union of 20,000 Soviet troops and 1,000 tanks from positions in Eastern Europe. Although NATO has so far refused to be intimidated, Brezhnev's action demonstrates (and Dutch and Belgian reluctance to support the tactical nuclear reinforcement of NATO confirms its effectiveness) that the Soviets intend to exploit the fact of their military power to weaken NATO.

Asia. In Asia, the growing Soviet Pacific fleet and the declining size of the U.S. fleet are causing Japanese leaders to question American ability to defend their country. Political leaders in Japan, South Korea, North Korea, and China perceive a "diminishing American presence and an increasing Soviet presence," according to Makota Momoi, a staff member of the Japanese government's Defense Research Institute. Momoi[11] claims that "The American commitment to Japan is now a limited commitment. It is no longer the unlimited commitment Japan once thought it was."

Just as the Soviets have attempted to exploit their military muscle to intimidate the Europeans, they have also pressured the Japanese. In response to Sino-Japanese negotiations for a peace treaty, the Soviets conducted naval exercises off Japan and fortified the Kurile Islands. In effect, Moscow was signaling the

Japanese in no uncertain terms not to line up actively with the Chinese against the Soviet Union.

According to Momoi, the "diminishing U.S. presence and an increasing Soviet presence" in the Pacific is also being noted in China. Vice Premier Li Hsien Nien told the author in July 1977 that the PRC was concerned about U.S. indecisiveness and, in some quarters, "the Munich mentality."[12] Vice Premier Teng Hsiao-ping in January 1978 said that the U.S. military strength vis-à-vis the Soviet Union and our willingness to back our allies concerned China more than did normalization of relations. The United States did normalize ties with China and China's relations with the Soviet Union have worsened. However, the Chinese probably remain concerned that "advocates of appeasement" in the West "hope they can divert the Soviet Union to the East to free themselves from this Soviet peril at the expense of the security of other nations."[13] If the Chinese conclude that the United States lacks the ability or the will to oppose Moscow effectively, they may well be tempted to make amends with the Soviet Union. If this were to happen, not the least result could be the shift to the European theater of some or all of the forty-six Soviet divisions now on the Chinese border.

Third World. The Soviets have long been eager to exploit Third World crises for their own political benefit. An undercurrent of anti-Americanism continues to bubble up. Since 1967 they have employed their navy skillfully to produce positive benefits.[14] Now they are beginning to use airlift and other military capabilities as well. With each success they gain the opportunity for further activity. Cuban cooperation has given them wide options for projecting their power. Examples of Soviet activism in the Third World are legion: Afghanistan, Angola, Cambodia, Ethiopia, Iran, Iraq, Oman, Somalia, South-West Africa, Syria, Vietnam, Yemen, Zimbabwe-Rhodesia. These Soviet moves present the most immediate threat to U.S. interests.

Moscow's willingness and ability to exploit Third World crises have complicated U.S. efforts to maintain stability in the Third World. Washington's difficulties in maintaining strong ties with the oil-rich states of the Persian Gulf in face of Soviet activism are particularly evident. Soviet successes in Ethiopia and South

Yemen have obviously weakened the confidence of Saudi Arabia and other Persian Gulf states in the U.S. willingness to protect them. As one Saudi minister put it,[15] "Why is the United States stepping from one fiasco to another? In Ethiopia, in Somalia, in Afghanistan the United States left the field to the Russians without as much as an attempt to stop them." This, in turn, has complicated U.S. efforts to secure a Mideast peace settlement and to assure continuing access to Mideast oil. Feeling the need to accommodate pro-Soviet states like Iraq and Syria, the Saudis, after the peace treaty between Egypt and Israel, went along with much more stringent sanctions against Egypt than originally expected.

Soviet activism clearly complicated U.S. efforts to maintain stability in Iran. Soviet radio broadcasts helped inflame popular feeling. In warning the United States against intervening on behalf of the legal government of Iran, the Soviets were flexing their military muscle in an attempt to intimidate the United States. Even though the United States did not get involved in the Iranian revolution, Moscow's warnings and U.S. inaction represented a Soviet political victory in the eyes of many in the Persian Gulf area. If we had decided to become involved, we clearly would have had to take Mr. Brezhnev's warnings into account. Soviet military might gives such warnings a weight that prudent decision-makers cannot ignore.

Soviet arms shipments to Syria, Iraq, Libya, and the Palestine Liberation Organization (PLO) made it very difficult for the United States to achieve further progress toward a peace in the Mideast. Soviet actions in Afghanistan have been especially disturbing. They gave direct military support to revolutionaries in a bloody coup against an established government. They proved willing to intervene with combat troops on behalf of a new Marxist government facing popular unrest. The availability of this kind of support means that the attitudes of governments like Libya and Afghanistan toward accommodation and reconciliation will be tough and unyielding at best. The emergence of a neutral—and still less, a pro-Western—government becomes most unlikely.

In the Persian Gulf, the government of South Yemen gives the Soviets a toehold on the Arabian peninsula. The South Yemenis in the past have supported the Dhofar rebels against the conservative government of Oman. In 1979 South Yemen launched a mili-

tary attack on North Yemen, acting as willing agent of Soviet subversion in the area. The lesson was not lost on North Yemen; after
accepting U.S. arms to halt the invasion, it sought and won rap-
prochement and arms from Moscow. Across the Red Sea, the
Soviets support the Marxist-oriented military government of
Ethiopia. Although still attempting to suppress the guerrilla warfare of the Eritreans and the Somalis, the Ethiopians give the
Soviets a large pool of potential proxies for intervention in Africa
and the Persian Gulf. For example, if revolutionaries operating
out of South Yemen engineered the overthrow of the Saudi
government, Ethiopian proxies with Soviet help could be used to
sustain a hypothetical revolutionary government. (It was reported
that a small number of Ethiopian troops were in the People's Democratic Republic of Yemen during the Yemeni border war in
March 1979.)

In southern Africa, the Soviets have succeeded in complicating
Western efforts to achieve a smooth transition from the white-
dominated minority governments to majority rule. Through pro-
Marxist governments like those of Mozambique and Angola, the
Soviets have influenced the succession struggle with arms and
training.[16] They have also encouraged the guerrilla struggle in
Namibia (South-West Africa). So far, however, the Soviets do not
appear eager to play a direct military role in these struggles. The
Cubans are hampered by their inability to extricate themselves
from Angola. At this time the Soviets probably lack a proper in-
vitation, for the Africans remain wary of Soviet aims. The Soviets
may also fear South African intervention in the Zimbabwe-Rhode-
sian struggle if they act. Therefore, the British government has
had time to achieve what appears to be a transition to majority
rule, though it may scarcely mark the end of the guerrilla war.

However, the ultimate problem for the West lies with the Republic of South Africa. South Africa's mineral resources are a
great economic stake. South Africa's military capabilities and 20
percent white population probably guarantee the current regime's
survival to the end of the century. (After all, the struggle in Zimbabwe-Rhodesia, with only a 5 percent white population, has been
going on for fourteen years.) Western access to South Africa's
mineral resources, however, may be impeded by a protracted guerrilla war which the Soviets are likely to support with arms aid and
military training.

In Southeast Asia, the growing economies of Taiwan, South Korea, Hong Kong, Singapore, Malaysia, and Thailand have been an unexpected source of strength for the United States following the Vietnamese war. Their prosperity, however, is fragile. Dependent on exports for growth, they are vulnerable to dislocations in the international economy that might result from instability in the Persian Gulf. Social and political tensions generated by industrial growth would be exacerbated by a decline in growth. They could trigger unrest for the area's generally authoritarian regimes.

With the help of Vietnam, the Soviet Union could exploit such unrest and sustain any radical government that might emerge out of it. Vietnam has become the preeminent military power in Southeast Asia. However, it is now tied down by war in Cambodia and the threat of war with China. Vietnam also faces severe economic difficulties and political problems related to the absorption of South Vietnam. These many difficulties increase Vietnam's dependence on the Soviet Union for political, military, and economic support. Moscow thus might find the Vietnamese willing to support Soviet efforts to exploit political unrest in Southeast Asia. This fact and Vietnam's concern to destroy all Cambodian opposition could tempt Vietnam to invade Thailand.

In the Caribbean, the Soviets almost certainly will continue to probe U.S. reaction to incremental steps in their military presence in Cuba. The Soviets probably recognize, however, that their scope for action remains limited. They understand that Cuba is still an extraordinarily sensitive issue for the United States. They are therefore not likely to encourage too much Cuban activism in the Caribbean or Central America. More likely, Castro will confine his activities to subversion. Nevertheless, Cuba's acquisition of Soviet short-range transports is a worrisome development since it gives Castro the capacity to airlift troops to trouble spots.

Summary. The trends in the military balance have clearly given the Soviets an exploitable superiority, an advantage they have been using as a shield to protect their political and sublimated aggressions at every opportunity. Our primary alliances with NATO and Japan are long-established relationships with major industrial areas. They are now badly shaken but will not be easily destroyed. But the United States must show leadership in these relationships. They will not endure indefinitely if the United

States proves unwilling or unable to reverse the perilous trends in military capabilities. Nor will they endure if the United States lacks the will to counter direct Soviet pressures on our allies or indirect pressures from Soviet adventurism or anti-American sentiments in the Third World.

The Soviet drive for dominance can be seen most clearly in Asia and Africa. Sometimes Soviet activism in these areas seems piecemeal and opportunistic. This appearance should not distract our attention from the brilliance of that very strategy—probing on many fronts with prompt exploitation of opportunities thus revealed. The result is a determined and long-term effort to reduce our ability and our will to resist Soviet expansion. The immediate focus in on the Persian Gulf, long a traditional Soviet interest and a prize of immense value in the East-West competition. The Soviets see success here as the best way to achieve their overriding strategic political goal of Finlandization of NATO. The next most important Soviet goals seem to be (1) to deny the West's access to the resources of Southern Africa, (2) to achieve a significant foothold in South America. The 1970s have seen major moves directly and through Cuban proxies. So far these have not been answered directly by the Western alliance.

Though the Soviet's proximate goals are in the Third World, their ultimate goal is the subjugation of the free world. They aim to achieve this by threatening our access to raw materials and breaking down our alliance. They have vast military capabilities, but they threaten us more by indirection and subversion than by direct attack. Consequently the political effects of the changing military balance become of paramount importance.

Economic Assessment

The military and political developments of the 1970s illustrate the nature of the struggle between the United States and the Soviet Union. The fundamental rivalry is, so far, an indirect one whose end is not in sight. In this competition the United States and the Soviet Union invest economic power in military forces for global political effect.

To assess staying power in this unending competition, it is necessary to examine economic strengths and weaknesses. Can the massive Soviet efforts of the 1970s be sustained in the 1980s? Are higher U.S. military expenditures economically supportable? The answers to these questions depend on many factors—resources, technology, economic organization, and the willingness to apply economic power to national security purposes.

Economic strength is the United States' great advantage. If we can pull ourselves together and apply our economic strength appropriately, we can reverse the trends of the 1970s. This will require not only renewed military strength, but coordinated economic and diplomatic moves as well.

Economic strength. The best way to gauge the strength of a nation's economy is to evaluate its total production, called its gross national product (GNP). By this measure, the U.S. economy is the largest in the world; the Soviets are second, well ahead of Japan. Over the long haul, the Soviets have been closing the gap. Soviet GNP in 1955 was 40 percent of ours; by 1965 it was half ours; today Soviet GNP is about 60 percent of U.S. GNP (figure 5).

Figure 5

U.S./USSR: Trends in Relative Size of GNP
(Soviet GNP as percent of U.S. GNP)

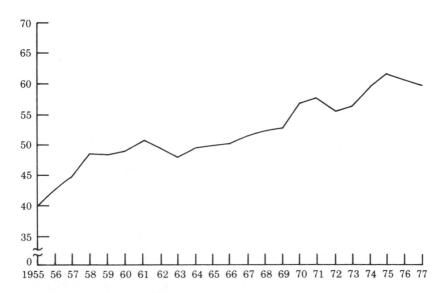

Source: I. Edwards, M. Hughes, and J. Noren, "U.S. and U.S.S.R.: Comparisons of GNP," *Soviet Economy in a Time of Change* (Washington, D.C.: Govt. Printing Office, 1979).

The implication of this narrowing gap is that the Soviet economy has been the faster growing. Soviet economic growth exceeded ours throughout the 1950s and 1960s. By the late 1970s, however, the U.S. economy was growing at a slightly faster rate. Both nations, though, faced a slowdown in the growth.

These aggregate differences in GNP conceal some important details. First, in the United States about 70 percent of output goes to consumption; in the Soviet Union just over 50 percent is consumed. Second, the Soviets have been allocating about 30 percent of their output to investment while investment in the United States uses only 15 to 17 percent of GNP. As a result, the amount the Soviets invest is greater than U.S. investment in recent years. Finally, the United States devotes a much smaller share of its total output to defense—5 percent versus about 15 percent for the Soviet Union.

Soviet economic potential. The slowdown in Soviet growth reflects serious economic problems. Earlier rapid growth was fueled by Russia's vast natural resources. But the costs of natural resources have been rising, the best sources have been used up, and more remote supplies must be developed. Energy costs are rising and the Soviets face serious energy problems in the 1980s. Agriculture continues to lag. The Soviet labor force cannot be expanded further; well over 90 percent of the working age population is employed and the size of the young adult population will decline in the 1980s. As a consequence of all this, productivity has declined and growth has slowed. The Soviet system seems unable to put new technology to use to alleviate these problems. Soviet economic growth is likely to slow further in the 1980s.

On top of this, Soviet economic managers are pressed to provide more consumer goods. A Soviet citizen consumes less than half the goods and services a U.S. citizen does. But though more resources have been put into consumption programs, the results have been disappointing; no significant increase in the availability of consumer goods has been achieved.

Given these economic problems, can the Soviets sustain the momentum of the military programs in the 1980s? A "command economy" such as the Soviet Union will produce what its leaders demand. Soviet leaders want "guns, butter, and growth," but butter clearly takes a back seat to guns and growth. Soviet leaders exert enough control over Soviet society to maintain those priorities in spite of consumer pressures.[17]

Soviet management skill may be weak, but the country's leaders remain determined. There is no sign that the Soviet drive for world supremacy is abating nor is there evidence of slackening in the efforts of Soviet defense industries. The Soviets have long borne the burden of a defense establishment that takes a share of output two to three times larger than that of the United States. Official forecasts predict that Soviet defense spending will continue to increase in real terms:

Soviet defense spending—and spending for military procurement in particular—will continue to increase in real terms at least through 1985. . . .

[Moreover,] we project a continuing across-the-board improvement in force capabilities as new, costly weapon systems are introduced. These will include new land-and sea-based strategic missiles, tactical and air defense aircraft and missiles, ground forces armaments, and general purpose naval ships. . . .

We think it unlikely that economic problems will force the Soviets to reverse their commitment to continuing improvement in their military forces.[18]

There is no reason to doubt the accuracy of this assessment. We cannot count on Soviet economic problems to reduce the threat to our security. We must do that ourselves.

U.S. economic potential. The United States emerged from World War II with its industry intact and it dominated the world economy for twenty-five years. American generosity contributed to our leadership, but most of our influence flowed from the diversity and the technical superiority of the products and services that poured forth from American industry.

Our economic superiority began to erode in the 1970s. Improvement in labor productivity virtually disappeared and economic growth began to slow. Efficient competitors appeared in the international scene. Inflation and unemployment became chronic problems that economic management seems unable to overcome.

Increasing dependence on foreign oil underlined the erosion of U.S. economic power during the 1970s. Our inability to put a coherent policy into effect leaves open a major economic vulnerability, one that our enemies are already exploiting. We are now—and for the unforeseeable future will continue to be—vulnerable to the embargo weapon.

This vulnerability is not limited to oil, though that is the weakest point. We also import a high proportion of other raw materials—aluminum, chromium, cobalt, manganese, nickel, tin, and titanium, for example. Access to these raw materials—at reasonable prices—is necessary to keep our industrial economy functioning.

To preserve our economic strength, we must insure our access to the energy and minerals of the Third World. To accomplish this requires that we contain Soviet military presence and political activism there. This calls not only for larger U.S. military forces, but also for the will to employ them when our interests are being challenged. If we are going to acquire and operate larger forces—and we must—we shall need to devote a larger share of our nation's economic output to national security programs.

Can we do so? We have in the past, and we can do so again. The proportion of GNP devoted to defense has fallen steadily (table 2). The defense outlay in the 1980 budget is less than 5 percent of GNP for the first time since before the Korean War. And it is a smaller portion of the federal budget than at any time since Pearl Harbor.

The Soviets recognize the power of our economy. They know that if we are aroused we have the capacity to regain military superiority. They recognize that as a great threat to their drive for world power. And so they proceed accordingly. They probe and

Table 2
Proportion of GNP Allocated to U.S. Defense

Year	Defense as Percent of GNP
1964	8.2
1968	9.3
1975	6.0
1980	4.9
1984 (projected)	4.7

push and stall and negotiate and feed our delusions. They move cautiously so as not to push America into rearmament. We must recognize a more subtle threat and arm against it.

If the proportion of GNP allocated to national defense could be set at a pre-1975 level—7 percent—about $50 billion more would be available to meet the vital military needs detailed elsewhere in this volume. This would clearly be a good investment. It would yield a high return in protection for our citizens and our interests. The military capabilities acquired would pay off in more certain access to the raw materials our economy needs. But, most important of all, a substantial boost in defense spending would signal our allies or enemies alike that the United States has the staying power for a long conflict.

Conclusion

As the Chinese curse would have it, the 1980s promise "interesting times." The trends in nuclear and conventional forces are moving against the United States. The shift in military power towards the Soviet Union threatens to weaken our alliances with Western Europe and Japan. It has also encouraged Soviet adventurism in the Third World, where we have vital political and economic stakes.

Indeed, it is in the Third World where the danger is most immediate. For the time being, the United States is dependent on petroleum and other mineral resources in Third World regions. Our allies in Western Europe and Japan are even more dependent. Soviet adventurism in Southern Africa—and especially in the Persian Gulf area—threatens our access to those resources. This activism may well grow as Soviet economic difficulties increase in the 1980s.

In the coming decade, leadership in the Soviet Union will pass to a new generation. This generation may well be less cautious and even more impressed with Soviet power than Moscow's present leadership. The Soviet Union's new leaders may be tempted to use their military power directly or through intimidation to gain greater access to Mideast oil resources in order to ease energy shortages at home.

In doing so they might underestimate our will and capacity to resist such a direct threat to the West's security and prosperity and thereby precipitate a general conflict. Or our own perception of our weakness might make deterrence or resistance seem futile. If so, our allies may see no choice except accommodation with the Soviet Union. Western economic cooperation and economic growth would collapse into cutthroat competition. A new dark age, presided over by the Soviet Union, would have begun.

7

WENDELL JOHN COATS, JR.

The Ideology of Arms Control

The anti-nuclear movement portrays Americans as confronted in
the nuclear age with a stark choice between peace and all-out
nuclear war. Indeed, the movement's appeal has flowed in large
part from the dramatic clarity with which its leaders have posed
this choice for the public. Yet contrary to the impression sometimes conveyed by the movement's spokesmen, this way of viewing the problem is not new. Far from articulating a fresh departure in American thinking about nuclear arms, the outlook of the
peace movement can be said to represent the logical culmination
of a doctrine that has dominated U.S. strategic thinking for the
past twenty years—a doctrine in no small measure responsible for
the dilemma in which we now find ourselves. At its heart, the
stance of the peace movement is a reformulation of the modern

This originally appeared in the *Journal of Contemporary Studies* (Summer 1982).

ideology of arms control, which has always sought to avert war by narrowing the alternatives to a choice between nuclear war and peace.[1]

From the outset, the overriding problem with arms control doctrine has been the divergence between U.S. and Soviet views of the problem posed by nuclear weapons. In the 1960s, the United States abandoned for its conventional forces the goal of victory in war on the grounds that such a goal would destabilize the nuclear "balance of terror." Conventional forces were to be used only as a catalyst to negotiations. It followed that they must never be victorious in any decisive sense but rather that they should simply force us back to the alternatives of nuclear war or peace. By the late 1970s, it had become apparent to a number of American observers that the Soviet Union had never accepted this formulation of the military alternatives available to a nation in the nuclear age. Soviet military doctrine continued to permit its conventional forces to aim at decisive victory in tactical operations, and thus the Soviets were able to justify a continuing conventional and nuclear arms buildup. The Soviets persisted in pursuing a third alternative—defeat of Western forces and dissolution of Western political will short of nuclear war. What is of interest here is not the Soviet view, which is quite traditional, but the American view that victory is an obsolete idea.[2] How did we come to this view of all (peace) or nothing (spasm nuclear war), but never victory?

The Arms Control Logic

The doctrine of arms control has implied from the beginning an entire perspective on national security.[3] Under the arms control perspective, the emergence of nuclear weapons is seen to have rendered obsolete the traditional conception of the defense of the state as understood from the time of Xenophon to that of Clausewitz. In the view of arms controllers, the use of force, directed toward disintegration of an opposing political will, and structured by the idea of victory—i.e., superior mass at a decisive point in time and space—is no longer a serious possibility at any operational level. Since nuclear war is not winnable for any side, national security (in lieu of national defense) must be based upon avoiding the use of nuclear weapons—a goal attained by deterring large-scale aggression through the credible threat of unacceptable, punitive retaliation.

Since no sane administration in either the United States or the Soviet Union (the smaller countries are a different problem) would ever intentionally initiate nuclear war, the gravest threat facing all of us is the possibility of accidental nuclear war, arising from the breakdown of communications, misperception of intentions, loss of political will and authority, etc. While for past ages the future was always uncertain, in the nuclear age certainty must become a major goal. Technical assurances, insulated insofar as possible from human error, must be found in order to guarantee that nuclear weapons will never be used. The delicate balance of terror must be kept stable by the establishment of essentially equal weapons levels on both sides through ongoing negotiations aimed at commensurate weapons reductions.

Use of military force in limited areas is permitted, but only for the purpose of returning concerned powers to the negotiating table, where collective bargaining can resume. Any use of force for traditional military goals such as victory or local territorial control is "destabilizing" of the nuclear arms balance and could link together a chain of events leading to an essentially "accidental," all-out nuclear war. In short, like the Hobbesian political theory based upon fear of violent death, United States security policy must continually take its bearings from the worst-case hypothesis—the possibility of accidental nuclear war leading to the destruction of, at least, Western civilization.

This viewpoint had direct policy effects from the mid-1960s, under Secretary of Defense Robert McNamara, through the early 1970s, under Secretary of Defense James Schlesinger. It is still a very influential point of view, although parts of it are not popular with the Reagan administration. As a policy perspective, arms control doctrine can account for a number of various and apparently unrelated developments in United States defense policy since the mid-1960s.

To begin with, it can account for the shape and composition of our nuclear forces with intercontinental range. On most of our land- and submarine-based ICBMs we have relatively small warheads, initially intended to be used against cities, not against other missiles. Cities can be destroyed with smaller weapons than are necessary to destroy hardened missile silos. In the view of arms controllers, to have built large warheads or highly accurate guided missiles would have been destabilizing of the nuclear arms balance because it would have provided us with the capability actually to *defend* the country, properly speaking, rather than simply to assure an unacceptable, "punitive" second strike. (In other words, in the logic of the arms controllers, it might have led to the use of the weapons.) In addition, the several hundred B-52 bombers that make up the third leg of our triad of nuclear forces are now so old (more than two decades) that most U.S. Air Force pilots train in computer simulators to extend the life of the planes. The canceling of the new B-1 bomber in 1977 was consistent with the arms controllers' view that bombers are highly destabilizing due to the fact that they can be sent out to threaten and then be called back, thus contributing to the kind of misunderstanding that might lead to accidental nuclear war. Even the placing of multiple warheads (MIRVs) on our Minuteman III missiles was consistent with the arms controllers' requirement for technical assurances that the weapons will never be used. If you put several warheads on one missile, it follows that you cannot afford to let it remain in its silo during attack. Thus, your opponent is assured of your instantaneous retaliation, and supposedly does not attack in the first place.

The failure to develop means to protect the American people against attack by nuclear weapons is also consistent with arms control doctrine. The absence of any serious civil defense and complete lack of ballistic missile defense, is a product of the view that the ability to defend your population against nuclear attack is itself destabilizing. Stability is best preserved by the mutual assurance of your own and the opposition's destruction. To maintain shelters might encourage the belief that nuclear war could actually be fought: better to leave your population unprotected and thus assure that you can never use the weapons without the destruction of the American people. One consequence of this posture is the almost automatic assurance of political opposition to any leader who dares to confront or finds it necessary to create an atmosphere of confrontation.[4]

Arms Control and Vietnam

Our conduct of the war in Vietnam is also illuminated by the logic of arms control. Fighting was directed by economic models. The aim was to inflict pain upon the enemy incrementally, up to a point of diminishing marginal returns on our investment in lives and money. Our handling of the war made plain to the whole world that American firepower would be used only to bring the concerned powers back to the negotiating table, where collective bargaining techniques would be used to solve differences. There was never a serious attempt to achieve victory in the traditional sense or to undertake the measures that victory would have required, such as sustained interdiction of enemy supply lines outside of South Vietnam and consolidation of territorial gains. All these measures would have been, in the arms control model, destabilizing of the nuclear arms balance and might even have mobilized American sentiment behind the war. The trick was to walk a tightrope between mounting American casualties and formulation of serious war aims.

The logic of arms control can also account for changes over the past fifteen years in American tactical doctrine, away from the idea of victory in the land battle as the basis for tactical operations, toward the view of warfare based on the technical problem of "targeting."[5] Behind this shift lies the view that war is ultimately a technical, not a practical or strategic, problem. Again, according to arms control logic, the idea of victory as a guide for the conduct of operations is destabilizing of the nuclear arms balance. It encourages a broad perspective and the tendency to link the use of force to attainment of political goals. Preferred is a compartmentalized, technical approach to warfare viewed as simply a series of discrete problems in targeting, going nowhere in particular (except toward mounting casualties).

The effects of arms control policy can also account for the general ill repute into which United States armed services have fallen, at least until the present administration. In brief, the real enemy becomes one's own military forces, since they are the ones likely to escalate hostilities and call up the specter of all-out nuclear war. At the same time, they are expected to perform certain minimal military functions. Yet since conventional forces cannot be allowed to attempt victory by massing decisive force, but instead must serve only to pressure adversaries into negotiations, in the end they must always lose. Thus they are caught in a double bind: when they lose, they fall into disrepute; but if they show signs of winning they are feared, for then they threaten to escalate the conflict into nuclear instability.[6] Finally, when negotiations themselves force another "graduated" U.S. withdrawal because (1) in our own doctrine we cannot afford to leave the bargaining table without a settlement lest we be guilty of destabilization, and (2) we generally refuse to pressure opponents with military force once negotiations begin, the disrespect originally attached to the uniformed military spreads to the government's diplomacy as well.[7]

Finally, the prevalence of the arms control perspective in and out of government can make sense of three otherwise puzzling recent developments: (1) the rejection of the SALT II treaty (which could never have been accomplished by conservatives alone); (2) "Presidential Directive 59," which authorizes targeting of Soviet military and Communist party command structures; and (3) recent calls for conventional troop buildups in NATO as a substitute for deployment of intermediate-range nuclear weapons in the European theater.[8] The key to the puzzle is the requirement for an *assured* second strike capability to inflict unacceptable damage on an aggressor and thus deter aggression.

The development and production of over three hundred large, new Soviet missiles (SS-18s)—made very accurate through sale of American ball-bearing technology, and soon to be armed with up to ten large warheads apiece—threatens the land-based U.S. Minuteman force, the bulk of our second-strike capability. Since the SS-18 missiles were permitted the Soviets under SALT II, those arms controllers who accepted the argument that our second-strike capability was threatened or made less credible could and did oppose the treaty. To allow our own retaliatory force to become vulnerable is to generate instability in the nuclear arms balance by *inviting* attack. Also permitted within the arms control framework was a publicly articulated targeting doctrine directed toward Soviet Communist party and military targets, making punitive, second-strike retaliatory capability credible in the face of the SS-18 threat. (This is still not the same as building larger, accurate missiles capable of destroying Soviet missiles in their silos.)

The recent arguments to forego upgrading NATO intermediate-range nuclear capabilities in Western Europe, and go to a stated "no first-use" nuclear weapons policy while strengthening conventional forces, are also consistent with the arms control perspective. Such missiles in Western Europe, which could reach Soviet targets in six to eight minutes, will make the Soviets nervous about their own second-strike capability and generally destabilize the nuclear arms balance, on this view. The call for strengthened conventional forces in NATO still suggests no traditional military uses for them, such as trying to win the land battle. Conventional forces are intended primarily to "stretch out" the time for negotiations to end incipient hostilities (most likely through further U.S. accommodation) and thereby to avoid the use of nuclear weapons. This move also aims to placate the European and American peace movements. The point, in arms control, is to get domestic populations to see the alternatives as nuclear war or peace, so that they will put pressure on their political leaders not to confront or escalate—while maintaining a sense of moderation that prevents the same domestic populations from becoming so excited or frenzied that they contribute to instability through sustained unpredictability or even demands for complete, unilateral disarmament.

To summarize, arms control aims to be a full national security policy for the nuclear age. It substitutes the idea of security, through technical assurances and formal weapons agreements issuing from international collective bargaining, for the idea of defense *per se* as the capability to eliminate the adversary's ability to commence or continue hostilities. In short, it attempts to substitute a technical solution (assured retaliation and arms reductions) for what is essentially a political problem, arguing that the possibility of accidental nuclear war makes this a necessity. Displays of resolve and political will must not be permitted, since they might establish the destabilizing link between force and national sovereignty. Finally, by linking the conduct of local military operations to the chain of events that *could* set off accidental nuclear war, it forces both U.S. diplomacy and military policy continually to take their bearings from a possible worst-case scenario.

Yet the new science of arms control is making a serious miscalculation about how to avoid the instability that might lead to use of nuclear weapons. In its obsession with absolute certainty and control, it is backing into the very thing it has sought to avoid—destabilization of the nuclear arms balance. While the goal of deterring the use of nuclear weapons is worthy, the accompanying loss of nerve (reflected in the attempt by arms control advocates to eliminate the political resolve in American leadership that might lead to confrontation with the Soviets) is contributing to a genuinely destabilizing loss of American practical military and diplomatic skill. Not only is this worrisome in the face of a continuing Soviet nuclear and conventional arms buildup, but it forebodes the enervation of political will and resolve in American politics—a development that Alexis de Tocqueville repeatedly warned us to guard against if we would preserve our political freedom as we become more democratic. I shall begin with the discussion of our loss of practical military and diplomatic skill and then take up the problem of our paralysis of political will. Although I believe the former derives initially from the latter, after a time they begin to feed (or starve) one another.

Critique of Arms Control

Each profession has its own ends and means. While there is some room for tinkering with the means of a profession—for instance, exchanging one tool for another—there is not much latitude for altering ends or general goals without fundamentally altering the original profession or replacing it with something else. Furthermore, the attempt to change the end of a profession without changing its means can result in loss of practical skill as the profession wrestles with the problem of determining its fundamental purposes. Something like this happened as arms controllers tried to change the *end* of the military profession to the civil police function of keeping order in South Vietnam, while continuing to demand from it the sacrifices associated with military, not civil police, duties.

Until the new science of arms control, the aim of the military profession was to provide the nation with the least inhumane solution to external problems of force by developing and practicing the expertise necessary to dissolve the ability and will of the opposing force to continue hostilities. The basis of this expertise was tactics, the art of fire and maneuver directed toward massing superior force at a decisive point in time and space known as victory. The art of tactics saw itself as providing a way to end hostilities skillfully and short of eliminating the entire opposing force (and the civilian population it defended). Although tactical operations were conducted with loss of life, the losses were redeemed by translating military sacrifice through strategy into meaningful political achievements.

In addition to this emotional requirement, especially in the face of mounting casualties, there was a practical and even logical requirement for the idea of victory. It was the goal that ordered all the other efforts. All principles of fire and maneuver, whether direct or indirect, were ultimately directed toward massing force to break the enemy's will and ability to continue to fight. It is not clear that anything else has ever been able to justify in men's minds the kinds of sacrifices war demands. (Can even mercenaries be expected to fight for long in the face of mounting casualties without the motivation of political goals?) Once an army begins to take casualties it is forced into either (1) withdrawal, (2) surrender, or (3) offensive actions to eliminate the ability of the opposing force to continue hostilities. Yet under the arms controllers' direction, almost all powers fighting the United States have become relatively equal to it, since we refuse to take the offensive on grounds that it is destabilizing. Thus, we can only accept losses and continue to withdraw militarily and diplomatically.

Victory vs. "Body Count"

It is instructive to scrutinize the confusion of ends involved in the direction of the Vietnam war by arms controller Defense Secretary McNamara and his advisors. Given the overriding goal of avoiding nuclear war, the argument was made that military science could no longer be the science of victory, since the resulting escalation might lead to expanded hostilities with the People's Republic of China or the Soviet Union, and eventually to the use of nuclear weapons. Yet, initially anyway, there was a desire to wield

influence in Southeast Asia to check the expansion of the North
Vietnamese communists and their proxies in South Vietnam. This
meant that force would be used in a limited and controlled way to
inflict pain incrementally in expectation of "marginal" political
aims. Although use of force was to be limited, there was still a
need for some way to measure "success," short of victory. This led
to a measure of "military" success that was able to be quantified
and controlled by the science of economics—the "body count,"
dramatized nightly on television screens across America as a
legitimate military aim. Additionally, arms control introduced
logical muddle into the military vocabulary so that theory would
not contradict practice. The words "strategic" and "tactical" were
redefined as budgeting categories, the former referring to funding
for nuclear weapons with intercontinental ranges. Formerly, the
relationship between strategy and tactics had been hierarchic,
strategy referring to the art of linking together tactical or local
successes in such a way as to defeat the enemy forces. Now the
logical link betwen the two had been severed and the terms given
technical, compartmentalized meanings with no special connection to one another.

In brief, the arms controller calculated that the way to prevent
escalation of military activity in Vietnam was to induce mutation
of the defining principles of the U.S. military profession. (It is far
from evident that any communist army has been willing to accept
the arms controllers' view of tactics.) The link joining tactics,
strategy, and victory was severed, and the body count was introduced as a new measure of military success. The effect on the
professional U.S. officer corps (and in turn on the conscript army
and the American people) was devastating. In short, the purpose
of the military profession was debased. Rather than attempt to
achieve victory through application of tactical expertise, com-
manders were expected to kill as many of the enemy as possible.[9]
Morale, self-esteem, and military effectiveness all suffered as a
result.

The drop in military effectiveness was ultimately a consequence
of the faulty and incomplete presuppositions of the economic approach to warfare employed by the arms controllers. Instead of
looking at human nature as they found it, these men argued back-
wards from what they considered to be the moral imperative of

our times—the necessity to avoid any development that might lead, even accidentally, to the use of nuclear weapons. Human beings would be changed because they had to be changed. A method of employing force in a graduated fashion would simply be imposed universally upon the human psyche: if we killed enough Viet Cong gradually, the will of surviving Viet Cong would diminish, commensurately. But *homo economics* is not the whole man. There is still in us the "spiritedness" spoken of by Plato's Socrates—this thing in people that, when properly channeled, will drive them to make all sorts of sacrifices for political goals, beyond any calculus of utility. Thus the "graduated" inflation of casualties on the Viet Cong simply heightened their resolve to fight.

If this had been done in a decisive and sustained way, in combination with serious interdiction of enemy supply lines outside of South Vietnam, it might conceivably have resulted in a U.S. military victory. But this was not what the arms controllers had in mind, for it would have been an admission and allowance of "spiritedness" and political resolve on our part, a destabilizing eruption. The economic psychology of the arms control model will not admit the existence of a part of human beings not subject to incremental measurement and control, since this would be to concede an impermissible uncertainty in human affairs in the age of nuclear weapons.[10] Yet spiritedness persists in the human breast despite the efforts of arms controllers, and when U.S. casualties began to mount in Vietnam, the spiritedness and political resolve that were not permitted to erupt on the battlefield erupted, as it were, back home in the form of protest *against* the war.

The effects of anti-war protest at home, the limited success on the battlefield (combined with steady casualties), and the arms control approach to bargaining in general all congealed to lessen our diplomatic effectiveness in negotiating even a measured withdrawal during the Nixon presidency. Yet the drama itself unfolded within the script initially written and directed by the arms controllers. Avoidance of nuclear war requires that we avoid confrontation or demonstrations of political resolve. Thus all differences must be open to negotiated settlements; not to reach a settlement is itself destabilizing of the nuclear arms balance. Armed force will be used only to return adversaries to the negotiating table, not to pres-

sure them once they are negotiating, however outrageous or un-
compromising their demands. In time, the direction of diplomatic
negotiations parallels the direction of events on the battlefield—
graduated withdrawal and concessions, with flashes of resolve permitted only to stop a complete rout (itself destabilizing). There is a
cumulative and reciprocal loss of military and diplomatic skill and
effectiveness as both professions are forced to take their bearings
continually from avoidance of any action that might conceivably
destabilize the nuclear arms balance. (This approach to bargaining
reappears in the unequal terms of SALT II. Since in our own models
we could not afford *not* to reach a settlement, we were continually
ratifying the Soviet arms buildup, especially in the form of the
SS-18 missiles and the Backfire bomber.)

The requirement for absolute certainty and control over all
facets of external policy in the interest of avoiding accidental
nuclear war, manifested in the attempt to eliminate anything
resembling spirited independence and resolve, not only results in
our doing poorly in activity requiring the ability to confront (e.g.,
tactics and diplomacy) but also augurs ill for the future of political
freedom in America. It was Tocqueville who, in alerting us to the
conflict between freedom and equality, warned that expanding
equality might well lead to a loss of political balance and resolve as
we were pulled more and more into the realm of things that can be
equalized—material comforts. The hope of preserving our political resolve, according to Tocqueville, lay in preserving the tension
between the democratic desire for material comfort and formal institutions requiring public-spiritedness. Tocqueville suggested
that our political will might gradually be enervated or slackened
as we slid into a kind of benign, unspirited, materialistic despotism. If we cherish political freedom, he cautioned, we must
preserve our political will and resolve. Could Tocqueville have
foreseen that it would be a variation on the Hobbesian theme of
fear of violent death in the form of arms control doctrine that
might exponentially advance the enervation of our political will?

Need for a New Policy

Spiritedness—this opaque, irrational force in us that makes us
angry, and when properly channeled makes us courageous and

leads us to make sacrifices of comfort and even life for family, friends, and country—has always been the political "problem." Whatever its dangers, it is also the basis of our political freedom because it propels us to fight tyranny, or the desire of others to dominate us. Arms control doctrine has chosen to ignore this part of the human psyche and base its calculations on those of our motivations that can be controlled and directed with certainty, treating all motivations as variations of consumer demands, subject to the laws of economic rationality. Perhaps the arms controllers believe privately that spiritedness, and political orientation in general, can and must be unlearned if we are to achieve the stability necessary to survive the nuclear age. And perhaps in private they might admit that some loss of political resolve and freedom is a small price to pay to avoid nuclear war.

But what if they are wrong, as I believe they are, about how to avoid nuclear war? What if the economic psychology on which their model is predicated is faulty and partial? What if political resolve and spiritedness cannot be unlearned at all? Or, what if they can be partially tamed or unlearned, but unlearning them on one side (ours) while not on the other side contributes to instability? In short, how are we to deal with the Soviet SS-18 threat bequeathed us by the arms controllers in such a way as to maintain a stable balance of power?

We might begin by formulating a foreign and defense policy predicated on the understanding that spiritedness is a part of our humanity, and that to avoid nuclear war we must *work with* political resolve, not attempt to exterminate it. To open the way for such a policy, it is first necessary to sever the mythical, automatic link in our policy thinking between instability in the nuclear arms balance and the conduct of tactical operations with conventional forces, and to allow the directing idea of victory to again form the basis for tactics. There is nothing automatically "escalatory" in this aim. A political decision to stop hostilities can still be made; it is not victory itself that is vital, but the *idea* of victory as the integrating concept at the level of tactical operations. This decision might also help to avoid the kind of civilian adventurism that got us into the Vietnam war—the misguided belief that one can use incremental pain infliction for the achievement of incremental political goals. A return to an understanding of the rational use of local force is the best hope for achieving genuine arms control. Such an understanding would assume that (1) even local war is not to be entered into lightly, and (2) if it is entered into, we must be prepared to win locally.

Second, it is essential that we sever in our policy thinking the mythical, automatic link between failure to reach a diplomatic settlement and instability in the nuclear arms balance. If we are to be effective negotiators, we must be able to sit down at the negotiating table and get up without a settlement without violating our own strategic doctrine.

Finally, we must sever in our policy thinking and in the public mind the mythical, automatic link between the capability to defend ourselves and the paralyzing specter of accidental all-out nuclear war. The international instability that is beginning to follow from Western vulnerability to Soviet strategic forces is sufficient testimony to the bankruptcy of the theory that stability lies in never confronting our adversaries and in never demonstrating the political resolve to defend ourselves. In fact, demonstration of the political resolve to defend ourselves is the best hope of avoiding war.

These measures might help dissolve or disassemble arms control as a comprehensive security policy—a policy that leads toward gradual accommodation up to a point either of great instability or of surrender. They would allow negotiations with the Soviet Union on genuine arms reductions to take place within the context of a stable balance of power. Finally, they would remind us that a technical solution to avoid war can never replace a political solution to achieve peace, and that a balance of power has always been the closest approximation to justice achievable in the international realm.

8

ROBERT CONQUEST

The Human Rights Issue

"Human rights" constitute the central crux of the whole relationship between ourselves and the Soviet Union. The suppression of undesirable political, economic, or religious ideas; the persecution of those who express them, by imprisonment, pseudo-psychiatric incarceration, and expulsion from the country; the refusal to allow the circulation of foreign books and periodicals; the banning from their homelands of the million-odd Crimean Tatars, Meskhetians, and Volga Germans; the harassing of the Jews. All this is profoundly distasteful to those who cherish the principles of the Western culture.

There are areas of the world in which tyranny, however distasteful, is not a direct threat to the West; others where the hostile regime lacks any power to harm us, or—itself under threat—might arguably help us. Areas, in fact, where the matter is purely, or almost purely, a moral one. Human rights in the USSR, however, do not concern us simply on principle, but also—and

---

This essay originally appeared in *Defending America: Toward a New Role in the Post-Detente World* (1977, co-published with Basic Books, Inc.)

overwhelmingly—as regards our interests. I shall here be less concerned with the humanitarian aspect than with its profound significance—even on the most cold-blooded calculation—for Western foreign policy.

First, the Soviets' conduct on human rights gives us the clearest understanding of the essentials of their political attitude; and without such understanding our own foreign policy must lack its necessary foundation. Misunderstanding of the nature—and even the existence—of the differences between the essentially divergent political cultures which divide our planet is the central problem of politics today. We are all prone to inappropriate and parochial presumptions about other political cultures and about their deepest motivations. It requires a constant effort of the intellect—and not only of the intellect but of the imagination too—to keep us free from the habit of making these unconscious assumptions about the present thoughts and future actions of the Soviet leaders.

Apart from anything else, the concept of détente seems based on the assumption that those leaders have the same "natural" interest as the West in lessening tension. Western policymakers have thus failed to grasp the basic differences, not so much of opinion as of motivation. Political Man is seen as a sort of android robot, programmed with one or another "opinion"; if the opinion is removed and another substituted by demonstration and argument, his total behavior will change. It is thought that we may thus "rationalize" political conduct by applying criteria of reason and reasonableness which seem natural to our own culture but are quite alien to others. In reality Political Man in different systems is not just basically the same creature holding different theoretical opinions, but rather a life form which has evolved into radically different phyla, each with deep-set attitudes historically determined over long periods—and subject to natural selection as between different temperamental groups. In the USSR the present Marxist-Leninist ruling elements are actually unable to see the world in terms other than their own.

We may conveniently make a basic distinction between the "civic" and the "despotic" cultures. In the former, the policy is articulated and decisions are made in accord—in principle at least— with a balance of interests and views, through consultation with and acceptance by various sections of the community. In the "despotic" culture decisions are made by a single man or group regarded as uniquely qualified, and the population is merely a passive element.

The despotic form of culture divides naturally into two general types. In the traditional "imperial" system it is assumed that the true form of the state has already been achieved; the messianic revolutionary type seeks by an act of will to bring history to an eschatologically predetermined conclusion. The two varieties have much more in common with each other than they do with the Western culture. But above all, the present Soviet regime amounts to a fusion of the two.

Human Rights and the Russian State Tradition

In the Russian tradition, since Mongol times, the state claimed absolute control over society as a matter of principle. The revolutionary countertradition which developed in it was equally total in outlook: the elect, with their perfect doctrine, would seize power with an absolute claim to rule over the population. Even before the revolution, the Polish revolutionary Rosa Luxemburg had noted how the idea of the infallible Bolshevik Central Committee was no more than a mirror image of tsarist autocracy. It is true that from about 1860 there had been the rise of a Europeanized civic attitude, with courts, juries, eventually a fairly free press, and a duma; but this development was crushed between the millstones of traditionalist and messianic despotism. In fact, the main achievement of the October revolution may be seen as the destruction of the fruit of two generations of precarious civic development.

Not all traditional despotisms had been expansionist. But tsarism, as Marx noted, carried a tendency to universal expansion; while communism was explicitly a world-idea, and Lenin and his successors ruled that only the Soviet model would serve. Similarly, both traditions held the same view of the unofficial thinker; and Brezhnev's Russia resembles the Russia of Nicholas I far more closely than, for example, Britain resembles the Britain of 1830.

This is to say that the Soviet rulers are the product of a long tradition, a deep-seated political psychology. They are not to be converted to new ideas by argument; hardly by experience. Though some of them are also deeply involved in the exegesis of ideology, that is not the point. The others, who may not spend their time reciting or studying the texts of Marxism-Leninism, are nevertheless soaked in that tradition and determined by it. And this background is likely to weigh more heavily with them than the syllogisms of Western statesmen.

The important thing is not so much the wickedness or otherwise of their culture as its strangeness, from our point of view. We can see this, for example, in the agricultural problem, which is a gross and inefficient burden on the economy. They are unable to change it, for reasons of doctrinal habit alone. They are similarly unable to grant the legitimacy of any non-Soviet regime—even a Communist regime, as we saw in Czechoslovakia in 1968. They are unable to abandon the world claims intrinsic to their whole psychology.

The Soviet attitude to mere truth would make them very uneasy company among the nations. It will be remembered that one of the great issues between the Brezhnevite repression and the dissenters was not merely that the latter were expressing intolerable opinions, but that they were also trying to discover and publish the true facts about Soviet history. We are used to the nature of the regime, for otherwise it would—as it should—strike us as quite fantastic that no account, true or false, is now available about the Stalin terror, which was the vastest and most determining event to have moulded the country in modern times. The political struggle, the great trials, the enormous death roll, the archipelago of camps, have simply disappeared from the public prints. The period is filled instead with industrial construction. The only explanation for this is that the leaders are psychologically unable to countenance truth, or to abandon the idea that the past is freely to be manipulated at their behest. And, of course, these overweening rights extend also to the present and the future.

Thus, when it comes to human rights, their refusal of free opinions or free movement of their subjects is no mere accidental or temporary willfulness on the part of the Soviet rulers. On the contrary, it is something that characterizes the essence of their political attitudes. For them society, and members of society, have no rights against the state. And all other attitudes on the part of individuals or foreign states are not merely mistaken, but wholly damnable and subject to extirpation as a simple duty, wherever and whenever tactically possible.

The single issue of human rights tells us the essential nature of the Soviet political culture and its attitude to aberrant nations as well as individuals. And therefore the human rights issue is the crucial test when it comes to establishing peace in a durable sense. Human rights is the one demand—the only essential demand— we can make, and the degree of its fulfillment is the one true criterion of progress to peace.

The Helsinki Agreement, 1975

This understanding, particularly on the part of certain Northern European leaders, led to the inclusion of Basket Three in the 1975 Helsinki Agreement. Its formulation was, of course, in terms of the free movement of people and ideas—which, expressed in concepts suitable to international relations, emphasized the liberty of the subject and freedom of thought.

Of the two, the first, though of vital importance, does not have the scope of the second. Although it is a pity that the principle of free movement has become reduced in many Western minds to the free emigration of Jews (who are of course not specified in either the Helsinki Agreement or the Jackson amendment), that principle is an indispensable last sanction by the oppressed against the claims of the state, and once secured, even in part, would be an enormous first step to civilizing Russia. But the free movement of ideas goes to the heart of the matter. When Milton wrote "Give me liberty to know, to utter, and to argue freely according to conscience, above all liberties," he implied the truth that while freedom of thought does not contain all the other things we would list as human rights, it contains their potentiality, and they cannot be realized or sustained without it.

Moreover, the free movement of ideas is not some parochial fad of the Western culture. It is what distinguishes a society with the possibility of change and progress, even of peaceful progress, from one without it. It is what distinguishes an articulated social order, with its compromises and consensuses, from a barracks or a prison. It is what distinguishes a country able to live in a world

with various state forms and ideas, from one based on the principle of the imposition everywhere of received truth. It constitutes,
in fact, all that can be meant by political civilization; and it provides the criterion of an essentially peaceable, as against an essentially aggressive, state.

The Soviet interpretation of détente places the emphasis
elsewhere. The Soviet leadership are frank in their public
speeches in describing détente—or "peaceful coexistence," as
they have till very recently preferred to call it—as itself a form of
struggle; and in emphasizing that the "ideological" struggle continues, that the "class struggle" on a world scale cannot be
stopped. But just as class struggle on the world stage does not
mean supporting the aims of genuine proletariats but merely of
any political forces whatever who serve Soviet interests, so
ideological struggle does not consist—as some Westerners seem to
interpret it—of a harmless campaign of honest argument about
ideas, with the best man winning. On the contrary, its main components are: (a) a stepping-up of anti-Western propaganda by pro-
Soviet groupings in the West and Soviet radio broadcasts abroad;
(b) an intensification of anti-Western "vigilance" and militarist
propaganda in the USSR; (c) the suppression of pro-Western (and
indeed pro-Maoist, pro-Islamic, pro-non-Soviet) voices wherever
possible; (d) a soft-spoken, weasel-word "dialogue" with any
Western elements—Christian, trade union, or whatever—who
may have failed to notice (a), (b) and (c) and in spite of everything
still present pathic targets to the surprised and delighted Marxist-
Leninist. Thus for the Kremlin, détente is simply a matter of tactics comparable to that adopted by the Sun in Aesop's fable: when
the Wind's attempt to make the Traveller shed his coat by violent
blasts has failed, and the tactic of friendly warmth proves more
successful.

Distinguishing Two Aspects of Negotiation

At this point it will be appropriate to disentangle the two different
aspects of negotiation with the Soviet Union which have been
lumped together under the détente label. First, the consultations
for mutual reductions in and control of armament, and for arrangements on "crisis management." Even if the two blocs remain

in principle in a state of complete hostility, it is still sensible to seek arms reduction, both for economic reasons and to lessen the purely military danger. While it may be argued that these considerations will prove inadequate in the long run without some measure of goodwill, at least it cannot be denied that some progress might be made. The Soviets maintain, of course, that such progress cannot be made unless we accept their intransigence on human rights and other matters; and they have had some success among short-sighted Westerners. But in fact, it is plain enough that, regardless of other issues, they will not come to any agreement on armaments unless they conceive it in their interests to do so—in which case they will.

Such agreements could somewhat reduce immediate risks, but they could not destroy long-term dangers, a solution to which must be sought by other means. Moreover, the disarmament problem itself is affected directly and in detail, as well as in basic principle, by the Soviet stand on state control of the movement of people and ideas. For the refusal of adequate *in situ* inspection is a product of their hostile siege mentality. Moreover, arms control becomes in principle more difficult if there is a well founded general distrust of the bona fides of one of the negotiators. At the same time, crisis management becomes more refractory if crises are continually provoked on the principle that, in Brezhnev's words, détente does not apply to "class and liberation struggles in the capitalist countries and the colonies."

It is sometimes urged that the denied goodwill and mutual tolerance, the "mellowing" of the Soviet system, are in fact gradually being achieved as by-products of piecemeal trade, cultural, diplomatic, and other bonds—somewhat as the Lilliputians sought to bind Gulliver with a thousand weak threads, each strengthening the last. In this way, it is hoped, direct confrontation on the human rights issue can be avoided, since *apparatchik* resistance will eventually be outflanked in a painless manner.

Cultural exchange, it is true, clearly has some minimal effect in eroding the rigor of monopolistic party conviction in a limited circle of Soviet citizens; and it even implies, in fact, a very small contribution to greater movement of people. The Kremlin has indeed made this small payment under fairly careful conditions, and partly motivated by the necessities of scientific progress. Still, the

controls are definite, and even if it does produce a certain increase
in alienation on the part of some intellectuals, that alienation is
already present in the USSR—the whole *raison d'etre* of the dic-
tatorship is the containment and suppression of the alienated. The
state and party machine built by Stalin and his successors is a
mechanism for that purpose. And the central question is precisely
to ensure that that state and party, rather than suspect subjects,
develop a tolerance of the outside world. Naturally, in the long
run, one must rely in part on social and intellectual pressures
within the USSR to secure the evolution or elimination of the
regime. But as dissidents so often tell us, these pressures are impo-
tent without active Western encouragement and support, in the
sense of firm pressure on our part too.

Many people believe that the import of technology itself implies
the import of ideas. No doubt, again, a certain penumbra of
unorthodox thought may penetrate with the technological trading.
But, again, it seems untenable that this peripheral seepage has
any tangible effect on—or that it presents any but the slightest
and most readily containable threat to—the ruling apparat.

There is nothing new in this. Russia's rulers have always aimed
to import Western technology for the purpose of strengthening the
old system—especially in the military field. Such was the principle and practice of Peter the Great, Catherine the Great, and
Stalin the (in his own way) equally Great. On each occasion the in-
flux of Western technique, though inseparable from a minor drift
of ideas, was accompanied by an intensification of serfdom and a
general tightening of despotism.

Moreover, when it comes to trade, and indeed other aspects of
negotiation—if we omit in this context the military aspects of détente—it is clear that on the face of it the Soviets have virtually
nothing we want. While the Kremlin is fully conscious of its need
for Western computers and, on occasion, for Western wheat, it has
very little, economically speaking, to give in exchange.

The same argument applies to the questions of legitimation of
the Eastern European status quo, and other problems discussed at
Helsinki. And while it is true we would wish for some measure of
liberty in Eastern Europe, it is clear that our statesmen will not
press for it with the same militancy the USSR uses to extend its
own system. Détenters tell us we should not cause trouble in the

area. But, again, the liberties of Eastern Europe are primarily part of the human rights issue, which remains our only substantial demand and bargaining counter in negotiation.

The Need for "Psychological Disarmament"

Thirty years ago, in an article published in the *New York Times* magazine (10 March 1946) and in the London left wing *Tribune,* Arthur Koestler argued that world peace must remain precarious without "psychological disarmament." He had no objection to

criticism directed by one country against another. This democratic right is as vital on the international as on the national scale.... But it becomes poisonous if the country attacked is deprived of the right of defense—as the Western countries are at present.... A country which builds a Maginot line of censorship from which it fires its propaganda salvoes is committing psychological aggression. Since the end of the War the USSR has raised certain claims.... The Western Powers, who have no territorial counterclaims to make, should table instead a demand for psychological disarmament, including: free access of foreign newspapers ... to the USSR; such modifications of the Russian censorship ... as to permit the free circulation of information about the outside world throughout Soviet territory; ... the abolishing of restrictions on travel for foreigners in Soviet territory, and Soviet citizens abroad.... No one in his senses will expect the Soviet leaders to agree to this easily. Hence the suggestion that psychological disarmament should be made a bargaining object in all future negotiations, and given high priority on the political agenda. The demand for the free circulation of ideas across frontiers, for restoring the arrested bloodstream of the world, should be raised at every meeting of ... the Security Council, the Committees and Assembly of the United Nations; it should be made the precondition of concessions in the geographical, economic and scientific field. To get it accepted, the use of all levers of pressure, political and economic, would for once be morally justified.

The crises of the 1940s were solved by military strength and a staunch political will, now alas lacking. But since the root of the problem was not after all dealt with, it has continued over the decades to bear the bitter fruits of psychological aggression. The danger of war has remained in being.

Helsinki and the Betrayal of Human Rights

At Helsinki some effort was made to come to grips with the essential. But the Soviet Union has in effect welshed on this one part of the Helsinki accord—the issue of human rights—from which the West and the world really stood to gain. No serious attempt has been made to secure Soviet compliance. The few token gestures they made on the issue—usually concerning individuals only—have been tacitly accepted. Which is to say that the Western détentists have effectively welshed on Helsinki too.

Soviet inaction has been justified by the theory that the rights granted at Helsinki should be implemented only to the degree that they do not contradict "national sovereignty," which in this case signifies the Soviet right to treat their subjects as they wish, regardless of their international undertakings. Of course, the visits of Suslov and Ponomarev to the congresses of Western Communist parties devoted to the Sovietization of Western society do not, on this view, constitute interference in the affairs of other states. Nor does the often virulent output of Radio Moscow on international channels—unlike the generally factual or serious output of the Western international broadcasts. But, to take an even closer parallel, the appeal to national sovereignty is incompatible with, for example, United Nations and Soviet-supported campaigns against apartheid in sovereign South Africa, which is precisely a violation of human rights in the same sense as the Soviet violations they now declare sacrosanct.

In any case, on this reading, in merely obtaining Soviet signatures to international documents on human rights the West has obtained nothing. The problem remains that of enforcement. Indeed, a default on a signed guarantee—on the grounds that treaties only apply when the USSR finds it convenient—may seem to prove the total unreliability of the Soviet signature to any document whatever. (It is certainly true that Soviet guarantees of the independence of the Baltic States and—in the peace treaties and at Potsdam—of the freedom of operation of all antifascist parties in the Balkan countries and East Germany meant and mean nothing.) Yet our negotiators probably did not insist on the provisos of Basket Three being made watertight because they thought the USSR would not then sign; and they had some vague hope that the evadable phraseology might nevertheless produce some minuscule result in exchange for the substantial Western concessions on other issues. Now that we know this sort of bargain to be pretty well worthless, perhaps future negotiators will insist on some element of genuine substance—or alternatively, refuse the Russians a *quid pro nihil* and abandon the appeasement.

For here, as ever, one is driven to the position that the Soviets will do nothing unless they are refused the benefits they seek under other items of the various agreements they have obtained. The advantage of the Jackson amendment is that it insisted, with safeguards against nonfulfillment, on the human rights *quid pro quo*. It did not grant benefits without a mechanism for checking on Soviet performance of their own side of the bargain. In these cases, if the Russians comply, well and good. If not, we have avoided giving something for nothing, and the inducement to—or pressure for—more civilized and peaceable conduct remains. Russia never had a tradition that trade or negotiation can lead to mutual benefit: the first true merchant bank in the country was only founded in the 1860s. The Communist contribution to this outlook was Lenin's basic principle *"Kto kove?"* ("Who—whom?"): the idea that every act is part of a struggle in which one side loses and the other wins. The Soviets will not make any concession unless it is made absolutely clear that they can gain no benefit by defaulting.

We should note, moreover, that the attempts to secure an improvement in the Soviet attitude have not been—as one might gather from some critics—anything like an all-or-none, bullheaded demand for instant total compliance. On the contrary, it was mere minima which were at issue. Just as Koestler speaks not of the abolition of censorship but only its relaxation, so the Helsinki Agreement is in terms of "gradually to simplify and to administer flexibly the procedures for exit and entry," "to ease regulations," "gradually to lower," "gradually to increase," and so on; and Senator Jackson did not demand immediate full freedom of emigration, merely an improvement to the extent of allowing a "benchmark" of some 60,000 exit visas.

The Russians did not, in the end, accept the terms of the Jackson amendment. They did accept those of Helsinki, including, for example, "To facilitate the improvement of the dissemination, on their territory, of newspapers and printed publications, periodical and non-periodical, from the other participating States." Nothing of the sort has taken place. On the contrary, the Western failure to press the issue has gone with—no doubt partly been the cause of—a notable increase in repression over the past year. If one believes that present Western tactics may begin to have some effect, as promised, one must surely ask for at least the beginnings of fulfillment of Basket Three. It was recognized that change is hard, and liable to be fairly slow at first, especially in rigid cultures; but this is not to say that we must accept gestures barely visible to the naked eye, without any sort of genuine and substantial improvement. A Western statesman who puts these human rights clauses into a treaty and then makes no attempt to see to their fulfillment seems, on the face of it, to be collaborating with the Soviet Union in deception—and so to be deceiving his own constituents. This is particularly the case if he adduces Soviet willingness to accept such clauses as an authentic sign of change in the Kremlin. Indeed, such inculcations of delusion can only confuse and weaken the Western will to resist.

The Importance of Human Rights

To secure no change on human rights must be disastrous in the longer run. It is true, as we have said, that the differences between political cultures are as persistent as they are profound; that they have enormous intrinsic momenta and cannot be rapidly turned in new directions. But they can be turned. There have been despotisms in transition to civicisms, as in prerevolutionary Russia. Even apart from the possibility of a catastrophic breakdown—by no means impossible—slow and firm pressures and inducements from our side might eventually lead first to the abandonment in practice of the Soviet struggle *à l'outrance* with the West, and later to its virtual abandonment even in principle. But our situation is dangerous, and a slow erosion through trade and cultural contacts while giving up all attempt at serious political leverage, could not conceivably have any adequate effect in the period of international danger which looms immediately ahead.

Ideologies do evolve. They evolve under pressure. When the disadvantages of pursuing aggressive policies are clear, and the advantages to be gained by concession are present as a continual bait, then and only then is there any reasonable prospect of slow but substantial change. Lack of firmness is a certain guarantee that the Kremlin, having no inducement to change, will retain its present condition of hostility in both principle and practice. Those who call themselves "realists" and argue that the rulers cannot be expected to make concessions and so should not be pressed to do so, surrender in advance and thereby encourage aggressiveness, while failing to erode in any way its continuation through the foreseeable future. One is tempted to say of them, as Orwell said of appeasement-minded intellectuals in another context, that one doesn't know which to despise more, their cynicism or their shortsightedness.

What one asks of the Kremlin, after all, is no more than we practice, or are willing to practice, ourselves. So long as they maintain a siege mentality, in a state of declared and active hostility to all other ideas, the fuse of war remains primed. A siege mentality is, moreover, no more than the obverse of a sortie mentality.

We can exert pressures by effective military and political blocking of aggression while maintaining the constant offer of true peace. Above all, we may chart any progress of the Soviet rulers away from their total hostility by their attitude toward human rights. For the USSR will indicate its cooperative membership in the world community when its rulers cease their intransigeant intolerance of all that the West stands for. Their progress can be most easily checked in the one area where they are free to tolerate or suppress our ideas as they feel fit—the USSR itself. For the present the answer is clear. "Détente" has been accompanied by repression.

The West's only sane attitude remains one of military strength and diplomatic unity and forcefulness adequate to deter and rebuff expansionism—of which every successful example serves only to encourage more. We must refuse simply to strengthen the Soviet economic (and therefore military) machine without any return; and we must maintain a constant vigilance—combined with a continual offer of real détente as soon as the Russians prove their bona fides by implementing Basket Three. Meanwhile, a stable truce based on mutual distrust is preferable to delusions of friendship accompanied by and encouraging political and military initiatives by the Kremlin, which increase the dangers of both war and totalitarian victory.

The human rights issue remains the key test of their animus against *us,* a test of the basic motivations of their foreign policy.

9

ROBERT A. GOLDWIN

Common Sense

vs.

"The Common Heritage"

When President Reagan's decision was announced in March 1981 that the United States would not continue negotiations and would instead begin what turned out to be a lengthy review of the Law of the Sea Treaty, proponents of the treaty in the United States and elsewhere in the world were incredulous. Two years later, after completion of the review, after announcement of the "six objectives" that the United States sought and other nations did not agree to, and, finally, after announcement that the United States would not sign the treaty or participate in any future preparations or activities, the proponents of the treaty are still incredulous. They do not believe, they cannot accept the thought, that the United States will not be a signatory.[1]

This essay originally appeared in *Law of the Sea: U.S. Policy Dilemma*, edited by Bernard H. Oxman, David D. Caron, and Charles L. O. Buderi (1983).

To them the benefits to the United States, as to the world, seem so obvious that they can offer only three possible explanations for President Reagan's actions: that he is ignorant,[2] that he is a rigid ideologue,[3] or that he is both.[4]

The argument I shall put forth suggests the reverse: it is the critics of the Reagan policy, the *proponents* of the Law of the Sea Treaty themselves, who have allowed unthinking commitment to ideology to blind them to dominant facts that lie at the heart of the controversy over whether to sign the treaty.

Let us turn directly to the questions that matter: What, if anything, is wrong with the treaty? Is there reason not to sign it? If we do not sign, what should we do?

"Law of the Sea" and "Law of the Seabed"

To begin to see what is wrong with the treaty we must make a distinction so obvious that almost everyone either ignores or overlooks it. The treaty deals with two significantly different kinds of subject matter: one has to do with *the sea*, the other with *the deep seabed*. It deals with the former tolerably well, and by acceptably sensible means. The latter it botches incredibly, in ways that are simultaneously excessive, irrelevant, and potentially oppressive. The parts having to do with the sea—fishing, navigation, shipping, pollution control, marine research, and the like—are familiar subjects of international maritime agreements and are properly called "law of the sea." The provisions having to do with the deep seabed, on the other hand, are unprecedented in international agreements; they are an international novelty and should go under a different name, for the sake of clarity and truth: "the law of the deep seabed." These provisions pertain only to the seabed of those waters beyond territorial limits or economic zones of any nation, beyond the continental shelf, and to the nonliving resources lying on the deep seabed. The specific nonliving resource that has been the object of attention of the negotiators for more than a decade has been the manganese nodules, presumably worth billions of dollars, just lying there at great depths, presumably waiting to be scooped, pumped, or sucked up, then to be transported, refined, and sold for immense gains.

This distinction between *the sea* and *the deep seabed* is the essential starting point for understanding what the problem is and what is at stake. *All* of the controversy over whether to sign the treaty centers on the law of the deep seabed, *none at all* on the law of the sea. If the treaty dealt only with the law of the sea, the United States would have signed long ago. If the treaty were now stripped of the deep seabed provisions, and no other word in the treaty were touched, the United States would sign without delay. There are provisions in the sea portions with which the United States is not especially pleased—some having to do with fishing, others with marine research—but on balance the spokesmen of the United States, including especially President Reagan, have expressed themselves repeatedly as not merely satisfied but even pleased with that major part of the text of the treaty.

There is nothing surprising in this. Few other nations have as much of a stake in the law-abiding, peaceful use of the oceans as has the United States. Use of the oceans increased too rapidly in recent decades. As a result, new problems were generated and old ones were intensified. It was obvious that some wholly new rules needed to be formulated, some existing rules needed strengthening, and in certain very important situations long-standing customary rules needed codification. The United States made useful, major contributions throughout these negotiations and was not unhappy with the results. President Reagan affirmed this in his statement announcing that the United States would not sign the treaty. He explained that the provisions dealing with the law of the sea contained "positive and very significant accomplishments." Most of the provisions, he said, "are consistent with United States interests and, in our view, serve well the interests of all nations."[5] In short, the United States would be a willing signatory if the law of the sea were the full subject matter of the Law of the Sea Treaty. But it isn't; the law of the deep seabed is a part of it, too.

It should also be noted that to implement the provisions of the treaty dealing with the principal activities of the world's oceans—fishing rights, navigation and overflight, pollution control, marine research, and similar matters—not one new international agency had to be brought into existence. But everything is quite different when we turn to the other part, the troublesome part of the treaty, the part that deals not with the sea but with the deep seabed and

the inanimate things that rest on it. This part of the treaty an-
nounces a new doctrine of international control, if not international ownership, of hitherto unowned territories, and it establishes new institutions that rival the United Nations itself in size,
scope, complexity, powers, and numbers of employees. There
would be an Assembly, a Council, a Secretariat, a number of expert commissions, courts of various sorts called disputes cham-
bers, and a mining company called the Enterprise that would—on
paper, at least—be equal in size, funding, and activity to all of the
competing private sea-mining consortia of the world *combined.*

Ill-Founded Hopes

The obvious justification for a new law of the sea is the greatly intensified use of the seas by the nations of the world, which generates new problems that must be addressed in a constructive manner—and which by and large, on balance, have been so dealt with
in the treaty. But what is the justification for the new law of the
deep seabed? The answer given by treaty proponents is that the
manganese nodules present a new problem and a new opportunity
for global development and international economic justice.

To understand the deep seabed provisions of the treaty, it is
necessary to try to recapture the aspirations and expectations of
the negotiators in the 1960s and 1970s. The assumption was that
the manganese nodules represented tremendous riches and that,
unless strict precautions were taken and enforced with energy
and vigilance, only the most wealthy and technologically advanced
nations would profit from this new source of raw materials. This
gave birth to the doctrine of "the common heritage of mankind,"
interpreted to mean that the unowned and unacquired nodules
already belonged to "mankind as a whole" and that each
sovereign nation owned a share of the common property. By
carefully drawn rules to be made, administered, and adjudicated
by novel international agencies, the poorer nations would get a
fair share of the immense profits, would acquire advanced technology, and would assume a new role in actually managing vast
enterprises that would dwarf the most optimistic possibilities in
their own smaller and poorer national economies. It sounds won-
derful but there are two things wrong: the theory and the facts.

Three hundred years ago the argument was made that a "universal commons" (based on a false analogy to the familiar village commons) is impossible. A village commoner can help himself to much of what is common without seeking the consent of his fellow commoners, but the commons itself is property, joint property that excludes others who may not take what they please without permission. There can be no property, no ownership, without excluding others. Where others can take what they want without another's consent, there is no property. In short, to speak of the deep seabed as a universal or "global" commons either is nonsense, literally, or it means that *no one owns the seabed* or anything on it, which is where matters stood *before* the treaty was written.

That the deep seas are unowned has been the principle underlying freedom of the seas for centuries. A doctrine that seems to proclaim that they are now "owned" by "mankind" is used in the treaty to claim the right of an international authority to control and regulate uses of the seas. This theoretical nonsense jeopardizes one of the great foundations of international peace and prosperity—freedom of the high seas.[6]

Not only is the theory wrong, but the factual assumptions underlying the treaty provisions are even more obviously wrong. Some experts probably knew from the beginning that it was all a pipe dream. It was certainly known by many in 1981.[7] For example, in May 1981, spokesmen of the Kennecott Consortium, in a detailed report to the House of Commons, described how calculations based on surveys in the 1950s and 1960s misled mining companies to think that nodules could become profitable, but that "estimates of the total resource of nodules have little significance since they take no account of the economics of recovery," which had been grievously miscalculated. "Only a very small fraction of the total resources of nodules can be classified even as potential reserves—a term that implies that they can be mined profitably." The report contends that the provisions of the treaty are a disincentive for investment in mining, but then adds that "even with no legal, economic, or financial restraints a nodule project is unlikely to be in operation before 1990. Market considerations . . . may postpone the first project even longer." Finally, they say, "Whilst it cannot be denied that the total content of manganese, nickel, copper and cobalt in all the nodules in the oceans may be vast, most of this resource will be uneconomic for many decades — *possibly centuries*" (my emphasis).[8]

Two great errors underlying treaty negotiations were that there were useful minerals lying there for the taking and that production of the metals from the nodules would be profitable. The reality is that obtaining the nodules would be very costly and hazardous, refining the metals twice as costly as retrieving them, and the prospects for return on investment sufficiently dismal to bring almost all operations to a complete halt. But starting as they did from these two massive errors, the proponents decided that great efforts were justified to regulate the increased activity that would develop—that new courts were needed to judge disputes, that commissions were needed to control production and prices, and that legislative bodies with new principles of representation were needed to assure that the wealth that would be pouring in would be shared fairly. Dreams of untold wealth are not a new phenomenon in human history, nor are they easy to give up, but in the case of the nodules there is no alternative.

No Market for Seabed Minerals

The chief minerals in the nodules are manganese, copper, nickel, and cobalt. All have been selling at unusually low prices. For example, the nominal price of nickel in early 1983 was the same as in 1974, despite a decade of high inflation. Manganese is used almost entirely in steel production, and steel production is 50 percent or less of plant capacity around the world, with many steel mills closed down, perhaps forever. Not only are cobalt prices low compared to recent years (about one-fifth of 1979's all-time high), but the volatility of its price and the uncertainty of supply are encouraging consumers to be wary of using it. The Congressional Budget Office (CBO) issued a study urging a review of cobalt stockpiling.[9] The existing stockpile goal is considerably higher than needed, according to the CBO study; it urged that care should be taken not to reduce incentives for development of cobalt substitutes by industry. In short, as *The Economist* wrote of the main ingredients of the deep seabed nodules, "nobody wants these minerals."[10]

Most reports indicate that copper would not be the major factor if there ever were commercial nodule mining, but recent developments in technology make expensive new sources of copper seem even less important commercially. Copper pipe has been replaced by plastics in many applications. Copper wiring is being replaced by fiber optics for much, if not all, of communications traffic. Not only can this glass product take the place of copper wiring, it will provide a new source of scrap copper to compete with copper from land mines or nodules; one analyst contends that the obsolete copper communications cables will be the biggest new reserve of copper in the world. To add to the indignities being heaped on this splendid metal, once so highly prized and profitable, the U.S. Mint now produces annually more than 13 billion pennies that are 97.5 percent zinc (less than half the price of copper), plated with 2.5 percent copper, saving the mint an estimated $25 million a year in metal costs.

Pessimism about the future of many metals seems justified when prices are depressed, but of course those with long experience remind us that prices and profits fluctuate in all commodities, and no one can be sure of the future. The prudential rule, partaking of the character of a natural law, is that whatever goes up must come down, as for example petroleum prices in early 1983 after a decade of huge increases. But nothing in nature or experience says that what is down must go up. The example of copper is instructive. The fluctuations are not simply cyclical or the result of the worldwide recession; the causes are in large part technological innovation and substitution, and of such a nature that, although unforeseen new uses may be developed, some major uses of copper are unlikely ever to return.

Similar dire prospects exist for steel, and (since over 90 percent of manganese is consumed in the steel industry) as steel goes, so goes manganese. The Ford Motor Company says it is testing an automobile with a body made of plastic described as lighter than aluminum and stronger than most steel. KYOCERA Corporation (Kyoto Ceramics) has developed a ceramic diesel automobile engine. It is lightweight, thermal-efficient, estimated to give a 30-percent reduction in fuel consumption, and would practically never wear out.[11] Though one cannot know when or if it will be put into production, an advance model can be driven now. U.S. Commerce Undersecretary Lionel Olmer has driven it in Japan and is quoted as saying, "It's an experimental model and it idles sort of rough—but it works, that's the main point."

The development of substitutes for metals brings a deep uncertainty that demand, and hence prices, will rise enough (relative to future prices of everything else) to justify the huge investment costs of retrieving and refining metals from deep seabed nodules. Without significant growth of demand, mining nodules for profit makes no sense. "Production of metals from nodules now would cost more than from virtually all existing producers and there are still many undeveloped deposits of these metals on land from which they could be produced at lower cost than from nodules."[12]

Irrelevance of the Production Provisions

There has always been an internal contradiction in the mining provisions of the treaty. On the one hand, there was a desire for production and profit, especially for the Enterprise, to produce the revenue to sustain the Authority. On the other hand, there was a powerful tendency to protectionism, to prevent production sufficient to affect adversely the price of minerals from land-mining countries. A major concern was protection of the prices of the metals produced by less-developed land-mining countries, heavily dependent on export income, like "the three Zs"—Zaire, Zambia, and Zimbabwe.[13] Canada, too, perhaps alone among the developed nations, was more concerned with devising and enforcing production controls on deep seabed mining than on developing and facilitating the mining. Canada had in mind, of course, its preeminence in nickel mining. Complicated formulas, practically unintelligible even to many experts, were written into the text to empower commissions to regulate production and thereby prices.

But in the last few years, without any deep seabed mining, prices of these metals were affected by a combination of factors— worldwide recession, inflated dollars, oil price increases, high interest rates, currency fluctuations, energy conservation measures, discoveries of extensive new land-based mineral reserves, development of substitutes for several metals, and technological advances—unpredicted but powerful in their effects.

In short, the architects of the treaty thought they were designing protections, through production controls, for price stability in commodities. But the kinds of events that happen all the time in the world economy—and that happen with greater intensity and rapidity in our time than ever before in history—were occurring with a complete disregard for the concerns or the powers of the treaty drafters. The forces at work were, in relation to human lawmakers, anarchic; they could not be controlled by anyone's fiat— not by the United Nations, the International Seabed Authority, or solemn words on the heaviest parchment, no matter how many heads of government put their pen to it.

Many proponents of the treaty continue to argue that an international agreement is necessary to give adequate legal security to miners, and that without the treaty it will be impossible for them to get financing for mining operations. Without denying the logic of their argument (and leaving the legal niceties to others who know more about them), I think it sufficient to respond that there will be no financing and no investing in deep seabed mining of manganese nodules for profit in the foreseeable future—"possibly centuries"—with or without the treaty. C. R. Tinsley (in 1981 the vice-president, Mining Division, Continental Bank of Chicago) has written that the treaty's set of mining provisions "brings forth a higher degree of *uncertainty*" (his emphasis) than he had seen in over 250 mining projects worldwide that he had reviewed. His study of the treaty led him to conclude that his bank would not, and probably no bank would, finance deep seabed mining ventures. He added:

But if a bank is unwilling to "take" or to absorb certain risks, which it traditionally has been able to do in mine project financings all over the world, then we can be safe in anticipating that the companies themselves are not going to take on these risks either.[14]

This view is borne out by the fact that current work and expenditure of the mining groups is negligible, and has been for several years now, with no prospect of change.

Some Americans support the seabed provisions for reasons other than profit—for example, for the sake of assured American access to some strategic mineral, or the chance to develop new technology. Such activity would probably be limited, but it would surely produce no revenue such as was dreamed of for sharing with the poorer nations. Profitless mining activity will not sustain the Enterprise, nor will it cover the expenses of the Authority and its hoped-for thousands of employees.

Doubts about Practical Purposes

Where does that leave the law of the deep seabed? It was designed to assert ownership over the nodules, set up agencies to license and regulate their retrieval, resolve the anticipated controversies characteristic of a rush for gold or other precious metals, profit from the Enterprise's sale of the metals, and distribute some of the profits to those who need help most. All of this was to be done from a headquarters financed from license fees and the rest of the Enterprise's profits, for the grand purpose not merely of producing the revenue to support the entire establishment, but especially of taking into its hands, on a supranational basis, the task of aiding the developing world. The aim was to take a giant step in the direction of a new international economic order.

None of these expectations was justified, and none will come to pass. For the foreseeable future there will be no financing (with or without the treaty), no investing, no mining, no licenses, no fees, no disputes to settle, and no contributions from the United States (and no assurance of participation from most of the other nations with a deep seabed mining capability). Thus there is no prospect of funds for the Authority, the courts, the expert commissions, or the Secretariat; no technology or capital to transfer to the Enterprise; and no revenue to share with the poorest countries.

If I am right (and I will, later, consider objections to the argument presented here), a question arises that goes beyond the details of metals and their markets. Why have the proponents of the treaty persisted in trying to have it signed and ratified? That is, if the expected activities are not going to occur, why continue the effort to generate new agencies to guide and control them? If there is going to be little or no production, why persist in establishing the mechanisms to control the levels of production? If the activity will be so limited and the likelihood of disputes so remote, why establish specialized new international courts to adjudicate? If there is going to be no revenue, why continue with plans for an expensive establishment that will be equal to or perhaps greater than the United Nations itself? Why, when there is no practical purpose to serve, do the proponents of the treaty persist?

Unkind answers come immediately to mind. One is that the treaty negotiators have spent a decade and more in a tight world of their own (a world of their own making, one might say) and cannot bear to see it fall short of realization. It would not be the first time that negotiators have become so committed to their own handiwork that they lost touch with the interests of their countries (especially when the matter is of so little interest, as in this case, that few governments have more than a handful, even in the foreign ministry, who know or care anything about the treaty).

Another unkind explanation is concern about careers: many of the diplomats have devoted a major part of their professional careers to the law of the sea. Some of the younger ones have never done anything else. It is *their* subject, their expertise; if the treaty organization does not come into being, they have no way of knowing what other assignment may ever come to them. A test of the validity of this explanation would be to propose one brief addition to the text of the treaty: that no one who has participated in its writing may hold any position of trust in the Authority or the Enterprise or any of its agencies. It is unlikely that such a provision would receive support, but if by some magic it were made a part of the text, support for the treaty would decline sharply among the diplomats. This explanation, I repeat, is unkind, and surely not the basic factor. Nevertheless, diplomats would have to be inhuman for it to be of no significance whatsoever.

There is, finally, an explanation of a different sort that is much more convincing, the one we started with—ideology. Serious professionals who care about the work they do, who are devoted to the principles that guide them and the causes they live for—and that is a fair and accurate description of the proponents of the treaty— do not expend great effort aimlessly. They worked unbelievably hard and very skillfully for a decade to produce the most complex international agreement ever devised. Along the way, either conditions changed or they emerged from obscurity to visibility only gradually. In any case, at some time—sooner for some than for others—all of the competent ones saw that the facts were not as initially described and that expectations were not going to be fulfilled.

In the face of these changes they agreed to some adjustments, but never to any basic ones. They never looked for the elegant reformulations that astute and proud professionals would make if they wished to. When it became clear, for example, that the production-level formulas no longer made sense, they made a "concession" to the United States by changing the formula so that it would have "no bite," but they would not even consider giving up the power to set production levels, nor would they eliminate the commission to exercise that power.

Again, they were willing to make a "concession" that had the practical effect of nullifying the mandatory character of the transfer of technology—but a suggestion that the word "mandatory" be deleted brought only amused smiles that said, in effect, there are some things more important than technology, and the word "mandatory," with all it implies, is one of them.

Again, the text of the treaty provides that the Assembly (not the Council) be the supreme body. Proponents sought to reassure by arguing that many provisions taken together demonstrate that the Assembly (dominated by Third World countries, because they are so numerous) would not really be, for practical purposes, supreme, but suggestions that the text be reworded to accord with their reading of it were not taken seriously.

What can the explanation be for insisting on going forward when no practical purpose would be served? Why, if some provisions for the deep seabed must remain in the text, did the conference refuse to make revisions, deleting unnecessary powers and agencies? The answer is ideology, the ideology of "the common heritage of mankind," the single most sacred of UN sacred cows. If one were to suggest that the deep seabed provisions now be deleted from the treaty, that the remainder—the true law of the sea treaty—be presented for signature and ratification and put into effect, and that the question of the law of the deep seabed be approached separately and anew on the basis of what is now known—if such a proposal were made it would receive the same response as recommendations that India increase its food supply by slaughtering and eating cows, and for a similar reason.[15]

"Common Heritage" vs. Common Sense

If there were no ideological barrier, if the law of the deep seabed could be approached now on the basis of common sense instead of "the common heritage of mankind" ideology, there are several things we could quickly agree on. First, we could agree that there is enough time to proceed sensibly; there is no rush and no crisis. Second, not much, if anything, in the way of new international structures or agencies is required. The level of activity related to the deep seabed will be far less than the activity on the seas, and the agencies and regulatory efforts should be minimal, commensurate to the low level of activity. The private mining consortia have already met; in a very short time they came to an agreement on procedures, by negotiation or arbitration, to settle any disputes that might arise over mining sites. Probably some simple system for registering claims for sites could handle all of the necessary work, since it is estimated that in all international waters there will be no more than five to twenty sites for mining nodules for the foreseeable future. But, most important, there should be no claim put forth of an *inherent right* of an international authority to regulate deep seabed activities.

One of the most fervent proponents of "the common heritage of mankind" doctrine, Elisabeth Mann Borgese, a leader of the world-government movement in the years after World War II (until that movement for global harmony destroyed itself by internal strife among rival world-federalist factions), agrees that ideology is the dominant factor. After listing some developments that have diminished "the value of the Common Heritage of Mankind, particularly of the manganese nodules," she goes on to say that that is not the main point. The main point is that "the creation of the International Seabed Authority . . . must be reckoned as a breakthrough in international relations. Here is an international institution," she writes,

unprecedentedly empowered to regulate and act on the basis of the new principle of the Common Heritage of Mankind. Here is a first attempt at a global production policy with due regard to conservation of the environment. Here is an opening to industrial cooperation between the North and the South based not on aid but on sharing. . . . The International Seabed Authority, a utopian dream of 20 years ago, is now a fact of international law. Something has been moving.[16]

What clearer evidence can there be that for many proponents of the treaty, ideology takes precedence over the explicit practical goals? And if one were to protest that Mrs. Borgese, no matter

how devoted and enthusiastic, does not speak for all treaty proponents, we are still left with the puzzle: why, when the stated practical reasons for going forward with the law of the deep seabed
have all dissolved, do the advocates nevertheless persist? My
answer is that the ideology of "the common heritage" is, as Mrs.
Borgese tells us, of overriding importance.

Reasonably Facing the Unforeseeable

I am aware that others might say my analysis is factually wrong,
that there are indeed untold riches out there, if not nodules then
something else, and that some form of mining and other activities
foreseen or unforeseen will indeed occur. Let me turn, then, to
these objections.

The very experience I have described teaches that we cannot
know what the future will reveal. New discoveries are being made
now—for instance, deposits of polymetallic sulfides containing
metals in much higher concentrations than in the nodules—and
it is considered a certainty that more and richer deposits of nonliving materials will be found in unexpected places and forms not
limited to metals. Proponents of the treaty say that for this reason
we must be prepared with agencies and regulations to assure an
orderly, peaceful, and fair exploitation of the sea's riches, whatever they turn out to be. Without a legal structure, they say, there
will be chaos or paralysis: either every claim an occasion for strife
and even violence, or no exploitation at all because those who
might be active would be intimidated by the uncertainty and
danger of an anarchic situation. These, I admit, are valid and formidable objections—but they are answerable.

The attempt to establish elaborate systems and formulae to deal
with every detail of the future turned out to be an extravagant
waste of time and human talent. The structure was static and the
subject matter was fluid. Sensible (rather than doctrinaire) action
to bring order to the extraction of raw materials from international waters may be based on several guiding principles:

• use existing international agencies, which are numerous
  enough already, rather than generate new ones;

• let the regulatory forces be commensurate with the activities to
  be regulated;

- insist on the principle of encouraging discovery and extraction of materials useful to all, rather than discouraging them;

- encourage nations to cooperate, without unnecessary and complicated international agency interference;

- if nongovernment, for-profit corporations are the ones capable of exploration and extraction, encourage them to function according to their nature and capabilities; and

- assert and impose on others no doctrines that are not necessary for the immediate task (that is, eschew imperious globalism and sweeping claims to powers that are potentially tyrannical).

In short, as an opponent of the present provisions dealing with the deep seabed and as a proponent of the present provisions dealing with the sea, I urge that steps be taken now to make a fresh start. Let the present deep seabed provisions be deleted from the text—Authority, Enterprise, and all. The United States would not delay in signing what would be left: a true law of the sea treaty. The two parts are not naturally linked and are severable; there is no reason why one part should be held hostage to the other. Deliberations could then begin to make simple and brief rules, if and when any are needed, commensurate with the level of activity at the time, utilizing existing entities, aiming to encourage activity, and adding provisions as they might be found necessary.

Provision could be made that a share of profits go to those less fortunate, but to make that possible the rules must be such that profit-making is not only permitted but encouraged. A small office with a dozen or so workers could be established to register claims and to keep records of disputes and their resolution through negotiation or arbitration.

The True Meaning of "Common Heritage"

And what of "the common heritage of mankind"? Can it have no place in new deliberations? My opinion is that a deep seabed treaty is not needed now. If and when one is needed, if the "common heritage" theme is then reintroduced, let us hope that this time, for the first time, it would be considered as seriously and as respectfully as it deserves. It would be a service to rescue "the common heritage of mankind" from the abuse it has suffered at the hands of its ideologues.

The word "heritage" has at least two meanings, one referring to material possessions that are heritable, the other to immaterial principles of good, civilizing truths and wisdom that are handed down from age to age, as expressed in phrases such as "the heritage of constitutional liberty."

Although it would be difficult if not impossible to explain just what sequence of steps led to the false conclusion that all of us have "inherited" the manganese nodules at the bottom of the sea, that meaning of heritage—the material inheritance of property— seems to have dominated the treaty negotiations. This is especially ironic because the initial intention, no doubt, was to elevate our thoughts about the human condition, to encourage us to regard all human beings as equally deserving of treatment as one "kind."

Instead, very quickly, there were enthusiasts speaking of metals as the common heritage, the area to be brought under control of the Authority as "the common heritage area," and the revenue that would flow in as "common heritage dollars." Even today, so high-minded a person as Mrs. Borgese worries about the decline of "the value of the Common Heritage of Mankind, particularly of the manganese nodules." One can see *how* it happened. But *why* do intelligent and principled people collaborate in the debasement of such a splendid phrase and allow thought-polluters to give ugly little rocks lying in the darkest depths of all creation the noble title of mankind's common heritage? Even if the nodules were pure gold, such usage would be desecration.

Mankind's true heritage lies in the great human accomplishments. I mean books, music, plays, paintings, buildings; I mean the search for the truth of things through philosophy, theology, poetry, mathematics, logic—yes, even rhetoric. This is not the place to attempt to describe it, but there is a connection, even a progression, from philosophy (seeking knowledge of the nature of things) to technology (the power to use knowledge to transform nature to improve the human condition). Sever the bond, separate philosophy and technology, and we are left with a defective "heritage," either formless *stuff* or airy abstraction.

Human beings are not capable of "creation," the divine power to make something out of nothing. We are bound to materials; that is why we explore ceaselessly to find them. But one aspect of the best in mankind, what is often called the divine within us, is the striving to make much out of little, progressively making more and more out of less and less. Sometimes the most advanced technology is spoken of as "miraculous," by which we mean that in the admixture of mind and matter, the matter is so lowly and the quantity of it so negligible (e.g., silicon chips from sand) that the combined product is almost immaterial, almost all mind, as if divinely made, just as we tend to call the best poetry or music "heavenly."

If most practical-minded diplomats would consider this a strange approach to useful thinking about the deep seabed, they would be right. But we must not forget that *they* are the ones who introduced "the common heritage of mankind" into the proceedings and never ceased to brandish it thereafter. Their failure to understand what they were talking about explains, at least in part, why a decade of their brilliant work has ended in contention, bitterness, and failure. In my opinion, nothing could be more practical than to reflect on the two different meanings of the "heritage" and to instill into the proceedings, should there be more of them, some of the higher meaning of the word. Let those who are unwilling or unable to rise to that level acknowledge, honestly, that they were never really serious when they used the phrase, and then let them get on with the job without singing anthems to "the common heritage of mankind."

What good might come from serious reflection in treaty deliberations on the human "heritage"? It might remind us that raw materials, whether low-grade ore or high-grade petroleum, are valuable only if we know what to do with them. Raw materials, *in themselves,* are worthless. The ability to reason and imagine, to learn what to do with raw materials, is what is common to us all, is what makes us, equally, all of one "kind." The only true resources are human understanding and the ability to make nature serviceable.

The great error of the treaty negotiators was to speak and think of the *nodules* as "the common heritage of mankind" and to ignore—worse, to shackle—the true heritage all human beings share, the rational power to make the most of what nature gives, for the betterment of all.

10

PATRICK GLYNN

The Moral Case for the Arms Buildup

That the Reagan administration has so far won most of the policy battles in the nuclear debate seems remarkable in light of the fact that it has lost virtually all the moral ones. Even as its defense programs have gradually gained approval in Congress, an enormous array of moral forces has mobilized against it. The press, the universities, even the hierarchy of the Roman Catholic Church— from nearly every institution vested with moral authority, powerful voices have been raised in opposition to its plans.

The ethical debate over nuclear arms has compassed a broad range of themes, but at its heart the moral case against the administration rests on two charges. First, and most important, is the claim that under Ronald Reagan American nuclear strategy has been moving from an essentially defensive posture to an essentially offensive one. It is this impression that has proved perhaps most dismaying to ordinary citizens. Occasionally the charge has shaded into the accusation that the administration ac-

This essay originally appeared in *Nuclear Arms: Ethics, Strategy, Politics,* edited by R. James Woolsey (1984).

tually "has come to plan," in the words of one antinuclear writer, "for waging and winning a nuclear war against the Soviet Union."[1] On the whole, however, few people seriously suspect the president of harboring the wish to launch a premeditated attack. What is more generally thought is that through a combination of factors—fervent anti-Communism, militarism, folly, incompetence—the administration, left to its own devices, could conceivably blunder into a nuclear confrontation with the Soviets.

The second charge, closely related to the first, is that the administration's program will inevitably spark a new round of the arms race. The arms race is deplored on the grounds both that it is wasteful, diverting resources that could be applied to more humane programs; and that it is provocative, increasing the risk of nuclear war.

Against these charges the administration has mounted only the most ineffectual defense, failing again and again to dispel the impression that it is significantly more willing than its predecessors actually to risk nuclear war. Even its active attempts to engage the opposition have tended to turn to its own disadvantage. Indeed, so badly has the administration generally put its case that it has often appeared to gain more from silence than from its maladroit efforts to persuade.

Yet in fairness to the administration, it must be acknowledged that the suspicions it has encountered do not spring solely from its policy formulations or even from its rhetorical ineptitude. The nuclear debate has been conducted in an atmosphere of deep distrust and mutual suspicion, and opposition to the administration's policies has come from two somewhat separate camps. The broad appeal of the antinuclear position has tended to obscure important differences between the moral perspectives of the two groups: while the grievances of one party might be said to find their root primarily in the "new" morality, the objections raised by the other party reach back to a much older moral consensus.

It is the first group that has formed the vanguard of the antinuclear campaign proper. Whatever concern nuclear weapons themselves may have provoked, the antinuclear movement has emerged partly as the product of a much broader sense of moral and political disillusionment. Critical to the movement's formation has been the experience of "demythologization" that touched so many lives in the 1960s and 1970s. For whole sectors of our culture, it should be recognized, moral thinking now finds its starting point in the *rejection* of received moral and political values. This loss of faith has had a profound effect on the perspective that many people bring to the problem of national defense. In particular, it has undermined in many minds the idea that the United States, at least as a political entity, is something basically good and worth preserving. Thus while protest is inevitably directed against the weapons, for many people it is the United States government that is the real object of distrust. At its roots, the contention of these people is not that the administration has a bad defense policy, but that in the end the United States, or at least the United States government, is hardly worth defending.

The strength of this view should not be underestimated, for among the young and the educated it enjoys extremely wide, if usually tacit, acceptance. Moreover, it has entered respectable discourse. Traces of this outlook can even be found in the Catholic bishops' pastoral letter on nuclear arms. "To pretend that as a nation we have lived up to our ideals," write the bishops, "would be patently dishonest."[2] Such moral judgments, whether warranted or not, cannot help but influence our thinking on the subject of our self-preservation. It would be no exaggeration to say that our sense of guilt has in recent years tended to prejudice us *against* the cause of our own political survival.

The Vision of "Assured Destruction"

Still, the most serious and powerful moral criticism of the Reagan administration's policies has come from people who believe strongly in our right to survive but who contend that the administration's policies far exceed any merely defensive requirement. The moral thinking behind this assertion is by no means new. The general conviction that Western nuclear strategy ought to remain defensive flows from a long-standing moral and strategic consensus, grounded in the doctrine of "containment" and forged in the wake of the Cuban missile crisis. This consensus has influenced both public feeling and government policy concerning nuclear weapons for upwards of twenty years. The most prestigious public figures who have risen in recent months to oppose the administration—including a number of famous men from the Kennedy administration—have done so largely in defense of this older outlook.

The convictions that constitute this older consensus are now very familiar: that nuclear war, once begun, will unleash a catastrophe of unimaginable dimensions, resulting, effectively, in the end of the world; that consequently nuclear weapons could have no conceivable military use; that we already possess many more times the weapons than we need utterly to annihilate the Soviet Union and even to obliterate the world as a whole. To most Americans these propositions have become nothing less than axiomatic. Indeed, so basic are these ideas to public understanding of nuclear weapons that their origins in actual strategic theories about nuclear war are now generally forgotten. It is widely assumed that they spring from the simplest common sense. But in fact the reigning public consensus on nuclear policy has its roots in a very specific theory of nuclear strategy, first articulated by the Defense Department under Robert S. McNamara in the early 1960s: the doctrine known as "assured destruction" or (as it eventually became) "mutual assured destruction." The public moral consensus on nuclear armaments is in large measure a somewhat simplified version of "MAD."

The outlines of this strategy are by now well known. In its original formulation, the theory of assured destruction stipulated that a deliberate nuclear attack on the United States could be deterred so long as the U.S. maintained the clear ability to inflict upon the attacker an "unacceptable" retaliatory blow. Deterrence depended, in the words of two of McNamara's civilian strategists, on "maintaining at all times a clear and unmistakable ability to inflict an unacceptable degree of damage upon any aggressor, or combination of aggressors—even after absorbing a surprise first strike."[3] "Stability" is the conflict between the nuclear superpowers would thus spring from the reciprocal vulnerability of their two societies—meaning chiefly their cities—to devastating nuclear attack. From these simple premises followed a number of important consequences. First, the attainment by the Soviet Union of a similar assured destruction capability was to be encouraged rather than opposed, since "deterrence" to be "stable" must be "mutual." Second, the United States would gain nothing from the attempt to acquire "superiority" in nuclear weapons, both because any effort to gain an advantage would be countered by the Soviet Union and because in the presence of assured destruction no real advantage can exist. Finally, defensive weapons such as an antiballistic missile system—especially when designed to protect civilian populations—were not to be sought but rather shunned as dangerous, for by threatening to rob one's adversary of an assured destruction capability they would "destabilize" the nuclear "balance."

From the standpoint of traditional military reasoning, these propositions have always appeared highly paradoxical, which may explain in part why over the years MAD has failed to find much support among the professional military. As Lawrence Freedman notes, it is among civilian strategists in the West that the doctrine of assured destruction has found its strongest adherents. Yet the challenge that MAD posed from the beginning to traditional military thought was made credible by the radically novel nature of the weapons at issue. Writing of nuclear weapons in 1959, Bernard Brodie expressed an idea that has since become commonplace: "The basic fact is that the soldier has been handed a problem that extends far beyond the *expertise* of his own profession."[4]

Moreover, whatever doubts may have been raised concerning its military validity, particularly in the past few years, MAD has persisted as a vision of imposing moral authority. This authority derives chiefly from two considerations: the inherent defensiveness of the doctrine, and its compatibility with the process of arms control. The strongest military argument against MAD—that it offers no guidance, in Benjamin Lambeth's phrase, "at the edge of war," that it is not in any operational sense a "strategy"—has tended to be the strongest moral argument in its favor. Precisely because it would be useless in war, the doctrine of assured destruction has seemed to many to strengthen the cause of peace. Even more important, MAD establishes a theoretical upper limit to forces necessary for deterrence and in doing so provides the strategic logic that permits arms control. It allows us to stop building even if the Soviets continue—so long, it would seem, as our assured destruction capability is indeed assured. MAD is valued in great measure because it seems to leave open a path to disarmament.

Beyond MAD

Nonetheless, it is fair to say that the doctrine of assured destruction has exerted a more enduring hold on public thinking concerning nuclear war than on government policy. Even in the
mid-1960s, when assured destruction was the official declaratory
policy of the U.S. government, actual military targeting priorities
remained at odds with MAD. Declaratory policy emphasized that
nuclear weapons would be used to make punishing strikes against
enemy civilian centers; but the Air Force continued to give
priority in its targeting to military sites.

From the mid-1970s onward, moreover, U.S. policy began gradually to move away from MAD. Contrary to the common conception, the Reagan administration is by no means the first to frame
its defense policy on premises at odds with assured destruction
thinking. In 1974, in response both to changes in missile technology and to new testing and deployments by the Soviet Union,
the Defense Department under Defense Secretary James Schlesinger moved from an assured destruction posture toward a policy
of "flexible response," or "flexible targeting." At issue were two
concerns: first, Schlesinger claimed that the threat that any
Soviet attack, however limited, would be met with retaliation on a
massive scale was losing credibility and no longer provided an adequate foundation for deterrence; second, he argued that it was
necessary to envision in more detail what might actually occur in
the event of Soviet nuclear aggression. Assured destruction
offered no guidance in the event that deterrence "failed." The so-
called "Schlesinger Doctrine" emphasized the need to develop
"sufficient options" between the "massive response" of assured
destruction and "doing nothing."[5] The goal was to limit escalation
in the event of a nuclear conflict by preparing to "hit meaningful
[i.e., military] targets with a sufficient accuracy-yield combination
to destroy only the intended target and to avoid widespread col-
lateral damage."[6] This strategic evolution was continued under
the Carter administration with the issuance of Presidential Directive 59 (PD-59) under Defense Secretary Harold Brown, which
sought to further extend the emphasis on military targets and on
increasing possible options for responses in the event of nuclear
attack. Both the Schlesinger Doctrine and PD-59 were attacked as

departures from assured destruction; the latter policy statement aroused particularly vociferous opposition. In this sense, the current debate is merely a continuation of a dispute that originated in the mid-1970s.

Thinking Morally about Strategy

But while the basic issues of the debate have not altered, its shape has been critically affected by the emergence of the popular antinuclear campaign. A kind of fissure has opened between the moral and strategic issues in the conflict, with one side in the debate (the administration) resorting instinctively to strategic arguments, while the other side (the peace movement) resorts habitually to moral ones. In the process, the complicated relation between these two kinds of issues has been obscured.

The chief beneficiaries of this development have been the advocates of MAD, for the view of nuclear deterrence based on assured destruction has come to be understood by many as, in effect, the middle position of the conflict. There is irony in this development, since for most of the 1970s MAD was not the center but rather one side in the controversy over nuclear policy. Yet in comparison with the more extreme antinuclear activists, with their unilateralist sympathies, their suspicions of the United States, and their ambitious dreams of a utopian future, the adherents of MAD, once seen as the "doves" in the debate, have tended to appear more and more as hardened realists. After all, next to outright nuclear pacifism, any form of belief in deterrence tends to appear tough-minded. Thus over the past year numerous articles have appeared "in defense of deterrence"—by which is usually meant a view of deterrence based on MAD. It is this outlook that to many seems to combine best the moral concerns raised by the peace movement and the strategic concerns articulated by the administration. One writer expressing this view has tersely divided the debate into three camps: a "party of peace" (the antinuclear movement), a "party of war" (the administration), and, in the center, a "party of deterrence" (the advocates of MAD).[7]

Thus in the name of MAD the specter of unilateral disarmament has been vanquished again and again, but in the process the deeper relation between the moral and strategic issues has tended to be lost to view. The relation between these two concerns is not merely additive; a strategy that existed merely as an ill-conceived compromise between our strategic necessities and our moral ideals would hardly provide an adequate foundation for our defense. Moreover, what would be true of any other strategic doctrine is also true of MAD: its moral value depends entirely on its prior claim to practical, strategic validity. It may well be desirable to prevent the unstinted growth of nuclear arsenals and to avoid the costs and risks entailed by a U.S. military buildup. It may well be desirable to leave open a clear path to disarmament. But it is moral to attempt this *only if it can safely be done*—that is, only if by taking this course we do not embrace the greater risk of weakening deterrence to the point where a nuclear war becomes more likely as the result of our well-meaning efforts. Thus whether MAD offers intrinsically a more or less moral outlook on the nuclear problem depends on whether it is strategically valid; for any moral claim the doctrine may have rests in the first place on the assumption that it will work. Thus to answer the moral questions raised by the conflict between assured destruction and its alternatives, it is necessary to grasp with some precision the strategic realities at issue.

The Soviet Factor

Critical, above all, is the significance of the imposing military buildup undertaken by the Soviet Union over the past decade. That the Soviets have added massively to their military strength in the last ten years hardly any knowledgeable person will dispute. Indeed, the administration's strongest moral and strategic argument on its own behalf has been that its actions constitute nothing more than a necessary response to measures taken by the Soviet Union. Yet the force of this argument has been constantly undermined by the repeated denial on the part of prestigious figures in public debate that the Soviet buildup poses any real threat to the security of the United States—or at least a threat strong enough to merit the administration's response.

What is not widely understood is that this denial is based not on any factual dispute with the administration, but rather on a certain conceptual understanding of nuclear strategy: on the MAD hypothesis. Thus the whole moral argument hinges critically on this fundamental strategic assumption, and it is simply impossible to make an informed moral judgment on the debate until its merits and demerits are sorted out.

At the heart of MAD, in its initial formulation, was a promise of convergence—in technology, in strategic doctrine, in military behavior—between the two superpowers. It is this convergence that opponents of MAD, including the members of the Reagan administration, argue has entirely failed to come to pass. As envisioned by the framers of the doctrine, the rationale for convergence lay in the unprecedented nature of nuclear weapons. The weapons had only to exist, it was felt, for new laws of strategy to obtain—the laws of assured destruction. In the nuclear age, strategy and politics would be shaped ultimately by imperatives embodied in the technology. As one group of analysts wrote in the mid-1960s: "Technology seems to have a levelling effect which subsumes political, ideological, and social differences in various political systems."[8] Whether or not the rather radical changes these analysts predicted would come about, it was felt generally that nuclear weapons forced certain necessary choices on the leaders of countries that possessed them.

One of the critical difficulties that proponents of MAD confronted from the beginning was the overwhelming evidence that Soviet strategists had no such view of nuclear technology; on the contrary, the Soviets seemed to assume even a central nuclear war to be "winnable." This is not to be confused, as it occasionally has been, with the implausible claim that Soviet leaders or military men approach the prospect of nuclear war in a spirit of light-heartedness. The Soviets presumably recognize as well as anybody else the horrors that nuclear war would entail. But this has not prevented Soviet strategists from persisting in the conviction that in practice there would be a difference between "winners" and "losers" in such a war, and that this outcome would not necessarily be random but could be affected by the weapons, the defensive preparations, and the strategies of the two sides. While public statements of Soviet leaders were gradually adjusted to take account of Western thinking on nuclear war, behind this facade of apparent agreement Soviet military thinking remained extremely hostile to the prevailing Western notion that nuclear war would mean "the end of the world." "There is profound error and harm," in the words of Soviet strategist Gen. Maj. A. S. Milovidov, "in the disorienting claim of bourgeois ideologues that there could be no victor in a thermonuclear world war. The peoples of the world will put an end to imperialism, which is causing mankind incalculable suffering."[9] Whereas in the West the emergence of nuclear weapons led to the radical break with traditional military thinking defined by MAD, in the Soviet Union nuclear weapons were assimilated to the traditional military understanding of operations in war: the ordering concept was, and still is, that of "victory." As a result, Soviet strategy has retained two emphases that for some time dropped out of Western military doctrine and certainly from public understanding concerning nuclear war: the primacy of military (as opposed to civilian) targets, and the utility of civil defense. Thus even when discussing massive nuclear salvos, Soviet strategists envision the strikes aimed not at civilians but at military and economic facilities.[10] Civil defense is also seen to play an important role, as explained in this passage from a 1970 article in a Soviet military journal: "Obviously there will be a mass evacuation of the population from densely populated cities, major industrial and administrative centers."[11] Some preparations would be made in peacetime (for example, the Soviets currently possess hardened shelters to accommodate 110,000 key party and military personnel), but the most significant efforts would become visible during the period when, as Soviet strategy put it, events indicated that "war is coming."

The fact that Soviet strategic thinking diverged from that of the West was apparent even at the time that assured destruction was formulated, but it was not understood to present an insurmountable difficulty. For one thing, as Lawrence Freedman notes, Soviet doctrine had undergone some interesting revisions in the 1950s when it was altered to accommodate the existence of nuclear weapons and missiles. It was assumed that it could change again, and more radically.[12] For another, the Soviets lacked anything approaching the military capability to bring about what their strategy proposed. It is important to recognize that McNamara explicitly conceived the formulation of MAD partly as an educative effort to wean the Soviets away from what were understood to be "primitive" and tradition-bound military notions. The early posture statements setting forth assured destruction were written with great care, partly with the intent of instructing the Soviets, and McNamara expressed satisfaction at the number of statements purchased by the Soviet embassy in Washington.[13] This idea of "educating" the Soviet high command has remained a remarkably persistent theme among adherents to mutual assured destruction. As late as 1977, for example, Paul Warnke, head of the Arms Control and Disarmament Agency, referred in an interview to the "primitive" Soviet concept of victory: "Instead of talking in those terms, which would indulge what I regard as the primitive aspects of Soviet nuclear doctrine, we ought to be trying to educate them into the real world of strategic nuclear weapons, which is that nobody could possibly win."[14]

To judge from Warnke's comment, Soviet leaders have proved to be pupils of more than average recalcitrance, since it would seem that in 1977 the U.S. was still "trying to educate them" regarding ideas that had been first explained to them almost fifteen years before. Still, in measuring the success of this effort of education, both sides in the American debate have tended to agree that progress should be measured more by deeds than by words. Whatever the Soviets may say about "victory" in nuclear war, it is their actions that count. But even here controversy arises, for while there is broad agreement concerning the facts of the case, there is great variance in their interpretation. Readings of Soviet behavior seem to be materially affected depending upon whether one accepts or rejects the premises of MAD.

The Case of the ABM Treaty

Proponents and opponents of MAD tend to diverge markedly in their interpretations of even specific Soviet actions. Take, for example, the antiballistic missile (ABM) portion of the 1972 SALT I agreement. The ABM Treaty has frequently been praised as the most successful single arms control agreement concluded to date, since the treaty actually prevented the deployment of a wholly new weapons system that would potentially have transformed the strategic balance. The treaty has also been cited as concrete evidence of implicit Soviet acquiescence in at least the essential elements of MAD. Prohibitions on defensive measures seemed to run counter to the strong bias in Soviet military thinking toward the utility of measures designed to defend both military installations and economic centers. Soviet willingness to accept such provisions therefore was understood as a significant adjustment to the "realities" of the nuclear age. As Jerome H. Kahan put it in a 1975 article: "That the USSR has now accepted the inevitability, if not the desirability, of a mutual deterrence relationship with the United States is suggested strongly by Moscow's preference for stringent limits on area ABM deployments in the SALT treaty." Kahan acknowledged that Soviet doctrine had not shifted away from its explicit "war-fighting" orientation. Nonetheless, he insisted on the basis of the ABM Treaty that Soviet doctrine was "somewhat comparable to ours."[15]

Yet there was an alternative explanation for Soviet behavior regarding the ABM Treaty that successive events have rendered ever more persuasive. It is that, far from acquiescing in some new technological imperative of the nuclear age, or accepting MAD, the Soviets in negotiating limits on ABM systems were simply seeking unilateral military advantage in a very traditional sense. Notably, the Soviets actively pursued the development of defensive technologies throughout the 1960s. These efforts resulted in the creation of the so-called "Galosh" ABM system that is deployed to this day to protect Moscow and in fact much of the western Soviet Union.[16] (Under the treaty, each side was permitted two area systems, reduced to one in the July 1974 protocol; our response has been to dismantle our last remaining ABM sites.) During the 1960s the Soviets spurned all suggestions by the U.S. that such defensive deployments be limited by treaty. It was only when Richard Nixon had secured Senate approval for the technologically superior U.S. "Safeguard" ABM system that the Soviets became eager to discuss ABM limitations. In Henry Kissinger's account:

In 1967, before we had an ABM program, President Lyndon Johnson had suggested to Soviet Premier Alexei Kosygin at Glassboro that both sides renounce ABMs. Kosygin contemptuously dismissed the idea as one of the most ridiculous he had ever heard. By 1970, after the Nixon Administration had won its Congressional battle for ABM by one vote, Soviet SALT negotiators refused to discuss any other subject. Only by the most strenuous negotiating effort did we ensure that limits on offensive, as well as defensive, weapons were included.[17]

In short, once the full political context of Soviet actions is considered, the ABM provisions and even the SALT I agreement as a whole take on a new aspect. What one sees is not, as has been portrayed, the involuntary Soviet acquiescence in MAD but rather the effort of a traditional great power to secure by negotiation the military advantage that it could not attain by its own technology. In the United States, where the chief preoccupation in the strategic debate has tended to be the validity or invalidity of mutual assured destruction, the American Safeguard ABM system was seen as a threat to the logic of MAD. In Russia, one suspects, the U.S. ABM system was seen as a threat to the Soviet Union. The problem with the American Safeguard system, from the Soviet point of view, was not that it threatened to invalidate MAD, which the Soviets had never accepted in the first place, but that it threatened to neutralize the military and political value of Soviet rocket forces as a threat to the West. If this characterization seems harsh, it ought to be kept in mind that Soviet behavior in this regard would be consistent with the behavior of most powerful states through most of history. It is America that, in its preoccupation with the MAD hypothesis, turns out to be the odd bird.

Subsequent Soviet actions have tended to confirm this interpretation of the ABM episode. The effect of SALT I in the United States was to extinguish political interest in ballistic missile defense; consequently, funding for ABM research in the United States dropped precipitously. In the Soviet Union, by contrast, such research has continued apace. The Galosh system was modernized, and new phased-array radars of the sort used by ABM systems, and covered by the treaty, have been deployed in six sites. In recent months, testing and deployment has even skirted violations of the treaty. SAM-10 and SAM-12 anti-aircraft missiles have reportedly been tested in an ABM mode; and the recent detection of a new phased-array radar installation, deployed near a Siberian ballistic missile field in an area prohibited by the treaty, has prompted a debate within the Reagan administration concerning the wisdom—political and otherwise—of raising the issue of Soviet treaty violations.[18] Whether the administration will press its case is not clear at this writing. In this connection, however, the presence or absence of violations is less important than the abundant confirmation that the Soviet Union is committed to a view of defensive measures totally at odds with MAD. The main evidence for tacit Soviet acceptance of mutual assured destruction would appear to have been misinterpreted.

The Apolitical Vision of MAD

It may be an overstatement to describe as "epistemological" the differences that result in such divergent interpretations of Soviet actions, but radical contrasts in perception are clearly at issue. Critical is the role assigned to politics. Opponents of MAD have tended to dwell more than their counterparts on the specific political character of the Soviet regime. MAD, by contrast, reflecting its intellectual origins, offers a fundamentally nonpolitical account of the conflict between the superpowers. Rooted in economic "game theory," MAD arrives at its analysis by viewing strategic adversaries simply as rational actors abstractly understood. Presumably the logic of MAD would apply equally well to any two states that found themselves in the circumstances of the United States and the Soviet Union — i.e., to any two politically opposed states in possession of nuclear weapons. While accepting political conflict as a kind of axiom or condition, MAD abstracts from the content of the political struggle, dwelling instead on the dimensions in which the outlook and circumstances of the U.S. and the USSR are rendered by virtue of nuclear technology "comparable."

Grand strategies, it has been observed, tend to reflect the character of the regimes that devise them, and from the outset there has been a close kinship between "assured destruction" and the nature of the American polity. MAD stands as a kind of partial reflection of the American ethos. In America, as in the MAD vision, technology is understood to be the decisive shaper of life, the modern fact *par excellence,* the ultimate supplier and limiter of human options. But even more important, the MAD doctrine is, like so much of American political thinking, essentially apolitical in orientation. In MAD as in American life generally, politics is treated as a sort of afterthought, an epiphenomenon of a broader "human" experience. The actors in MAD are essentially unaffected by ideology or value: whatever their beliefs or other goals, they respond predictably, almost automatically, to the imperatives embodied in the technology. In this portrait of strategic actors there is something of America's genial, ethnocentric self—a confident projection of *homo economicus*: the assumption that, once the deal is spelled out, everybody is bound to agree on the basics with everybody else, to evaluate the costs and the benefits in the same way. In the context of American culture, the primacy that MAD assigns to technological influences and essentially economic calculations of advantage hardly seems surprising.[19]

There is now good reason to wish that in the nuclear era Americans had possessed more of what the poet John Keats called "negative capability"—the ability, simply speaking, to put oneself in another's shoes. Despite mountains of evidence to the contrary, the overwhelmingly prevalent assumption has been that, at least in the essential respects, Soviet views of nuclear strategy were "somewhat comparable" to ours. To most Americans and even to many American "experts," it has been inconceivable that the Soviets might approach nuclear weapons with different goals, different priorities, a different understanding of how the weapons might be used and what they could be used for. Nothing the Soviets themselves might say seemed capable of shaking this hypothesis.

Yet if the comfortable assumption of Soviet "comparability" has persisted for a long time, that is partly because for most of the nuclear era it has been, in the literal sense of the word, a "safe" assumption. That is to say, during much of the postwar period, Soviet military capabilities—especially nuclear—were so inferior to those of the United States that it hardly mattered what the Soviets thought about strategy at any level.

There is an irony in the history of MAD, for this doctrine of "mutual" vulnerability was formulated at a time when vulnerability was anything but mutual. As late as 1966, it should be remembered, the Soviets possessed only 350 land-based and only about 30 submarine-launched ballistic missiles as compared with an American total in the two categories of over 1,700.[20] Yet our doctrine was predicated on "parity." By a trick of memory it now tends to be assumed that it was "parity" of weapons that ensured our safety in the past. It was nothing of the sort. At the time of the Cuban missile crisis, the United States possessed overwhelming superiority in both conventional naval and nuclear armaments.

Those present at the crisis have since argued that it was not nuclear strength but in fact conventional force locally applied—in particular, the naval quarantine of Cuba—that brought successful resolution to the crisis. But as Peter Rodman has shown, this is not at all self-evident.[21] The fact is that the Soviet Union was aware of U.S. strength at all levels, and it is difficult to argue that nuclear superiority did not play a role. At all events, it was overall *strategic* superiority that gave the United States scope to act—and it is crucial to recognize that this strategic superiority, whether in nuclear or conventional arms, is now a thing of the past.

Technological and Political Imperatives

The whole dispute over the validity of MAD and the nature of Soviet intentions might have remained what it originally was—chiefly a theoretical argument—were it not for certain troubling developments. Yet changes in both technology and military deployments have forced these issues once again to the fore. Notably, technology has moved in a direction exactly opposite to that predicted by early proponents of MAD. Rather than force a convergence of doctrine and strategy upon the superpowers, it has helped to pull them, strategically speaking, further and further apart. The crucial factor has been the emergence of highly accurate nuclear warheads capable of destroying hardened military targets and even hardened missile silos. These so-called "counterforce" weapons endow "war-fighting" strategies of nuclear war—such as those articulated in Soviet military writings—with a physical plausibility that they never previously had. Thus technology has introduced into the military arsenals of superpowers a physical distinction corresponding to the strategic distinction between war-fighting and assured destruction doctrines. MAD envisions a punitive strike at the *society* of the enemy; counterforce weapons make it at least physically possible to destroy missiles in their silos and thus to strike at the enemy's *weapons*, the adversary's physical ability to wage nuclear war.

Yet even these technological developments might have been weathered by MAD had the Soviet Union not moved so decisively to take advantage of them. It is critical to recognize that the Soviet

Union responded to the emergence of counterforce technology in a manner fundamentally different from that of the United States, though in a fashion totally consistent with its own understanding of the function of nuclear arms. At this point in the nuclear era— if not before—there was a clear divergence in the behavior of the two superpowers. Throughout the 1970s the Soviet Union moved unstintingly to develop and deploy as large a number of counterforce warheads as was practical. Faced at the same moment with the possibility of developing such counterforce capability, the United States deliberately decided to forego its option, in the interest of preserving the relationship of mutual deterrence. From 1969 to 1974 the United States exercised deliberate restraint in the development of warhead accuracy so as not to threaten Soviet assured destruction capability. Thomas Wolfe summarized the U.S. action in a well-known study for the Rand Corporation:

From 1969 to 1979, it was U.S. declaratory policy, backed up by budgetary controls, not to develop highly accurate weapons that might threaten hardened Soviet military targets. This policy was not universally applauded on the U.S. side, as indicated by news accounts in August 1972 of Pentagon plans to accelerate the development of more accurate warheads but not to deploy them. Congress, however, rejected appropriations associated with these programs, illustrating continued congressional adherence to constraints upon improvement of U.S. counterforce capabilities. It was only during [James] Schlesinger's tenure as secretary of defense that the declaratory policy against accuracy improvements was formally stopped with congressional approval.[22]

In a pattern that was to be repeated again and again during the course of the decade, the Soviets failed to reciprocate the United States' gesture of unilateral restraint—its "self-denying ordinance."[23]

That Soviet leaders would move in such a direction is hardly surprising in light of Soviet strategic thinking; at the same time, the deployment of counterforce weapons on a massive scale gave new credibility to the Soviet strategic formulations that had been long dismissed in the West as absurd.

The Problem of U.S. Vulnerability

Thanks to massive Soviet deployments of counterforce weapons, it began to become apparent in the middle of the last decade that by the early 1980s the Soviet Union would have deployed a sufficient number of such warheads to destroy 90 to 95 percent of U.S. land-based missiles in their silos, using only a small portion of its own intercontinental ballistic missile (ICBM) force. Since the U.S. submarine-based missiles that would remain intact do not currently possess counterforce capability, it seemed that the president might be left with the sole option of retaliating against such an attack with a "countervalue" strike against Soviet society, only to face far worse countervalue retribution in return. Thus the Soviet buildup was operating to deprive us gradually of a credible retaliatory capacity. That we would have survivable missiles was not in doubt, but since the Soviets would possess an equal number and since the missiles could be targeted effectively only at civilian centers, there would be no possibility of U.S. retaliation short of mutual suicide. Even the Soviet first strike could produce casualties in the millions; but if retaliation meant 100 million more Americans dead, it was felt that the president's hand would likely be stayed.

The plausibility of this scenario was widely criticized. But what is important to recognize is that ten years earlier, even the hint that the Soviets might be allowed to achieve such an advantage would have been greeted with an outpouring of public concern. At the same time it should be stressed that the controversy over the so-called "window of vulnerability" had to do with the likelihood that the Soviets would launch such an attack. Among knowledgeable people the technical reality of U.S. ICBM vulnerability is no longer a matter for dispute. It has been confirmed not only by the Defense Department but by the bipartisan report of the Scowcroft Commission:

While Soviet operational missile performance in wartime may be somewhat less accurate than performance on the test range, the Soviets nevertheless now probably possess the necessary combination of ICBM numbers, reliability, accuracy, and warhead yield to destroy almost all of the 1,047 U.S. ICBM silos using only a portion of their own ICBM force. The U.S. ICBM force now deployed cannot inflict similar damage, even using the entire force.[24]

This passage is especially interesting in light of the popular conception that in the Scowcroft report the idea of a "window of vulnerability" was dismissed. It needs to be noted that the United

States does not possess a comparable capacity vis-a-vis the Soviet Union. Because of the smaller size and lesser accuracy of U.S. warheads, it is estimated at present that even a full-scale preemptive American attack against the Soviet rocket force would leave about 65 percent of Soviet ICBMs intact.[25]

It is important to recognize that the military and political significance of the Soviet Union's newly acquired preemptive capability does not rest on any foolish or simpleminded assumption that the Soviet leadership is somehow eager to make actual use of it. It has become customary in the nuclear debate to point out that the idea of a Soviet preemptive strike is preposterous and to assume that with this single stroke the argument is done. What is critical to grasp is that the missiles do not have to be fired to be of significant military and political weight. To the degree that relations between opposing states remain peaceful, they are based on the calculation, rather than the actual employment, of military power, and it is this calculation that the growth of Soviet strength decisively upsets.

Throughout the postwar period the security of the democracies has depended decisively on the U.S. "nuclear umbrella"; that is, the freedom of the West has been predicated on American strategic superiority, and American superiority in turn on superiority in nuclear arms. (There is reason to lament the degree to which the West has neglected conventional military strength in favor of less expensive nuclear deployments, but that is a topic for another time and place.) To say that the American nuclear advantage has been canceled by recent Soviet deployments understates the case. What people are pleased to call "parity," on the basis of a definition artfully grown vaguer and vaguer over the years and months, is, from the standpoint of any operational military calculation, Soviet superiority—growing clearer and clearer almost by the day. To the degree that these calculations describe physical possibilities that could be made to come about, they cannot be dismissed. It is not necessary to assume that the Soviets want to wage nuclear war; indeed, hardly anyone in or out of the administration does. It is only necessary to assume that the Soviets wish to banish from *our* minds any hope that if they chose to initiate such a struggle we would have a chance to survive.

What tends to be forgotten, moreover, is that the whole controversy over Soviet nuclear "parity" takes place in a strategic climate of overwhelming Soviet superiority in conventional forces. Numerically the Soviet Union far outdistances the West in nearly every category of conventional weaponry, and in many areas the technological gap that once worked to the advantage of Western forces has virtually closed. Even if the Soviets were to succeed in shifting the strategic conflict entirely to the conventional level, they would gain an enormous advantage.

For a long time it was possible to explain the Soviet buildup as an effort to gain "parity." And yet it is now obvious that the Soviet Union attained rough parity in nuclear armaments at least a decade ago and attained an assured destruction capability some time before that. (The 1972 SALT I agreement, it should be remembered, allowed the Soviet Union a quantitative advantage of 800 intercontinental missiles, to compensate for what was understood to be American technological superiority and for the existence of 162 nuclear missiles in the British and French arsenals.)[26] Even now, the Soviets continue to construct powerful, counterforce-capable ICBMs at the rate of nearly 200 a year. In the past decade, the Soviet Union has built a total of 2,000 ICBMs. (For comparison, it should be noted that the U.S. built 350 ICBMs during the same period; and even the controversial Scowcroft proposal concerning the MX envisions the construction of only 100 of these missiles.) In addition, 350 new, extremely accurate intermediate-range missiles have been deployed by the Soviets against Europe and Asia in the past six years. Even in areas where the Soviet advantage is absurdly overpowering, construction continues at a fantastic rate. Warsaw Pact forces now enjoy roughly a 5-to-1 advantage over NATO forces in tank power; yet in 1981, for example, the USSR and Pact countries built a total of 5,040 new battle tanks, as compared with a NATO and U.S. total for the same year of 760.[27] From 1969 to 1975, U.S. defense spending actually declined in real terms, while Soviet spending grew at roughly a 4 percent real rate. For much of the later 1970s, the Soviet Union was outspending the United States by as much as 50 percent, on a much poorer economic base. To this day, in the wake of Mr. Reagan's "massive buildup," Soviet military spending substantially exceeds that of the U.S.[28]

Denying the Danger

In a democratic nation alive to the requirements of its own survival, such a series of dark developments might be expected to arouse a sense of emergency and call forth a new consensus. Nothing of the sort has occurred. The absence of a sense of crisis, moreover, is self-reinforcing; for if, as the public mood suggests, there is no real emergency, then why worry? It is not MAD alone, of course, that has prevented acknowledgment of these new developments. Most of the really obvious changes have occurred in the past ten and many in the past five years—precisely the period during which American public opinion was occupied with the denouement of Vietnam and the crisis of Watergate. But critical in annulling any sense of emergency has been the vocal denial of extremely prestigious public figures—nearly all of them longtime partisans of MAD—that any real danger exists. Yet what is not widely understood is that this denial is not *factual* but *conceptual* in character. No responsible opponent of the current administration denies the veracity of its reports concerning Soviet military buildup; *what is denied is that it matters*. The basis for this denial lies in the MAD hypothesis: for if the U.S. continues to possess an assured destruction capability—and submarine warheads alone would seem to constitute such a force—then no Soviet actions, under the logic of MAD, could fundamentally threaten our security. Yet this conceptual denial of the importance of recent developments has tended to become confused in the public mind with a factual denial of their existence, just as opposition to the theory of MAD has sometimes been confused with the disposition to risk, "hawkishly," embarking on a nuclear war.

Yet it is worth asking whether the MAD hypothesis has not survived over the years simply by turning increasingly circular, tautological. In retrospect, the history of assured destruction thinking since its original conceptualization appears more and more a history of denial and rhetorical retreat: denial, first, of the importance of Soviet strategic thinking; denial, next, of the military utility of ABM; denial of the unceasing Soviet buildup, both in its early stages and even now when the supposed goal of "parity" has long since been surpassed; denial even of the military and political significance of a Soviet first-strike capability. At the same

time, there has been a steady tactical retreat from confident
assertions that the Soviets could be made to think and act toward
nuclear weapons the way we do; to the qualified claim that it
didn't matter what they thought so long as they acted properly
(the ABM Treaty); to the current rather implausible avowals that
nothing they think or do could ever make a difference. Thus, after
all the revelations of Soviet strategic thinking, after all the rever-
sals in American hopes for arms control, after all the discredited
predictions that the Soviets would stop building once they
achieved assured destruction or "parity," such a man as McGeorge
Bundy can still write, without humor, that "on the nature of
nuclear danger serious Soviet leaders and experts have repeatedly
shown an understanding not essentially different from that which
moved the [American Catholic] bishops."[29] In Bundy's new formulation, mutual assured destruction has been transformed into
something called "existential deterrence"—merely the latest
name for the twenty-year-old idea of MAD.[30]

In short, events and realities that to less committed observers
might seem to have clear and definite implications for our
strategic circumstances have successively been gainsayed or explained away in the service of the single hypothesis that assured
destruction is enough. "The more of doubt," says one of Robert
Browning's characters, "the stronger faith, I say/If faith o'er-
comes doubt." Against a cascade of doubts, MAD has proved a
marvelously resilient creed.

Yet so preponderant has become the need to discount or explain
away Soviet departures from MAD that the logic of the doctrine is
no longer applied in public debate with any consistency. MAD depends on what Glenn Snyder has termed "deterrence by pain"—
as opposed to "deterrence by denial."[31] MAD strategists argue, in
essence, that given the horrendous power of nuclear arms, the
threat of pain—i.e., the threat of retaliation against an enemy
society—should be sufficient to deter attack. War-fighting or
counterforce strategies, by contrast, emphasize the importance of
"denying" the enemy the military wherewithal to attain a decisive
advantage or "victory" at whatever price. From the standpoint of
deterrence by pain, the distinction between countervalue and
counterforce weapons hardly matters, because both are capable of
inflicting horrible punishment. For deterrence by denial, however,

the distinction could become extremely important, since the emphasis is on attacking the enemy's *means* of doing battle.

On this basis one could argue, perversely perhaps but still consistently, that if as MAD suggests the threat of pain should be sufficient to deter war, then a buildup of U.S. forces should not prove inherently dangerous to deterrence. That is because whatever additional armaments we may deploy the Soviets will always possess the ability to inflict horrible pain in retaliation. Even the possession of U.S. first-strike capability would leave the Soviet Union with upwards of 2,000 submarine-based warheads with which to retaliate — an assured destruction capability if ever there was one. One could oppose a buildup on grounds that it was costly or wasteful, but not on the grounds that it would lead to war. In other words, for the same reason that we are counseled not to feel threatened by the Soviet buildup, the Soviets should not feel threatened by ours. If the logic of deterrence by pain is in fact valid, war should not be made more likely simply by a buildup on one side or another.

But conversely, if the mere belief by American leaders (however fallacious) that nuclear war were in some sense "winnable" would make war more likely — and this is the gravamen of the charge against the administration — then it follows that a similar belief by Soviet leaders (however fallacious) would have the same result. Our ability to inflict pain in retaliation — i.e., our "assured destruction capability" — would not in the final analysis be sufficient to deter. Moreover, if, as is also often argued, moral suasion is insufficient to wean American leaders from this belief — if they must be denied the physical capability to accomplish what they would set out to do — then it follows that Soviet leaders also must be denied this capability. In America, we can place political pressure on the administration not to build the requisite weapons. But in the Soviet case such pressure on our part is futile. Indeed, the Soviets have already acquired the basic elements of a war-fighting capability and continue to acquire at a fantastic rate weapons whose only purpose is manifestly not to inflict pain but rather to circumscribe or if possible deny our ability to retaliate short of mutual suicide. Moreover, it is well established that Soviet strategy envisions even central nuclear war to be winnable (a fact borne out by the nature of Soviet deployments). Our only option is thus to take the measures to render the hope of victory not just *humanly* but *militarily* implausible. This means, in the end, acquiring a capacity to inflict equivalent military damage and doing what we can to ensure the invulnerability of our retaliatory capability. In short, once one steps out of the logic of deterrence by pain or MAD pure and simple, it becomes essential to think about the operational capabilities of weapons that one never intends to use. The capacity to deter war—to prevent war defensively from occurring—becomes logically indistinguishable from the ability to fight one. The recommendation to meet the Soviet buildup with a buildup of our own, therefore, comes not from belligerence or "imperial ambitions" on the part of American leaders, but simply from the straightforward necessity of securing our safety.

Self-Deterrence

The logic of MAD, in other words, has been applied in recent years more and more one-sidedly—to deter us from acquiring weapons to match and counter the Soviet buildup. Thus well-intentioned people have endeavored to stop the "arms race"; but the arms race is not war, and in stopping the arms race we are taking measures that logic and history suggest are making war more likely by making it more "thinkable"—for Soviet leaders.

The thinking embodied in MAD and arms control has tended to skew our discussions of these matters, so that we have come to debate the decision to acquire new weapons as though we were debating a decision to use them—as though adding to our arsenal, even for avowedly defensive purposes, were equivalent to launching an attack. The peculiarity of this position needs to be appreciated. At a time when the Soviet Union is adding MIRVed ICBMs to its arsenal at the rate of 175 to 200 per year, building hundreds of new aircraft, scores of new naval vessels, and thousands of new tanks, public figures in the United States rail against the procurement of the MX missile—the first new U.S. ICBM to be contemplated in over a decade—as though it were a heinous crime. Indeed, the metaphors that we employ in political discourse routinely treat the mere procurement of weapons as an action equivalent to murder. Writing of the administration's plans for a buildup, Theodore Draper has commented that deterrence "may yet equal liberty for the number of crimes committed in its name."[32] But an important distinction is being overlooked here. The "sins" committed in the name of liberty involved the actual killing of human beings; what Draper is discussing is merely a U.S. buildup undertaken to counter Soviet deployments and to deter aggression— i.e., precisely to prevent such weapons from being used. Yet he speaks as if the mere procurement of a weapon constituted an atrocity. Even the Catholic bishops have contributed to this moral perspective, describing the "arms race" as an "act of aggression" against "the poor."[33] It may be that if defense spending were less throughout the world, there would be more spending for the poor. But the United States is arming with the intention of defending itself, and not of persecuting its less fortunate citizens. So remote has public discussion in the West grown from the life-and-death realities of politics that we seem at times to have lost the capacity to differentiate between maintenance of peacetime defenses and the actual waging of war.

Little wonder that, in this looking-glass moral universe where arming for self-defense tends to be counted as equivalent to murder, an American administration has difficulty making a persuasive ethical case for its defense policies. But it must be understood that the moral objections to the administration's stance arise chiefly because the proponents of MAD succeed again and again in explaining away the rather simple and obvious *strategic* justification for the administration's actions. As a result, the debate must be conducted on the basis of premises so remote from the military realities with which policymakers must cope that even the modest successes achieved by the administration in the public forum seem surprising. Our whole discourse about nuclear weapons is dominated by a moral vision rooted in discredited strategic assumptions—assumptions at best appropriate to the strategic reality of 1965 or 1972 and in any case wholly irrelevant to the vastly changed circumstances of the present. Yielding to the temptation to play to this pervasive "moral" outlook, the administration has ended up more often than not with a lame, self-contradictory compromise between its own straightforward strategic logic and the prevailing nuclear orthodoxies.

But what of the more common worry that the existence of a stronger American arsenal might conceivably tempt American leaders toward adventuresomeness or a dangerous confrontation, or the more serious charge that elements in the current administration would be willing, under certain circumstances, to initiate a nuclear war? The latter charge, in particular, is rendered simply incredible by the actual state of the American arsenal when compared with that of the Soviet Union. No nation would be contemplating war in such a state of military disarray. The United States has nothing like the superiority of forces that would allow it to envision attacking the Soviet Union, whether by nuclear or by conventional means. Moreover, as the current administration is well aware, nothing in its defense programs envisions such superiority or even, for that matter, "parity," if "parity" is very strictly defined. It is worth remembering that every major new strategic system advocated by Mr. Reagan — the MX missile, the B-1 bomber, the Trident submarine — was originally proposed by previous administrations.

The Shibboleth of Warmongering

Indeed, the notion that the Reagan administration is contemplating war, for all its recent popular currency, is in fact little less than ludicrous. Much is made of the administration's supposedly fervent anti-Communism. But a government that cannot even bring itself to declare default on loans to Communist Poland or to withhold sales of wheat from the Soviet bloc to gain political and military leverage is hardly in a position to make the enormous economic sacrifices that would attend upon the actual waging of war. Besides, whatever various U.S. economic interest groups may gain from the "arms race," the West has nothing economically to gain from a war with the East. (For the East, of course, the situation is quite the opposite; much of the Soviet buildup has been designed to gain economic access to the West, preferably by political threats based on military power rather than the direct use of military means.) Our historical interest is not in conquest, but rather in securing trading partners — so much so that we can hardly restrain our commercial men from trading with our chief adversary even when such trade helps to build the Soviet military machine. There is simply nothing in the makeup of the Western commercial democracies to lead them to want war with the Soviet

Union. That this needs to be said at all is a measure of how far we have fallen from basic self-understanding. What is ironic is that Soviet officials, for all their disingenuous protestations to the contrary, are more aware of these realities than many of our own citizens.

At the same time, there is a point at which refusal to confront amounts to open retreat, and it is here that we must face up to the implications of possessing nuclear weapons. The world is still a dangerous place, and the political freedom of the West rests in the final analysis on the strength of the American arsenal. The vast economic power of America and Western Europe avails nothing if at the critical moment this economic power could not be translated into military force. Yet we.seem at once too craven and too greedy to be willing to pay for our own defense.

Many in Europe and America appear to have convinced themselves that totalitarian rule would be tolerable. For these it is useful to remember that the combined casualties of this century's two world wars did not yet equal the number who died under Communist rule in Russia and East Europe before, during, and after World War II. Nazi Germany was responsible for the extermination of six million people; Communist Russia, by moderate estimates, for the murder of *ten times* that many.[34] To this day some two million people suffer in concentration camps in the Soviet Union. Hundreds are committed to psychiatric hospitals for "political" offenses.[35] And the worst horrors of the Great Purge are being reenacted today in Afghanistan, where thousands have been subject to summary executions and the most appalling tortures — to which the Western democracies, as is their wont, turn a deaf ear.[36] These — and not the "arms race" — are the real horrors of our time.

Yet there is one important step in addition to upgrading our nuclear forces that can be taken toward reducing the chances of nuclear war: it is to deploy conventional forces in sufficient numbers to deter aggression from Europe and other areas of "vital interest" — which is only to say where the Soviet Union may threaten the West itself or the very basis of the West's long-term survival. There is very broad support, in principle, for such a proposal. But unfortunately, many who have campaigned most vociferously against nuclear arms have also worked to close off this critical alternative. The American Catholic Bishops offer an emphatic critique of the "first use" of nuclear weapons in Europe, but are considerably less clear regarding the only viable alternative—namely, a buildup of conventional forces. Many senators and congressmen who campaign against the MX also consistently vote against increases in the defense budget that would expand conventional procurement. At a time when the conventional forces of the Soviet Union and Warsaw Pact nations outnumber those of the Western Alliance by several times, our legislators have set off on a crusade against "waste" in the Pentagon, whose inevitable effect is to erode already shaky public support for defense spending generally.

Moral Myopia

All this is done in the service of what are understood to be moral goals. Yet throughout this debate we have been tending to treat as "moral choices" what, in light of accumulated facts, barely appear to be "choices" at all, let alone choices in which ethical considerations could be held paramount. It is not merely that Soviet forces are gaining on the United States; it is that by every measure that could be counted meaningful, the Soviets have overtaken us. We talk as though the decision facing us were between maintaining parity and acquiring some kind of strategic "superiority," when the choice is in fact between bare parity and an inferiority in both nuclear and conventional armaments that increases by the month. We talk of "threatening" the Soviet Union, as though we had the comparative force to make that any more a real option. Given our history, it is only natural that we would conduct these discussions in an atmosphere of confidence, assuming that we had the ability to choose among a plethora of options. Through most of our postwar history such discussions have occurred in a climate of American freedom and strategic superiority. What Americans fail to understand are the implications of this era's having come to an end.

It has now become almost axiomatic in public debate that an adequate ethical response to the problems posed by nuclear weapons requires a heightened moral awareness. Yet so plain are the horrors of nuclear war and so inescapable are the problems facing us, that it is hardly clear that anything more than ordinary decency is required to form an adequate moral response. The fundamental moral imperatives of our time would seem both simple and clear: to prevent nuclear war, and to prevent at least the existing democracies from falling under totalitarian rule. One need not be a saint or a visionary or a moral philosopher to understand and embrace these goals. Indeed, it can be argued that from the beginning of the nuclear era, decent people in the democracies have never wanted anything else. In this debate the really critical questions facing us are not in the strict sense moral but rather political and strategic. It is on a clearer understanding of these latter issues that our survival now urgently depends.

IV

Social Issues

11

MICHAEL NOVAK

Choice in Education: A Problem of Social Trust

Almost anything that can be said about America must be said as paradox. A given assertion is seldom true, without its opposite also having considerable substance to commend it. To say, then, that we are a diverse people, proud of our diversity, requires correction. Our diversity has also made us fearful.

The central energy of this chosen nation and "almost chosen people," born in an act of revolutionary choice and living under constitutional procedures for choice, might be said to be the maximization of choice. Yet, as the essays in this book have shown, on both left and right there are serious constraints upon free choice in education. Patterns of conformity are strong.

Intellectual and social energies, however, have recently opened up new possibilities. During the past ten years, the context of dis-

This essay originally appeared as "Social Trust" in *Parents, Teachers, and Children: Prospects for Choice in American Education* (1977). References to other papers are to chapters in that book.

cussion has been subtly and deeply altered. We are free at last to walk away from the dichotomous thinking of racial contrast— "white" and "colored," "honky" and "black." This impulse to find a new language springs from reality itself. At home, the civil rights movement found itself increasingly involved in questions of "minorities" other than blacks alone—Native Americans, Chicanos, Puerto Ricans, Asians, and (in general) Third World peoples. Even along this axis, it soon became evident that the distinctive element of coalition is not racial but, rather, cultural. And from this the full revelation about American diversity begins.

For, on the one hand, among the most successful "races" in the United States (to use the term as it was employed in the U.S. Congress prior to the immigration legislation of 1924) have been a whole series of "colored peoples" (as they were then defined): the Syrian-Lebanese, the Armenians, the Jews, the Japanese, the Chinese, the Koreans, the Italians, and the West Indian blacks. On the other hand, while conditions of slavery and reconstruction imposed upon American blacks a severity of disadvantage experienced by no other, neither blacks nor other races of "color" stand alone in facing cultural, economic, educational, and occupational disadvantage. If statistical surveys are to be done about the proportional representation of blacks on the Chicago police force, they are with equal justice to be done about the proportional representation of Polish-Americans on the Chicago police force. (The situation of Poles is even more dismal in that and in other instances.) An examination of the patterns of disadvantage in the United States reveals no stark dichotomy, based on race alone, which would supply simpler ideological needs. It reveals, instead, a large spectrum of experiences, sufferings, strengths, and weaknesses. The glory and the agony are not neatly divided.

Ideologues express concern that this more complex picture, even if more accurate, will deflate feelings of guilt, urgency, and social change. Such engines of change are far more fickle, unreliable, and suspect than ideologues have the wit to notice. In fact, the more accurate picture relieves the isolation of blacks and other racial groups, and generates among others an awareness of analogous historical experiences. It also inspires ever more exact social analyses. On such sympathies and on such concern for the exact truth—and on these alone—can one ground long-lived political coalitions.

In the international sphere, events have forced similar cultural awareness into consciousness. Most conflicts do not occur along racial lines but, rather, within them. Americans, particularly those born in the American South, may be forgiven for exaggerating the salience of race in human affairs. Intraracial historical enemies, however, are frequent, turbulent, and bitter, as witness the tribal wars of Africa or the bloodlettings of European history. Arabs and Israelis are not of different races; nor are Protestant and Catholic Irish; nor are Nigerians and Biafrans, Katangans and Zaireans. The Germans annihilated some eighteen million persons in concentration camps—Jews, Slavs, and others—who, from the perspective of Africa, would appear to be "white races." Whites have never wreaked so much agony upon blacks as upon each other; and, in general, so with other races. This is an important, but not the only, international lesson: culture is deeper than race.

It was believed for more than one generation that the process called modernization would homogenize the planet. The spread of rational procedures, the development of identical tastes, and a planetary communications network, it was assumed, would bring the peoples of many cultures closer together. As a consequence, modernity would make them more the same. World order, it was hoped, would become more rational. Irrational factors like blood, soil, tribal loyalties, and even nationalism would gradually diminish. And there have, indeed, been signs that such expectations were not entirely false. Coca Cola, Brut, Esso, Shell, and other products are used in the most remote locations. Where such modern products go, can managerial habits and rational arrangements be far behind? The surprising factor has been, however, the re-emergent salience of ethnicity. Far from being diminished by post-tribal modernization, the energies of localism and cultural loyalty seem to have been reawakened. In Slovakia, in Scotland, in Katanga, in Quebec, in Vietnam, in Ukrainia, in Palestine, among Soviet Jews, and in many other places, the desire of cultural minorities for political recognition (for sovereignty, for the redrawing of boundaries, for linguistic and other rights, for representation, etc., in baffling variety) has made ethnic consciousness one of the most powerful forces in international affairs at the end of the twentieth century.

As an hypothesis, consider three reasons why this might be so: (1) Discontentment with the moral content of modernity and the "new man" of the modern type; (2) the overlooked role in the human psyche of a sense of historical rootedness; (3) the capacity of modern institutions, and of the kind of consciousness appropriate for living within them, to permit differentiation and even individualization without threat to powerful bonds of social unity. Rationalistic theories, once persuasive, now seem to have been too optimistic about the moral content of the humanism actually to be produced by the modern institutions. Human types like John Dean, Jeb Magruder, and others involved in "Watergate" and in similar corporate practices at every level, whether in socialist or in capitalist regimes, have not been as attractive in practice as the celebration of the secular, urban, pragmatic style had led us to anticipate.

Rationalistic theories seem also to have been too shallow in their view of human historicity. Human beings are historical animals, and the absense of a personal history is like a hunger whose filling can bring tears to the eyes: witness the emotion stirred by the TV version of *Roots*, watched by over 80 percent of all American blacks.

Finally, rationalistic theories failed to estimate the power of modern institutions—books, television, travel, the computer—to permit the individual to retain and to deepen cultural consciousness even while living among persons of a quite different culture. It is not necessary to live in a cultural enclave in order to retain one's cultural consciousness. Meanwhile, the great centripetal power of the modern state (and of other modern institutions as well) pulls so heavily in the direction of homogeneity and conformity that, as if by check and balance, individuals and local "mediating" collectivities feel freer to assert their own energies. Human liberty seems to demand it.

Historical process cyclically and slowly alternates—systole and dystole—between tendencies of unity and of diversity (Professor Lazerson's history [Chapter I] suggests as much). At some moments, the movements are toward the center, homogenizing; at others, the center becoming too strong, resistance tends toward diversification in many directions. A system of social fear may govern such motions. When fears of division dominate, assimilation is encouraged. When fears of conformity dominate, diversity acquires partisans. We seem now to be living, both domestically and in the world at large, in an age of unparalleled "interdependence." Central governments grow stronger under liberal, as well as socialist, systems. Mass communications reflect, incite, and impose national styles. In rebellion—we may hypothesize—those institutions that mediate between the omnipotent state and the lonely individual will become the focus of increasing energy: family, ethnic group, church, neighborhood and other local associations, unions, and the like.

It is in this intellectual context that one must place the discussion of education in the United States and, in particular, the question of vouchers. Since World War II, enormous changes have taken place in American school systems. (1) Vast social migrations have occurred, especially three: that from rural to urban areas; that of blacks out of the South; and that from cities to suburbs. (2) School systems have become more centralized, professionalized, and bureaucratized. (3) The horizons for children in school have been so broadened as to change the nature of their education; it has come to be mandatory that children finish high school, and expectable that half or more will try at least some college work; education seems less and less like a privilege or a means of liberation, and more and more like an oppressive necessity. At one and the same time, schools have taken on a more complex set of tasks than occupied them prior to World War II, and parents have come to expect more and more of the schools— while providing less educational help in the home. "Consolidated" schools seem in any case more distant from the home. Education has become a specialization left to the experts.

As "modernizing" institutions *par excellence*—the institutions of passage into modernity—the schools are subject to all the aforementioned disappointments with modernity. Their moral quality is disappointing ("permissive," "progressive"); their inability to touch the moral-cultural roots of children is protested; and their capacities for developing a sound "pluralistic personality" seems to be frustrated. In part, of course, the schools are victims of their own ideology. Propelled out of the optimistic, rational hopes of the end of World War II, they have seen their task to be that of a "melting pot" in two senses: first, to mold a new undifferentiated ("unhyphenated") American characterology; and, second, to prepare millions of youngsters for the prosperity of a technical, bureaucratic, corporate civilization. (Out went the classics; in came "modern" curricula.)

The power of the upper class Anglo-Saxon elite of almost every American city and region has, I think, been exaggerated, but one area in which its hegemony has been particularly strong is that of culture, from museums and opera societies to the public schools. It could hardly be an error to see in certain forms of "Anglo-conformity" a central motif of American schooling. A few examples may be cited to establish my meaning: this nation is the third largest Spanish-speaking nation of the world; it contains more blacks than any single African nation; it contains the third-largest Eastern European Slavic community, etc. Yet the idological slant of the curriculum looks out at the world inexorably and rather narrowly from the viewpoint of English culture in Europe and in America. Not only the language and not only the subject matter but, in addition, the emotional and spiritual style of the schools is rather more narrow than the possibilities within the population. Many millions besides blacks and Latinos have experienced discomfort in the classrooms of the "Anglo" majority. Still, recognizing that economic and political power are connected to cultural power, many parents have been grateful for the "Americanizing" efforts of the schools and have demanded such efforts. In order to notice the power of such efforts, indeed, one need not be wholly negative about them. (Although I now believe it sad, even slightly tragic, that the schools of Western Pennsylvania did not encourage me to learn the language of my grandparents, thus involving my grandparents in my education and me in Slavic culture so that in adulthood significant options would have been open to me in that direction, I am grateful for the confidence early given me that America was "mine" and that I could plunge into the stream of its language with delight.)

Three consequences, nonetheless, derive from Anglo-conformity in the schools. First, the real pluralism of American life has been lost to our view. Our eyes have been trained not to notice what they do in fact see. In fiction, the ethnic background of a character is almost always introduced, usually quite early, and is always regarded as significant. In real life (at least we tell ourselves) we do not notice; it would seem unenlightened to notice. Tolerance is a high virtue; it is higher when it is respectful without pretending to be blind.

Secondly, the nation's public language about values is impoverished. Values are learned instinctively and profoundly in the early life of the child, in families. The language for expressing values, as well as the rituals, prayers, and celebrations of the deeds of moral heroes and heroines, are passed on from generation to generation in cultural traditions. In a pluralistic society, however, in order not to give offense or to provoke division, it often happens in common endeavors that none feel free to articulate the full particularity of their own ethical commitments. "Common denominators" are sought. Refuge is taken in truisms and cant. Sentimentality triumphs over intelligence. The whole moral enterprise falls into a certain disrepute, and as soon as the ceremonies are over, the skeptical and intelligent are pleased to hurry back to their pragmatic activities.

A further result is that public language tends to be either pious, in a neutral sort of way (best exemplified by President Eisenhower's reputed observation, "Ninety-nine percent of Americans believe in God, I don't care which one you mean"); or else far more secular than are the individuals who actually speak it. Many hide their personal beliefs; the public language becomes secular by default. It seems at times to be a language that belongs to no one, with no real roots or power. Yet it has gained public dominance just the same. I am thinking here of the language that passes as "sophistication," that well-informed savviness not only of the talk shows and the celebrities, but even of college presidents, politicians, and serious journalists. Quite often in our society, public figures are not saying exactly what they themselves believe. They grope for what they take to be the consensus, for the idiom of a "sophisticated" national audience, for what "may be said." The supposed consensual audience, it turns out, can be a fiction, no single member of it being rooted in, or being fully willing to subscribe to, the consensus supposedly at work. In a pretended monoculture, false consciousness thrives.

Thirdly, the monocultural emphasis of the schools leads to profound dissatisfactions the moment the schools begin to raise serious moral issues. One citizen's enlightenment is another's subversive ideology. Let the topic be sex education, or the intellectual-moral counterculture of the urban left; or let the method of discussion exclude recourse to evangelical-biblical traditions, or to specific religious or cultural traditions, or to local mores—and one ought not to be surprised if mass meetings grow hot. In West Virginia, on such an account, school buses have been fired at. There are many different cultural traditions for the transmission of personal and social values, but under a monocultural system the schools seem oddly inept in dealing with them. Public options seem limited to whether to skip "controversial" matters entirely, or to run roughshod over minorities by ramming through a treatment of the issues, sterilized by the approval of the dominant factions. The very word "controversial," used so often in educational matters, gives away the problem. That values are nourished by contrasting traditions a thousand years (or more) old, one would think, ought to be a given of educational psychology. Naturally, people will disagree about profound issues and be uncomfortable about discussing such differences publicly; we do not have a public language for such discussions. Nonetheless, such issues are not (with its negative connotations) "controversial"; they are, rather, fundamental, instructive, and in need of exploration. Were they not so flammable, they would not be so clearly at the heart of the matter. It is a major intellectual task of our time to fashion "a public philosophy" that enables us to give tongue to our pluralism.

During a period like our own, involved in so many moral uncertainties for every tradition and yet obliged, willy-nilly, to cope with serious public problems that have a moral dimension, we should not be surprised that the cry for more "freedom" and "choice" in education should blare out over loudspeakers. When values close to the spine of a whole way of life are in question, few wish to entrust their children to just anyone. The public schools have not dealt well with problems of fundamental moral diversity. On the other hand, the public can hardly afford to permit fundamental moral issues to go by default. The educational dilemma, then, is cruel. Radicals in some places, conservatives in other places, and liberals in yet others have known what it is like to be in the minority. Evangelicals and mainline Protestants; liberal and orthodox Jews; liberal and conservative Catholics; blacks, Chicanos, and Asian Americans—nearly all Americans have had occasion to protest against the conformism of one time and place or another.

Before the advent of national magazines, the radio networks, and television, there was more reason than there is today to believe that the public schools ought to "hold us together" and to build up a "common culture." Homogenizing, rationalizing, centripetal forces are today infinitely more powerful. The inexorable formation of a "common culture" is ensured by the national merchandising of products of all sorts, by significant family mobility, and by the growing role of a national professional class (the collaborators in this book, for example). What is not so certain is how nuanced, subtle, profound, and wise that common culture will be. No doubt a law applies here: *The probabilities of creative outcomes are enhanced if the number of originating energies is very high.* Today there is less reason to fear diversity than there was. There is more reason to fear the shallowness of certain forms of homogenization. For fifteen years considerable progress has been made, at least in superficial ways, to develop "ecumenism" and elementary knowledge about each other. It is time to go deeper.

Nathan Glazer is right (above, Chapter IV) when he commends John Higham's notion of "integrative pluralism." As the generations go on, the American experience integrates all of us, through vivid memories and intense common pressures. Those who were outside the country—even for a year or so—during the assassination of John F. Kennedy or Martin Luther King, Jr., during the riots or anti-war protests, or during Watergate—have often remarked on their return how it seemed to them that they were stepping back into a culture different from the one they had left. Strong and swift is our culture, powerful and searing, impressing upon each of us from year to year indelible experiences. These experiences may not homogenize us, but they do bind us to one another through at least analogous feelings, memories, and traumas. No one who once heard the fulsome English spoken by Martin Luther King, Jr. (or Barbara Jordan, or Yvonne Braithwaite), or heard Peter Rodino, Jr., discourse on the Magna Carta during the House impeachment proceedings, or—on a less sublime level—watched "Rhoda" and "Mary Tyler Moore" embrace, can deny that we are building here, in both a profound and subtle way, a "common culture." When I called my own book *The Rise of the Unmeltable Ethnics* (1972), I intended to suggest that Americans previously hardly heard from in the common discourse were about to "arise" and to make an important assertion, making a distinctive contribution in return for what they had been given. I had in mind, without having formulated it, something like Higham's notion of "integrative pluralism."

Such a perception of American society justifies fresh attempts to maximize choice in education. But this can be done only on a strong philosophical basis. The danger in our era is that the spiritual and moral life of our people will become banal. An homogenizing national culture, carrying no one's true voice, becomes subject to ridicule. Meanwhile, the state has grown more powerful and individuals more isolated and vulnerable. Thus, the focus and force of the liberal task has changed. In 1935 John Dewey argued that, for the first time in the history of liberalism, liberals should look to the national state not as an enemy and not only as a neutral force, but as a moral ally. Four decades later we recognize some of the costs that have accrued in the wake of the extraordinary advances made according to that choice. As Dewey once changed the goals of liberalism, so the genuinely liberal temper will once again question, reflect, and perhaps imagine a sharply different liberal future. The most promising direction, it appears, is to strengthen those "mediating institutions" that stand between the individual and the state, checking the extravagances of both. Hedonism and bureaucracy are reverse mirror images, equally restrictive of the liberal spirit.

If I am correct then, a new form of liberalism is on the horizon (and has been exhibited in many essays of this book). Superficially, its primary characteristic is its willingness to criticize the assumptions of the old liberal spirit—its own spirit of a decade or more ago—and to be just as rigorous and critical about the left as about the right. Profoundly, however, its characteristic turn is to look to social agencies outside the state for sources of renewal and strength. It is governed by a sense of modesty about what the state may accomplish; by a learned mistrust of experts or, at least, of the *hubris* of experts; by a sense of the ironies involved in every social and political policy; and by a renewed respect for what people can do for themselves, once freed from crippling circumstances, or enabled by favorable conditions. Reinhold Niebuhr in his later years often described an amalgam of classical liberalism and conservatism that, he believed, constituted a new and wiser form of the liberal spirit: a combination of the liberal's distrust of the *status quo* and its illusions, and of the conservative's sense of the tangled organic connectedness of human affairs. This combination the new liberal spirit embodies.

The matter of educational vouchers, for example, introduces a preventive *laissez faire* against the reach of the state. The state commands that children be educated, and even establishes certain standards to be met; and the state empowers parents to send their children to schools by building the schools and by offering various forms of assistance. Yet, under the voucher system, the parents would choose the actual school in which to exercise this civic right and duty. The practical design of a voucher system is not, however, simple. Conscious of the tangled history of education in America, including serious strains of racism, nativism, and exclusion, the new liberals—conspicuously in James Coleman's essay (above, Introduction)—have tried to surround the practical use of vouchers with safeguards and provisos. Their aim is to maximize liberty, uniqueness, excellence, and equality.

To recapitulate the many good points made about vouchers in the preceding essays would be to carry unnecessary coals. Their main thrust is clear. It seems within our technical capacity to design a system of education less centralized and less homogenized than the one we have, a system integrated (not only racially) and yet pluralistic, a system more representative of and nourishing to the many sorts of constituencies it serves. We can afford to have confidence in the choices of parents for their children. As Thomas Sowell has suggested (above, Chapter VIII), to seek better schooling for their children almost half of all the blacks living in the South undertook their long, difficult migration northward and westward. Indeed, to focus on the role of families in education is now timely and astute.

It is timely because there has been a tendency in Anglo-American social thought to swing back and forth between the individual and the state, to the neglect of the family, the neighborhood, the cultural society, and other small-scale institutions. Conservatives have tended to lavish passion on the individual, liberals on the government. Both have tended to regard mediating institutions as sources of prejudice, passion, bias, and constraint—as obstacles in the way of their own purposes. Neither classical conservative nor classical liberal thought has bequeathed us a strong body of theory concerning intermediate institutions.

Yet the family, in particular, has a significant and even in-dispensable role to play in education. The family is the original and most efficient department of health, education, and welfare. The nutritional support of the child; the development of its IQ; its nervous and emotional habits; its early lessons on how to identify letters, to read, and to compute; its motivation to read and to learn; its moral values and habits—all these are best imparted in the family and, if not there, only with difficulty elsewhere. If the family fails, society only with exceeding difficulty makes up the loss. With every new study that appears, science seems to assign the role of the family higher significance. (No wonder, under all their austere and newly recognized responsibilities, so many young people fear marriage; in the old days did parents just *do* what they did, without such exquisite scientific awareness of their possible failures?) It has been, no doubt, an error of grave conse-quence to have entrusted so much education to the schools, and so to have overlooked the role of the family in education.

In this respect, it is necessary to push the argument for vouchers a stage beyond the merely technical and administrative task of providing financial assistance and choice. Much attention should be given to what families can do to teach their children not only before the children begin school but in conjunction with the school. The separation of the family from the school is not a healthy step for either party. It seems preposterous that parents should expect the schools to teach their children how to read with-out joining in that task themselves during and after their children's preschool years. (Still at ten and twelve, kids need motivation and help in continuing to read.) It seems equally pre-posterous that schools should attempt all by themselves, without clear and direct communication with the homes of their students, to carry on the work of education. Home and schools are, in fact, in symbiotic relationship. The more they can do together, the better for education. In order to improve the quality of education, indeed, interventions in the home may show far more effect, more swiftly and profoundly, than interventions in the classroom. Particularly among underprivileged children, educational interventions in the home spur progress, especially if adult males are helped to work with their children. But the general point holds: throughout society, at every level, the role of parents in the education of their children is critical. Why is it so neglected in educational theory?

The notion that parents should take responsibility for helping their children to choose among competing schools does not, then, contradict the notion that the parents' role in the education of their children is indispensable. It reinforces it. To underestimate the capacities and the concerns of parents is wrong. In many families the entire strategy of where to take up residence is governed by long-range designs for the education of their children. Of course, there are many other families, themselves from traditions of peasantry, or in any case from traditions of low educational attainment, who do not so value education and whose attitude towards the schools is one of diffidence or of indifference. Yet into such families, too, are born brilliant youngsters whose aspirations may carry them beyond their parents, and to whom the opportunity—through vouchers—of seeking out special schooling might provide a decisive breakthrough from neighborhood limits. What a scholarship once was (say) to Boston Latin for youngsters from Dorchester or Roxbury, vouchers might be today.

The California proposal by Stephen A. Sugarman and John E. Coons (Appendix A) is a further example of the new liberalism, in part because it assumes a certain basic social trust. (The "basic trust" that Erik Erikson sees as so important to personal identity has its counterpart in the "basic social trust" necessary for the health of societies; even, as St. Augustine noted, societies among thieves.) Instead of approaching integration in a punitive way, Coons and Sugarman seek an incentive, a sweetener, designed to attract citizens (and schools) to do what they would probably be inclined to do, and what in their ideal selves they would approve of themselves doing. This incentive gives them a practical spur to overcome both past injustices and the expectable inertia of social systems. By contrast, many of those involved in problems of integration have come out of evangelical religious backgrounds. Guilt is their rhetorical staple, and their proposals for remediation are tinged with a punitive character. But guilt feelings in political and social matters often have ironic effects, deepening the very condition they propose to heal. Neither coercion nor punishment is the ideal liberal instrument. Each generates effects counter to its intention.

The new liberals, then, while remarkably more modest than they were fifteen years ago about the capacity of governmental social policies, are more sanguine about the good instincts of many citizens. What they have lost in trust in massive government interventions, they have gained in basic social trust. They tend to seek ways of *enabling* and *empowering* individual citizens and small-scale mediating institutions to act for themselves. "Ask not what your government can do for you. Ask what you can do better than the government." The role of government, in this view, is less arrogant and obtrusive.

The new liberals thus tend to place government in a less salient role than did the old liberals. They prefer it to play the role of a *removens prohibens,* a secondary, supportive role. In a sense, they have borrowed a leaf from the movement toward "participatory democracy"; they define social problems as very largely enabling problems. Buried here, as well, is the ancient Catholic notion of "subsidiarity" which holds that each social problem should be addressed upon its own social level; a higher agency should be called in only when the lower has exhausted its possibilities. Higher agencies, simultaneously, must take care not to weaken local agencies by taking too much responsibility and too many resources from them.

In a word, a new direction for liberalism is in the air. Assaulted by radicals on the one side and by an assertive conservatism on the other, liberals during the past decade have by now had a chance to get a fresh grip upon "the liberal mind." Much wisdom has been wrested from the struggles of the last few years. In 1963 John F. Kennedy in an address at Yale suggested that, given modern social knowledge, we knew what needed to be done; all we lacked was will. Such *hubris*—and the buoyant programmatic manifestos that went with it—are absent now. The newly skeptical eye searches for the possible unintended consequences of proposed courses of action. Governmental initiatives are still promoted, but both in their design and in the tone in which they are presented distinctive notes are heard. Consider the qualities of mind and spirit exerted in the preceding essays. Running through each of them is an activism tutored by respect for the intricacies of social reality.

Perhaps at no point has the liberal mind undergone a more profound change than in its perception of cosmopolitan atmosphere and felt most at home in it. Such an atmosphere is usually urban and somewhat continental, as in New York, Cambridge, and San Francisco. Yet cosmopolitanism in some respects falls short of pluralistic consciousness. To be cosmopolitan is to be surrounded by and experienced in cultural variety. But to exhibit a pluralistic consciousness is to become more sharply aware of one's own finitude, of one's own particularity and unique roots, while (a) respecting the uniqueness of others and (b) recognizing the many diverse sources from which one draws one's own spiritual nourishment.

The cosmopolitan experiences the many, and yet remains rather vague about his relation to the many. The cosmopolitan may glory in a kind of tolerance and practice benign neglect of differences. A sense of world-weariness may well afflict him. He takes differences for granted and does not perceive the threat that arises among the managers and mass-producers. The new managerial class, equally at home in any of the world's major cities, is not really cosmopolitan. It carries homogenization like a virus. By contrast, the pluralistic personality is *changed* by contact with the many. It internalizes diverse insights and virtues learned from others, while remaining sharply faithful to the traditions of the self. The pluralist is aware of the many social influences upon the self; his own personality draws—and knows that it draws—nourishment from several streams. The pluralist knows, as well, that diversity today is threatened.

Another significant contrast emerges from the theme of relativism. Since the cosmopolitan has seen much and experienced much, he has a tendency, confronted with variety, to shrug his shoulders as if to say, "Everything is relative." The cosmopolitan is eager to differentiate himself from the merely provincial, the narrow, the inexperienced. But the pluralistic personality is concerned not simply with the contrast on that side, but also with the contrast on the other. The pluralistic personality fears the mush of mere tolerance, the flaccid sentimentality of homogenization, and the sheer potential evil of "anything goes." Hence, the pluralistic personality respects the finite human need to be who one is, to take a stand, to make commitments, to define the self— while grasping clearly the risks and losses inherent in free choices, in the necessary self-limitation, and in unchosen alternatives. A swift stream runs in narrow channels. This personality, deep in its own traditions and yet open to those of others, evokes a new form of morals and religion.

The pluralistic personality could only have come into existence in a nation like our own. It is the distinctive American type. It is the distinctive American gift to civilization. In a book far too criticized along merely partisan political lines, a book of vast conception, *The Cultural Contradictions of Capitalism,* Daniel Bell has written of the need for our civilization to make contact once again with the clear streams of its basic religious impulses. He is not thinking of an instrumentalist use of religion. He means that every vital civilization has an implicit historical scheme, some way of understanding its relation to other civilizations and to the future. It has, as well, some implicit sense of what is sacred, what is truly "being," and what is a waste of time or a diversion. It gives to individuals deep instinctive ("gut") feelings about what is good, right, fitting, appropriate. A pluralistic society like ours, of course, requires a most sophisticated and complex scheme of values, feelings, and visions. But Professor Bell's point is that we cannot pretend not to have such a scheme, or not to need one. We shall have one, willy-nilly. Either it will be profound, creative, and inspiring of life, or it will be shallow, destructive, enervating and confusing. Have one we shall.

No society as free as ours has ever existed before. The economic system is more open, the social system is more open, and the cultural system is more open than any the earth has ever seen. Consequently, the task of articulating a religious system as open to freedom and choice as our institutional life demands is no modest task. It must be attempted.

This attempt, moreover, cannot take the form of some all-embracing "religion-in-general." There is no such religion. Historical religions, which take history seriously, are particular, embodied, limited. The genius of our culture has been to elicit enormous dynamism out of our religious particularities. Atheist, Protestant, Catholic, Jew (each in several varieties) contribute

special impetus to the culture of which we are a part. We learn
from each other, without ceasing to be different from each other.
Each is check-and-balance to the others. Slackness in one injures
all. Massive indifference corrupts all together, and each individual
person singly.

It may be wise here to distinguish between two forms of atheism. There is a false form of atheism, which is really a hidden form
of belief disguised by dislike for religious institutions and traditions. Such atheists show confidence in progress, history, socialism, science, art, or moral enlightenment. Such atheism is a form
of deism. An editorialist's religion, the religion of commencement
speakers, its universe is benign and moral. (What do they lack,
such humanists, seeking justice and loving the poor and all the
rest, but Sunday collections to distinguish them from being Chris-
tians?) The religious impulse in American life runs close to the
skin among millions who call themselves nonbelievers. Such
atheists, in the words of G. K. Chesterton, "do not believe in
nothing; they believe in anything"—from Tarot cards, to the environment, to socialism, to the divinization of Me. Tremendous
religious energies roam America unmoored. By contrast, the genuine atheist has a sense of what he has rejected and its costs. Such
atheism, like true belief, is a long-term project, requiring painful
discipline, commanding a long scorching journey through the
desert. In such an atheism the human spirit can also be renewed;
it carries to the depths. (Between true belief and true unbelief
there are many dark parallels; as there are many between happy
piety and happy atheism.)

Liberalism can no longer allow itself to be confused with a
shallow cosmopolitanism, an easy tolerance, an inexpensive dis-
belief. The vital human spirit sharpens edges. If one fears
organized religion because it is narrow and "divisive," one should
also fear the power of the state to become a religion of its own. In
all nations, a kind of "civil religion" (Rousseau) develops through
the grandeur and ritual of state display. In democratic states, in
which church is separated from state—and in the United States,
where the sense of developing a "new man" and a "new woman" in
a "new world" is acute—this tendency of the state (and its accompanying culture) to develop its own religious symbolism is particularly strong. On the popular level, "the American way" carries

religious connotations. On a sophisticated level, moral outrage and the urge for moral reformation prove that the itches of the Puritans live on in consumer advocates, environmentalists, champions of sundry rights, and critics of the nation's failings. Those who evince disdain for organized religion appear to park their unarticulated religious passions wherever they find space.

The problem of values and moral vision in American life is directly related to the problem of choice in education. One's sense of values and moral vision is "grounded" in a world view (atheistic or theistic), not in the sense that a conclusion is "grounded" in a premise, but in the sense that a stage play is "grounded" in a particular cast, a set, a stage, a theater, and spoken lines. World views, like dramatic traditions, have a history. They are concrete. There is no "religion in general," or "ethics in general," or "drama in general." Human cultures in their variety display the record of human liberty, the particularizations that human imagination and ingenuity shape from the materials of human life. Every human being in every culture is born, suffers, loves, dies. There are constants in the human condition everywhere. Yet even the constants—pain, irony, tragedy—are differently experienced through each form of the cultural imagination, are given a somewhat different meaning and a different reverberation in the sensibility. A funeral is not the same in Sicily and in Des Moines.

The attempt of American schools to proceed as if diversity did not exist has deprived the nation of many sources of nourishment for the spirit. If students cannot explore in depth the particularities of the culture of their own homes and linked families, what will be substituted is the thin gruel of "lowest-common-denominator" piety. Students will be graduated morally illiterate. Worse that that, they will have learned no language appropriate to the history and tradition of their own roots. Their own instinctive aspirations and inhibitions will be shortcircuited, stunted, and struck dumb. The contradictions between what they have learned at home, often unconsciously, and what they learn from teachers and peers, television and cinema, will go unnoticed and unexamined. Many will collapse in moral confusion. The allure of whatever morality happens to sway their crowd or their surroundings is likely to seem to them compelling. Thus did Jeb Magruder and John Dean describe the moral imperatives they too easily obeyed, and thus, perhaps, are we to understand the phenomena of sudden conversions and counterconversions sweeping through a confused population.

An education in values and in moral vision can only be conducted if pluralism is respected. Such respect demands that its workings be clearly understood. The pluralistic personality has two strengths: (a) clarity and depth about its own roots and particularity; (b) openness to and interest in sources of strength beyond its own traditions. A system of education designed to nourish the pluralistic personality must itself comprehend the diversity of the moral roots of the American people. It should not attempt to develop a "common culture" that would represent a watering down of each participant culture, but rather a "common culture" that arises out of a shared, common knowledge of the analogies and the differences between moral traditions. To take a thoroughly complex example like abortion, for example: it is not necessary for everyone within the school system to hold the same views; nor for the view of the majority, nor the views of minorities, to be accorded higher status than any other view. But it would be appropriate for all students to understand clearly the history and the forms of life from which present positions on this important public issue derive. Both those in favor and those opposed to abortion would benefit by a clear understanding of the way the world looks from where the other stands. It is an old American tradition to "walk in the other's moccasins a moon" before casting judgment.

The question of choice in education, then, is not only a question of where one chooses to send one's own children to school. It is also a question of what sort of schooling in choice goes on in the schools. One ideal form, particularly appropriate for schools that belong to and serve the whole public, would strengthen two skills: (a) the ability of children to understand, to articulate, and to think critically about the traditions in which they have been reared (and thus to supply some continuity between the home and the school); and (b) the ability of children to detect, to penetrate, to learn from, and to respect the internal power of traditions not their own.

There is, we have seen, an unfortunate tendency in the American public schools to assume that the values and vision of the secular-Protestant upper class of the Northeast represent morality simply, and to imagine that the moral task consists of enlightening the others accordingly. (To speak of a "blue-ribbon" commission is to describe a commission composed predominantly of members of that class, whose presence *ipso facto* bestows moral legitimacy and public trustworthiness.) This tendency runs against the best intentions and traditions of that class, and could not succeed except for the fact that we are each so close to our own moral vision that it always appears to us as the countenance of reality itself; we do what we think is right without noticing how different that appears to others. The cure is *not* to become relativistic, *not* to surrender our values. The cure is to become self-conscious, articulate, and self-critical about our own moral vision; to see both its strengths and its limits; to assess its trade-offs and its losses, as well as its gains. We can be who we are without insisting that others be like us, and without dismissing our own highest standards. For our own most highly developed upper class, too, the pluralistic personality represents a moral gain. The choices of that class, too, need to be deepened and strengthened. The nation would not be served by its loss of nerve, weakening of faith, or lowering of standards. A renewed emphasis on choice in education will help the members of every social class.

This nation is slowly acquiring, then, a public philosophy proper to the composition of its own people. This public philosophy is not a common set of values imposed upon all. It is, rather, a world view patiently acquired through which each participant comes to recognize the diversity of the whole. Even the simplest and most basic of values are understood differently in the light of different traditions. But there are sufficient "family resemblances" among those diverse points of view for skillful citizens to learn a public language for understanding both the self and others. The writers in this book, for example, have not had to be unfaithful to their own visions and traditions in order to speak intelligibly to each other. As the decades go on, the many American peoples discover each other, learn more about each other, and build up, slowly, social devices for attaining a maximum of cultural unity consistent with maximal respect for differences. Unity in diversity is the highest possible attainment of a civilization, a testimony to the most noble possibilities of the human race. This attainment is made possible through passionate concern for choice, in an atmosphere of generous social trust.

12

THOMAS SOWELL

A New Agenda on Race

This is an historic opportunity. The economic and social advancement of blacks in this country is still a great unfinished task. The methods and approaches currently used for dealing with this task have become familiar over the past few years and they demand reexamination for at least two reasons.

First, the effectiveness of these approaches has been ever more seriously questioned in recent years. There is growing factual evidence of counterproductive results from noble intentions. Some of that factual evidence will be presented here in the sessions that follow.

In addition, numerous political trends in recent years indicate declining voter and taxpayer support for these approaches, to which some of the older and more conventional black "spokesmen" remain committed. The events of 4 November were only the most dramatic examples of this. They were not the only examples.

In California, we remember Proposition 13; across the country, the defeat of school bond issues and spending proposals. With

This essay originally appeared as "Politics and Opportunity: The Background" in *The Fairmont Papers: Black Alternatives Conference* (1981).

future elections, the shifting fortunes of partisan politics may change the party labels of those in power. But Camelot seems unlikely to return. And we certainly cannot bet the future of 20 million people on its return. So we have an historic responsibility implied. We cannot simply run around claiming that the sky is falling—popular as that sometimes seems—because that implies that there is one approach which is the only approach. It implies that the partisans of that approach have some monopoly of either wisdom or virtue—which may be a convenient assumption to them, but no reason why the rest of us should take it seriously.

What is a more responsible approach? First, we need to recognize that many methods were failing even before they lost public support. We have to accept the challenge of reexamining why these approaches were failing. We need to accept the responsibility of seeking and devising new approaches for the decade ahead. That is why we are here—to explore alternatives, not to create a new orthodoxy with its own messiahs and its own excommunications of those who dare to think for themselves. The people who were invited to be presenters and discussants here are people who are seeking alternatives, people who have challenged the conventional wisdom on one or more issues, people who have thought for themselves instead of marching in step and chanting the familiar refrains.

The various speakers and discussants have varying philosophies and different areas of expertise. Some are Democrats, some are Republicans, and some like myself are neither. We are here to assess where we are, where we are going, and what are our alternatives.

We can start by looking at the present situation. We have come through an historic phase of struggle for basic civil rights—a very necessary struggle, but not sufficient. The very success of that struggle has created new priorities and new urgencies. There are economic realities to confront and self-development to achieve, in the schools, at work, in our communities. The sins of others are always fascinating to human beings, but they are not always the best way to self-development or self-advancement. The moral regeneration of white people might be an interesting project, but I am not sure we have quite that much time to spare. Those who have fought on that front are very much like the generals who like to refight the last war instead of preparing for the next struggle.

What are some of the pluses and minuses of our present situation? On the plus side, a dramatic economic rise of blacks during the 1960s, but which has slowed, in some cases stopped, in the 1970s. Many social problems are worsening. Continued disintegration of families; rising numbers of broken homes—one-third of all black homes now—a skyrocketing unemployment rate among black youths, five times as high in the 1970s as in the late 1940s; runaway crime rates of which blacks are the chief victims (there are more blacks murdered every year than whites, in absolute numbers). There is also a threat of a permanent underclass whose problems seem immune to prosperity, to equal opportunity, or to the advancement experienced by other blacks. We can see on the horizon the rise of racist groups such as the Nazis, the KKK, not only among the ignorant, but in places where you would never expect such groups, where they never had a foothold before. We can at least ask whether, or to what extent, the policies of our times have contributed to these problems of our times.

Looking to the future, one of the things that we need to focus on are facts about results—not rhetoric about intentions. We need to look not at the noble preambles of legislation but at the incentives created in that legislation. Very often, legislation intended to help the disadvantaged in fact pays people to stay disadvantaged and penalizes them to the extent that they make an effort to rise from disadvantage.

I mentioned that in the 1960s there was a dramatic increase in black income relative to white as well as a dramatic increase in numbers of blacks in high-level occupations. Much of this has slowed down, and in some cases stopped, in the 1970s. We need to ask whether the policies that were followed in the 1970s had anything to do with this. The question is not whether on the one hand "affirmative action" sounds better than "equal opportunity," but whether, in fact, the results show further progress or slowing down. There are some serious economic reasons why the latter would be so.

When we talk about rent controls, we need not be satisfied with cliches about affordable housing. We need to ask the factual question: will there be more housing or less under rent control? When we talk about minimum wage laws, we need to ask not whether a decent wage is a good objective, but whether there will be more jobs at higher pay or no jobs and no pay for increasing numbers of people. If we are going to talk about the future, we have to talk responsibly. We have to have a responsible dialogue with those who disagree with us. If you are serious, it means you are not concerned with scoring points; you are concerned with confronting the actual arguments, not straw men. We don't need to talk about "trickle-down" theories. I know of no one who has set forth a trickle-down theory. I know of many people who set that up as a straw man to avoid confronting the arguments that have been set forth by those who want to depend upon different mechanisms and different processes from the ones that are in fashion.

One of the other cliches of our times is the "bootstrap" theory: the notion that those who don't support the current political agenda believe that people should lift themselves by their own bootstraps, should be left to their own devices, that the government is doing too much to help them. There is no such theory. I have been around a few conservative economists in my time and I have listened but have never heard it. I have not seen it anywhere in history. But I see it as a convenient straw man for people who do not want to confront opposing views.

The issue is not that the government gives too much help to the poor. The problem is that the government creates too much harm to the poor. The cost of taking care of the poor is relatively small, compared to the cost of bureaucracy. Some years ago someone figured out how much it would cost the government to lift every man, woman, and child in the United States out of poverty by the simple expedient of giving them money. The amount that they came to was approximately one-third of what is spent on anti-poverty programs. My fellow economist Walter Williams has figured out how much the welfare expenditure in this country comes to per poor family. It is $32,000. Very few poor families get $32,000.

Another device that is often used to avoid taking unpopular arguments seriously is to argue that those people who are opposed to the welfare-state approach are simply middle class. I wish I had a dollar for every time I have been asked whether I came from an affluent background, and if that is why I have such an unfeeling heart for the problems of the poor. I have never heard that question asked of Andrew Young, who indeed did come from an affluent background.

Some time ago I met with a well-known TV newsman, and I asked him why it is that I look on television and see black spokesmen saying diametrically the opposite of what I hear in the black community and what I see in Gallup polls and other polls. For example, blacks in this country support voucher systems two to one; blacks in this country prefer more strict enforcement of crime laws, are opposed to quota systems in employment or college admissions, and have never had a majority in favor of busing. And yet when I look at the TV news, an entirely different world is created before my eyes on that tube. And he said to me, "Well, we can put Ben Hooks or Jesse Jackson on TV, but we can't put the Gallup poll on TV."

One of the consequences of this is that we are having, in addition to the usual conflicts among groups that any multiethnic or multiracial society has, artificial polarization. We are having polarization between a handful of black leaders and a handful of white leaders, many saying things which have very little to do with the beliefs of the people in whose name they are speaking.

If we are looking at the future and looking responsibly, we can learn much from the experience of others—which does not mean blind imitation; sometimes it means avoiding the mistakes that others have made. Many of the various policies that I hear being urged as the royal road to salvation for blacks today are policies which were tried and failed repeatedly by the Irish in the nineteenth century.

It is true that the black history is unique. But of course, you would have to make comparisons even to know that. And uniqueness is never sufficient reason to avoid learning at someone else's expense rather than your own.

One of the problems that I see is the problem of the political interventionist state. I pose it in categorical terms, as if there is some noninterventionist state. We are really talking about differences of degree. There seems to be a notion that political interventionism that produces earmarked benefits for this or that group necessarily makes those groups better off. But when you think of it, no politician gets elected by sacrificing 90 percent of the voters for the benefit of 10 percent of the voters. One thing that all politicians can do—whatever the party—is to count votes. They may create the illusion that they are helping 10 percent. Indeed, the ideal politician creates that illusion ten times. But since the government is not generating any wealth, government programs mean nothing more or less than robbing Peter to pay Paul. Now, there is no political capital to be made by robbing Peter to pay Paul if you get Peter's vote and lose Paul's vote. The real trick is to rob Peter to pay Paul on Monday, Wednesday, and Friday, and rob Paul to pay Peter on Tuesday, Thursday, and Saturday and get *both* their votes. Fortunately, the government is closed on Sunday.

By following this strategy, you can give a little bit to this group, a little bit to that group, and none of them ever ask if what is given to A is taken from B and what is given to B is taken from A.

Let's look at some of the losses that blacks suffer from the interventionist state. I think the greatest single loss is that the minimum wage laws promoted by labor unions protect their members by pricing black young people out of the market. There is no way to rise up a ladder if you can't get your foot on the ladder in the first place.

Environmentalism, to use the word they like to use—I call it the recreational-land-use special interest—means that, for the benefit of a relatively small group of people, we have set aside vast areas of the United States, an amount equal to one-third of this country, which is to say equivalent to all of the United States east of the Mississippi. Clearly, you cannot set aside that much land, take it off the market, without having the price of the other land rise and having that rise reflected in rents and mortgage costs all across the country. Of course, the government can come to your rescue with projects and subsidies. But, of course, these don't begin to add up to what you have lost by this vast giveaway to a handful of affluent people.

One of the great coups of the whole environmental movement is to avoid talking about people and tradeoffs. You would never dream that there are people who have alternative demands for the same resource by reading the environmental literature. You hear about protecting the environment and preserving "fragile areas." It is very touching. You would never dream that what that means is that one group of people will use the power of the government to put those vast resources at their disposal far below cost and keep them out of the hands of other people who have other uses for them. The recreational land that is set aside is land from which you do not build homes, from which you do not get energy, from which you do not create jobs. We have a protection of endangered species act that is concerned with every weed and reptile. We also need to recognize that human beings are an endangered species, and especially those who are poor.

There seems to be a notion that Darwinian evolution may have been a good idea at one time, but we are going to bring it to a screeching halt in our generation. Despite thousands of years in which all sorts of creatures have come into existence and gone out of existence, in which all sorts of ecologies have evolved, totally different from one another, for some reason the particular creatures that we have seen — even if there is only a handful of us who have ever actually seen them — those creatures are to be preserved forever, at all costs. The particular kind of ecology that happens to exist at this moment must be frozen for all future time.

One of the problems in dealing with the politics of poverty, and the programs for the disadvantaged in general and blacks in particular, is that vast empires can be built on these programs. These programs definitely prevent poverty among bureaucrats, economists, statisticians, and many others. The poor are also very useful as an entering wedge for programs which ultimately benefit other people who, by no stretch of the imagination, are poor. In New York City, for example, open enrollment was hailed as a great way by which blacks and Puerto Ricans could get into the free municipal universities. It became, instead, a means by which middle-class people who were paying tuition at NYU and Long Island University could now put that cost on the taxpayers. It is true that a handful of blacks and Puerto Ricans did, in fact, get in, but they were swamped by many others.

There's another serious problem, closely tied to the issue of state interventionism, and that's the notion that the poor, that blacks, are guinea pigs. They are subjects out there for every "innovative" idea that pops into the head of some academic. That they are there to provide raw material for surveys and schemes of various sorts. Above all, that their freedom of choice is to be denied in order to correspond to the grand designs of people who think they know better.

One of the more remarkable editorials that I saw a few years ago appeared in *The New Republic* as an argument against vouchers. The argument was that if you had vouchers, then those black parents who were most concerned about their children and most knowledgeable would pull their children out of the public schools, leaving behind only those whose parents didn't care. *The New Republic* thought that was a terrible thing to do. While every other group in this country has risen layer by layer as different people began to seize opportunities, blacks alone must all be held back until such time as the very last person in line has understood the value of education.

What this betrays is a proprietary conception of blacks somewhat at variance with the spirit of the Thirteenth Amendment. Insofar as we are going to enlist the intelligence, the desires, and the commitments of black themselves, we have to do so by offering more choice in more areas to let them decide what is best for themselves and not turn that job over to academics and government officials.

13

PETER W. GREENWOOD

Controlling the Crime Rate through Imprisonment

With respect to the use of imprisonment, the American criminal justice system is at an important crossroads. At the same time that a dissatisfied public is pressing vociferously for greater protection against violent crime and prisons are overflowing with new inmates, the concepts on which we formerly based our decisions about the sentencing and release of offenders have undergone a major revision. Most of the existing sentencing laws in the U.S. were written at a time when a principal goal of imprisonment was thought to be rehabilitation. In recent years, however, a growing body of research has questioned the efficacy of rehabilitation programs and called attention to the inequities produced by sentencing policies based on this goal. As a result, the emphasis on rehabilitation has been largely set aside, and the latest revisions in sentencing policy have begun to stress the role of imprisonment in simply punishing offenders and keeping them off the streets.

This essay originally appeared in *Crime and Public Policy,* edited by James Q. Wilson (1983).

The most conspicuous consequence of this shift has been the unprecedented growth of the number of offenders going to prison.

Yet the question remains: given the limited resources of the system, how can we best use imprisonment to contribute to the control of crime? The research reviewed here suggests that a more selective approach to sentencing—the use of so-called "selective incapacitation"—offers one potentially effective method of crime reduction. Modern research on criminal careers has shown that fewer than half of all active criminals are continually engaged in serious criminal behavior at rates high enough that their incarceration could lead to significant reductions in crime. In addition, researchers have been able to show a strong correlation between career criminality and certain conspicuous traits—prior convictions for serious crime, involvement in serious crime as a juvenile, drug use, etc. In combination, these findings suggest that by sentencing the predicted high-rate offenders to longer prison terms, while reducing the terms of low-rate offenders, we could secure a significant reduction in serious crime without any increase in the overall level of incarceration.

This chapter reviews the relevant research findings and discusses the potential advantages—and hazards—of a selective incapacitation policy.

The Impact of Incarceration on Crime Rates

There are three basic means through which incarceration can affect future crime rates: (1) the incarceration experience can change the propensity of those incarcerated to engage in crime when they are released; (2) the threat of incarceration can deter potential offenders from engaging in crime; and (3) incarceration prevents those crimes that would have been committed by inmates during their period of incarceration.

Rehabilitation. Prison may reduce the tendency of an offender to commit further crimes through either rehabilitation or what is termed "special deterrence." It is also possible that criminal propensities of some offenders will be intensified by prison experiences, either because inmates, having been labeled as criminals, will come to behave as such; because prisons are "schools for crime"; or because long periods of incarceration may inhibit an inmate from learning to function in an open society. Whatever the cause, the basic measure of the outcome is the recidivism rate.

For most of the past century, the criminal justice system attempted to control the crime problem through efforts at rehabilitation. Research and experimental programs were focused on developing improved methods for diagnosing the underlying problems that led to an offender's criminal behavior and developing programs that could respond to those problems. Probation, presentence investigation reports, reception clinics in prison, indeterminate sentences, and parole services are all legacies of this faith in the rehabilitation ideal.

By the 1970s, the picture had changed considerably. None of the numerous approaches to rehabilitation tested during the preceding decade was found to produce consistently significant reductions in recidivism rates, particularly for the more serious offenders. The view that "nothing works" has since become the conventional wisdom among most corrections practitioners and researchers.[1] It is now universally recognized that a substantial number of inmates will not recidivate after their release, but there is little faith that the size of this fraction can be increased by rehabilitation programs. Whatever residual hope remains for rehabilitation is focused on juveniles and the least sophisticated adult criminals.[2]

The same research tends to contradict the claim that prisons intensify criminal behavior. There is no compelling evidence that incarceration either extends the length of the criminal career or leads to increases in crime severity. In all likelihood, imprisonment has a positive effect on some inmates and a negative impact on others, with the two effects canceling each other out. Until a way is found of predicting in which category any given offender falls, a prediction that many practitioners continually attempt to make—apparently in most cases unsuccessfully—neither rehabilitation nor special deterrence effects can provide a useful basis for sentencing decisions.

Research on deterrence. Although general deterrence has historically been recognized as a major objective of the criminal justice system, it is only in the past twenty years that researchers have begun to explore its effect in detail. At its simplest level, deterrence theory holds that criminal behavior is influenced by the same types of cost/benefit incentives as any other type of economic activity. As the costs or risks associated with a particular type of crime are increased, the attractiveness of that type of crime to potential offenders should decrease. As a matter of public policy, the cost of engaging in crime can be increased by increasing the probability of apprehension, conviction, and incarceration, or by increasing the length of terms.

There is little disagreement that the criminal justice system does deter many would-be offenders. Debates about the impact of deterrence are concerned with the effects of marginal changes in sentencing patterns on particular types of offenders.[3] For instance, there is considerable disagreement about the ways in which risks are communicated to offenders. Do they respond to the language of a statute or to the ways in which it is applied? If a law is passed requiring a prison term for every defendant who is convicted of residential burglary, does it matter whether the law is strictly applied or whether a number of defendants are allowed to plead guilty to lesser counts? There is considerable debate about the relationship between the severity of sanctions and the certainty with which they are applied. Will longer sentences for robbery deter potential offenders if fewer than 5 out of 100 robberies result in conviction? Should more offenders be sentenced to prison for shorter periods of time? There is also debate about how sanctions may affect offenders differentially, at different points in their career. Some would argue that young, unsophisticated offenders, who are not yet fully committed to a criminal way of life, are the ones who are most easily deterred by sanctions. Yet this view directly contradicts those who argue that criminal processing only reinforces the criminal identity of these marginal offenders by labeling them as criminal, and that they should be diverted out of the criminal justice system to be treated by community-based programs.

Unfortunately, empirical studies have done little to resolve most of these disputes. Quasi-experimental studies, which attempt to measure the impact of changes in sanction severity over time, and cross-sectional studies, which compare crime rates across jurisdictions that differ in their sanction severity, are both plagued by a number of methodological difficulties. A recent review of these studies by a panel established by the National Academy of Sciences concluded that while the findings of the research are generally consistent with the deterrence hypothesis—i.e., jurisdictions with high sanctions generally have lower rates of crime—the data do not prove the existence of deterrence effects or indicate their magnitude.[4]

Of course, criminal justice officials do not have the luxury of postponing sentencing decisions until the final evidence on deterrence questions is in. Officials must establish or support sentencing policies that, in effect, conform to or depart from deterrence theory. For instance, deterrence studies suggest that the marginal impact of changes in certainty is more important than the effect of changes in severity. If a jurisdiction convicts, on the average, about 1,000 robbery defendants per year, this finding would argue that sending 1,000 defendants to prison for one year would deter more crimes than sending only 500 to prison for two years—the kind of policy now followed in most jurisdictions. Thus deterrence theory turns out to produce policy guidance that is in direct conflict with theories of rehabilitation or incapacitation, both of which would focus resources on those offenders thought to represent the greatest risk to society.

Incapacitation and crime rates. The third method through which incarceration can affect crime rates is called incapacitation. For any offenders who would have continued to commit crimes after their conviction, incarceration prevents the crimes they would have committed during their period of confinement. The amount of crime prevented by incapacitation is obviously directly related to the rate at which inmates would have committed crimes if they were free. The higher the crime rates of individual inmates, the greater the incapacitation effects of any given period of imprisonment.

But this general observation must be qualified. Incapacitation effects will occur only if the period of incarceration is subtracted from the total length of a criminal's career. If a one-year sentence simply extends an offender's career by one year, then the incapacitation effects are zero; his crimes are merely postponed. Similarly, if the incarceration of one robber leads his partners to recruit another offender to take his place, then the incapacitation effect of his sentence will be offset by the crimes attributable to his replacement.

Just as is the case with deterrence theory, there is currently no practical way of measuring the aggregate incapacitation effects of a sentencing policy, or of marginal changes in it. Crime rates are affected by a number of other social, economic, and demographic factors that are difficult to measure, and whose precise relationship to crime is unknown. Even the amount of crime occurring in any specific time period is subject to considerable measurement error. In reponse to these quandaries, researchers attempting to study how prison sentences might affect crime rates have turned increasingly to analysis of individual offenders.

Research on Criminal Careers

Information about the characteristics of criminal careers comes from a variety of sources. Between 1930 and 1950, when the emphasis of criminal justice research fell on prevention and rehabilitation, a number of studies collected extensive information on family backgrounds and social environments of young offenders, but did not focus explicitly on criminal activities.[5] Other studies from this period used extensive interviews to describe the activities of particular adult offenders, but did not try to draw a representative picture of adult criminality.[6]

Recent research on criminal careers has been more responsive to current sentencing issues and has followed three different approaches. The first is the cohort study, an approach pioneered by Marvin Wolfgang and his colleagues at the University of Pennsylvania in 1972[7] and replicated by Lyle Shannon and David Farrington.[8] Researchers in these studies assembled criminal justice and social (school, employment, etc.) records for all youths born in a given year in a given geographic area who continued to reside there through a given age (usually 18). The Philadelphia cohort studies by Wolfgang consisted of all males born in 1945 who resided in the city from ages 10 to 18. This form of study is the most accurate means of determining the prevalence and distribution of criminal activity, as reflected in official records, across the general population. It also provides a useful means to examine such issues as the age of onset of criminality and the age of desistance as a function of socioeconomic and other behavioral characteristics.

The second method of studying criminal careers involves collecting self-reported information from a sample of known offenders, usually while they are incarcerated. This method of research was pioneered at the Rand Corporation in a 1977 study of 49 incarcerated robbers,[9] a 1981 study of 624 California prison inmates, and a 1982 study that involved 2,190 male jail and prison inmates from California, Texas, and Michigan.[10] These self-report studies have the advantage of providing a picture of an offender's criminal activities that is more complete than one drawn exclusively from facts known to the police.[11]

It has been shown that while there is considerable variation between self-reports and official records (i.e., police contacts or convictions), there is no systematic bias toward either over- or under-reporting across different types of offenders, as categorized by age, race, or conviction offense.[12] The primary problem with self-reported studies of incarcerated populations is the sample bias inevitably introduced by criminal justice processing decisions.

The third approach to criminal career studies involves the analysis of longitudinal data on criminals' contact with the justice system (arrests, indictments, convictions) for a sample of known offenders in a given geographic area. This form of research has recently been pursued in a 1979 study at the Institute for Law and Social Research (INSLAW) and in an analysis by researchers at Carnegie-Mellon University. The use of arrest histories has the advantage of avoiding the expensive data collection required for self-report studies (all of the studies to date have used computerized files) and also avoids the problems of respondent veracity (although criminal justice records have their own reliability problems). The disadvantage of this approach is that criminal justice data provide information on only a fraction of each individual's crimes and usually say nothing about his social background.

In general, of the three approaches, cohort studies provide the most complete picture of criminal career development. But when data collection costs are limited, studies based on self-reporting and official records provide a clearer picture of the most serious types of offenders, who are rarely encountered in cohort studies.

A number of models have been proposed for estimating the incapacitation effects of imprisonment on individuals.[13] The most generally accepted model[14] was developed by Shinnar and Shinnar.[15] They assumed that there is only one type of crime and that all offenders commit crimes at random intervals at the same average rate (λ). They further assumed that all offenders are subject to the same probability of arrest and conviction (q) for any one crime and have the same probability of being incarcerated upon conviction (J). It was assumed that the sentences served by the various offenders have an average duration of S, with the sentences ranging exponentially around this mean.

With this model, the average or expected time served for any one crime is qJS—i.e., the probability of arrest and conviction multiplied by the probability of incarceration and by the average term. The fraction of time that an offender will be free to commit crime is:

$$\eta = \frac{1}{1 + \lambda qJS}$$

This formula also represents the amount of crime that will occur under sentencing policy q, J, S, measured as a fraction of the crime that would occur if no offenders were incarcerated.

The difficulty with this model lies in estimating the offense rate of individual offenders—λ. At the time the model was developed, estimates of λ, which were either assumed or inferred from aggregate data, ranged from less than one index crime per year[16] to ten crimes per year.[17] Within this range of estimates, the predicted crime reduction effect from incapacitation could range from less than 10 percent to more than 30 percent of the violent crimes that would occur if no offenders were incarcerated.[18]

The first serious attempts to estimate individual crime rates were undertaken by Mark Peterson and Harriet Braiker in 1981,[19] who based their estimates on self-reports by prison inmates, and by Alfred Blumstein and Jacqueline Cohen in 1979, who based their estimates on arrest history files.[20] These two studies produced remarkably similar estimates of individual offense rates for several specific crime types: between 2 and 3.5 offenses per year for robbery; 6 or 7 offenses per year for burglary; and 3 to 3.5 offenses per year for auto theft.

In addition to providing estimates of individual offense rates for specific crime types, these two studies also produced several other findings that bear directly on the measurement of incapacitation effects. First, it turns out that most offenders are largely unspecialized, engaging in several different types of crime during any one time period; second, the distribution of individual offense rates is highly skewed toward the high end, with most offenders committing crimes at fairly low rates. The first observation implies that the sentences given to convicted burglars, in addition to reducing burglary rates through incapacitation, will reduce other crime rates as well. The second suggests that the average offense rate for any given group of offenders is heavily influenced by the offense rates of the few high-rate offenders out in the right tail of the distribution. This second finding raises the possibility of focusing the use of imprisonment on the high-rate offenders as a means of increasing the incapacitation effects of imprisonment—if such criminals can be identified.

There are two basic methods for attempting to identify dangerous or high-rate offenders. One is subjective and relies on expert evaluations of an offender's background, behavior, and psychological characteristics. The other relies on actuarial data. The subjective approach has been the traditional method used in sentencing. A convicted defendant may be referred to a panel of court-appointed psychologists or psychiatrists or to a reception clinic within the correctional system. The evaluations of the panel or clinic are then considered by the court in determining the sentence. If a defendant is sentenced to an indeterminate term, periodic evaluations will be made to determine when he is suitable for release. Recent evaluations of these procedures have shown that they have very little predictive accuracy.[21]

The second method of prediction, based on actuarial data, has been used most frequently in the form of parole experience tables to guide release decisions.[22] These tables, which use a variety of factors to predict an offender's chances of success on parole, have been shown to be more accurate than diagnostic studies.

The most recent Rand survey of nearly 2,200 jail and prison inmates in California, Michigan, and Texas provided an opportunity to determine how accurately high-rate offenders could be identified using the actuarial approach.[23] For the convicted robbers and burglars in this sample, a seven-item scale was developed using variables that could conceivably be obtained from official records and that might be appropriate for selective sentencing purposes.[24] The seven binary variables selected were:

1. Incarceration for more than half of the two-year period preceding the most recent arrest.

2. Prior conviction for the crime type that is being predicted.

3. Juvenile conviction prior to age 16.

4. Commitment to a state or federal juvenile facility.

5. Heroin or barbiturate use in the two-year period preceding the current arrest.

6. Heroin or barbiturate use as a juvenile.

7. Employment for less than half of the two-year period preceding the current arrest.

An affirmative answer to any of these seven questions adds one point to an offender's score. The total scale can range from 0 to 7.

In order to simplify later analysis, this scale was used to distinguish between low-, medium-, and high-rate burglars or robbers. Offenders who scored 0 to 1 on this scale were predicted to be low-rate; those who scored 2 or 3, medium-rate; and those who scored 4 or more, high-rate. The distribution and mean offense rates for each group, in each of the three sample states, are shown in table 1. In most instances, the average λ for the predicted high-rate offenders exceeds that of the predicted low-rate group by a factor of 4 or more.

Of course, average or mean offense rates are not the only measure of the accuracy of this scale. While the mean rates are useful in practice, there is a methodological problem: as simple averages, the figures are greatly affected by the extremely high offense rates reported by the small fraction of high-rate offenders. But there are two other tests that tend to confirm the effectiveness of this scale. First, comparison of *medians*—which are not sensitive to the offense rates reported by high-rate offenders—shows a similar relationship: in every case, the median offense rate reported by the predicted high-rate group is at least five times greater than the median rate reported by the predicted low-rate

Table 1

Distribution and Mean Offense Rates for Offenders
in the Three Sample States

State	Predicted offense rate	Robbery		Burglary	
		N	λ	N	λ
California	Low	36	2.2	37	12.6
	Medium	58	11.0	69	87.6
	High	84	30.9	54	156.3
Michigan	Low	52	6.1	25	71.6
	Medium	72	11.7	65	34.0
	High	26	20.6	34	101.4
Texas	Low	49	1.4	70	6.0
	Medium	49	5.4	92	20.5
	High	19	7.7	41	51.1

Source: Peter W. Greewood with Allan Abrahamse, *Selective Incapacitation,* The Rand Corporation, R–2815–NIJ, August 1982.

group. Second, when one compares the accuracy with which offenders are classified by this scale with the accuracy of the predictions of their criminality implicit in the sentences imposed on them, one finds that the scale correctly classified 51 percent of the sample while their sentences were an accurate reflection of their offense rates for only 42 percent.

The analysis of these offenders was retrospective (i.e., focused on past behavior), and it relied on self-reported rather than official record data. Consequently, it does not provide a completely accurate method of determining how well high-rate offenders might be identified in the future on the basis of their official records. Nevertheless, the results that it achieved support the general supposition that it may be possible to distinguish among low-rate and high-rate offenders using actuarial prediction methods.

Selective Incapacitation

Suppose that the policymakers in some jurisdiction decided they would like to reduce the amount of some specific type of crime, say robbery, by changing their sentencing policy. In the past, this has been done either by increasing the proportion of convicted offenders who are sent to prison or by increasing the length of prison terms. Both approaches will lead to an increase in the prison population; both approaches will theoretically result in increased deterrence and incapacitation effects; and both approaches ignore any information about differences among offenders' individual crime rates.

The alternative would be to adopt a selective incapacitation policy—a policy explicitly aimed at ensuring that predicted high-rate offenders serve the longest terms.[25] In most jurisdictions it offers a means of increasing incapacitation effects without increasing the level of incarceration. In order to adopt a formal selective incapacitation strategy, a jurisdiction would follow a three-step procedure:

- Determine which of the many characteristics that have been shown to be correlated with individual rates of offending constitute acceptable criteria on which to base sentencing decisions.

- Using arrest histories for a large sample of offenders, estimate the distribution of individual offense rates and determine their correlation with the predictor variables.

- With the information developed and statistical information on current sentencing practices, estimate the effect of various selective sentencing policies on crime rates and on the size of prison populations.

The selective incapacitation approach described above also provides a means of determining how sentencing policies can be changed to *reduce* prison population levels with a minimal loss in incapacitation effects. This is particularly useful for jurisdictions faced with severe prison-crowding problems.

The key to any selective incapacitation policy is the ability to identify high-rate offenders. Yet in addition to the technical problems raised by this process, there are legal and moral issues. The concept of selective incapacitation is controversial, both because it conflicts with other theories of sentencing and also because it makes explicit issues that remain hidden by traditional sentencing practices. Traditionally the decision to incarcerate, the place of incarceration, and the length of confinement have all been predicated on an offender's "amenability to treatment" and his perceived response to treatment programs. Recent research findings notwithstanding, many practitioners continue to believe that an offender's susceptibility to rehabilitation should be reflected in sentencing practices.

To the degree that the theory of rehabilitation has lost ground in recent years, it has generally given way to sentencing based on the notion of "just deserts." Adherents of this view hold that the severity of punishment should primarily reflect the seriousness of the criminal act for which an offender is being punished.[26] The obvious problem with this approach, aside from the difficulty of determining how severity should vary among different types of offenses,[27] is that it ignores the potential impact that sentencing practices have on crime rates.

But perhaps the greatest theoretical barrier to the adoption of a policy of selective incapacitation is the idea that sentencing offenders to prevent crimes that they might commit in the future is on its face unjust. But of course courts and parole boards have always in practice considered future dangerousness in sentencing and release decisions, whether explicitly or not. Selective incapacitation does not alter this practice; it merely seeks to base predictions on objective evidence. All of the factors involved in the prediction scale described previously are routinely included in presentence or diagnostic reports, along with many more subjective assessments of an offender's current life-style and future risk. Moreover, to the degree that we use sentencing policies to deter crime, we are always thinking about the future; it is certainly no more just to impose sanctions on offenders in order to prevent crimes that *others* may commit than to prevent crimes they may commit themselves.

Selective incapacitation does raise the specific issue of which of the many potential predictive factors available will be allowed for selective sentencing purposes. The more restricted the set of allowable predictors, the less accurate the predictions will be. For most people, the use of prior adult convictions raises the fewest objections. When we move to include juvenile record, drug use, or employment history, more objections are raised, while most people would agree that such personal characteristics as race, social class, or education level should be excluded. It is not our point here to argue which of these factors should be allowed and which should not. Rather, we raise the issue to point out that they involve fundamental trade-offs in the effectiveness of sentencing practices that every jurisdiction must make, whether as a matter of conscious policy or on a case-by-case basis.

Potential Applications

Research on the prediction of individual crime rates could be used in a number of different ways. At the most informal level, it could be used by practitioners throughout the criminal justice system simply to focus their efforts on the most serious offenders. Police investigators could use it as a guide in deciding which cases or suspects should receive the most thorough investigation, since it is the quality of this investigation that largely determines the likelihood of successful prosecution. Prosecutors could use the information in case management decisions or in setting plea negotiation policies to ensure that high-rate offenders are convicted of appropriate charges, as many prosecutors already do with so-called "career criminal" cases today; selective incapacitation principles provide a basis for determining who should be targeted by career criminal prosecution units. Judges and parole boards could use the information in determining sentences on a case-by-case basis.

The information could also be used more formally to develop sentencing and parole guidelines or determinate sentencing laws that explicitly recognize the predictive factors as a basis for enhancing or reducing terms. It might be expected that the more formally these factors are embodied in specific statutes or guidelines, the greater the chance that they will be based on objective data and reflect informed decisions on the questions of judgment that this paper touched upon previously.

Any decision to adopt selective incapacitation principles as a formal basis for sentencing policies must begin with a clear idea of what these principles are designed to achieve and how they will interact with other policy concerns. For what types of crime are they to be applied? Are they to be used to limit the prison population, to reduce crime rates by some specific percentage, or to achieve some balance between these two competing goals? What other principles will be used to guide sentencing?

As a method of crime control, selective incapacitation will vary in effectiveness depending on the crime. For certain violent crimes—homicide, rape, and assault—selective incapacitation may have little effect. These crimes often involve people who know each other; moreover, arrest rates suggest that the commission of violent crime is so infrequent for any one offender that the overall rate cannot be influenced much by incapacitation policies. For these offenses, sentences will continue to be based primarily on the concept of just deserts, since the punishment deserved for any one crime will normally override any concerns about future offenses.

For the least serious property crimes such as larceny, fraud, or auto theft, very few offenders are now incarcerated. Therefore, any attempt to use selective incapacitation principles to reduce these crimes would place an additional burden on already overcrowded prison facilities.

The crimes for which selective incapacitation principles appear to offer best prospects are burglary and robbery. These are high-volume predatory offenses of which the public is most fearful. They are also the offenses in which career criminals predominate, and they are the crimes for which a substantial number of convicted defendants are currently incarcerated.

The 1982 Rand study previously cited used the survey data from convicted robbers in California, and the seven-item prediction scale, to estimate the incapacitation effects that would result from a number of different sentencing policy changes that differed in their degree of selectivity. Among the policy changes they investigated were four defined as follows:

1. *Nonselective increases in the prison commitment rate.* Under the sentencing policy in effect at the time of the study, 86 percent of all convicted robbers were incarcerated: 61 percent were sentenced to short jail terms (less than one year) and 25 percent were given longer state prison terms (an average of 52 months). Increasing the prison commitment rate would result in fewer short jail terms and a greater number of longer prison terms for all types of offenders. This is the least selective method of increasing the incarcerated population, since low-rate offenders are currently more likely to be sentenced to the shorter jail terms.

2. *Nonselective increases in prison term length.* Under this policy, the probability of being sentenced to jail or prison remained unchanged for all three types of offenders—i.e., those predicted to be low-, medium-, or high-rate. The only change was that the length of time served by those committed to *prison* became longer. This policy is somewhat more selective than policy 1 in that high-rate offenders are currently more likely to be committed to prison than low-rate offenders, who tend to serve jail terms.

3. *Selective increases in prison term length.* Under this policy, which is more selective than the previous two, only the terms of predicted *high-rate* prison inmates were increased; the probability of being sentenced to jail or prison remained unchanged.

4. *Imprisonment for only high-rate offenders.* This was the most selective policy tested. The fraction of defendants incarcerated in either jail or prison remained unchanged. However, all predicted low- and medium-rate offenders were sentenced to jail terms of one year and all predicted high-rate offenders were sentenced to prison terms.

The predicted impacts of these four different policies on robbery rates and incarceration levels are shown in figure 1.

Each line in the figure represents a specific policy and shows the expected adult robbery rate (vertical axis) that will result for a range of incarceration levels (horizontal axis). Both the robbery rate and prison population levels are expressed as a percentage of their current estimated value.

As figure 1 shows, the more selective sentencing policies result in lower crime rates for any given level of incarceration. Under policy 1, it would require a 15 percent increase in the number of offenders incarcerated to bring about a 10 percent reduction of the robbery rate. But by using the most selective policy (policy 4), it is possible to achieve a 20 percent reduction in the robbery rate with no increase in the overall number of offenders incarcerated. Note that in none of the policies would the terms of the predicted high-rate offenders be increased by more than a factor of two.

Figure 1

**Crime Rate/Incarceration Level Trade-Offs
under Alternative Selective Incapacitation Policies
(California Robbers)**

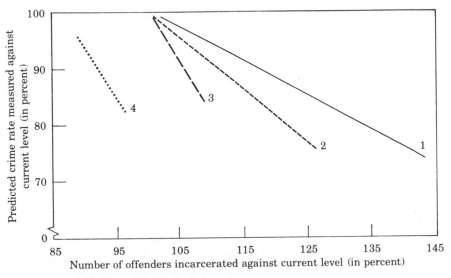

1 Nonselective increases in prison commitment rate
2 Nonselective increases in prison term length
3 Selective increases in prison term length
4 Imprisonment for only high-rate offenders

Source: Peter W. Greenwood with Allan Abrahamse, *Selective Incapacitation,* The Rand Corporation, R–2815–NIJ, August 1982.

Implementation

Any state that decided to use selective incapacitation in determining its sentencing policies would have to take a number of actions. It would have to begin by determining the distribution of individual offense rates among its offenders and identifying those factors that predict high offense rates. This could be done by using either arrest histories[28] or self-reports.[29]

It would also be necessary to estimate sentencing patterns for each different type of offender in order to estimate the total number of offenders and to provide a base for comparing alternative policies. Finally, one would have to evaluate the various alternative sentencing strategies.

Regardless of the policy adopted, it is unlikely that incapacitation will ever be the sole consideration in setting terms. Punishment and deterrence undoubtedly will play a role, even if their effects cannot be quantified. Some additional steps thus need to be taken.

First, the state must project both its future crime rates and its incarceration capacity on the basis of its current crime rates and incarceration levels (for both jails and prisons). (At this point, it would probably be best to ignore the effect of incarceration on crime rates, since incapacitation is unlikely to have much effect on such crimes as homicide, rape, and assault, which make up a sizeable proportion of the total incarcerated population.)

Second, the state must develop a pattern of minimum sentences based on just deserts and deterrence considerations alone, ignoring incapacitation. For instance, despite the fact that their recidivism rate is usually quite low, offenders convicted of manslaughter might be required to serve terms of six years, based on concerns of punishment alone. Similarly, the terms for unarmed and armed robbery might be set at eighteen months and three years, with an additional two years added for seriously injuring a victim.

Finally, in light of this pattern of minimum sentences and the expected crime rate, it will be possible to estimate the incarcerated population that would be generated by these terms. The difference between the population to be generated by the minimum terms and the predicted capacity is the amount of space available for selective incapacitation. In California, for instance, the projected population to be generated for minimum terms might be 30,000, while the available capacity might be 32,000. If it were decided to use all of this excess capacity to reduce robberies, and the projected minimum robbery population were 8,000, there would be room for a 25 percent increase in the incarcerated robbery population. Depending upon the sentencing policy chosen, one could obtain reductions in the robbery rate ranging from 12 to more than 30 percent. Of course, after one such cycle of estimates, it would be possible to go back and revise the minimum terms in order to provide more or less for incapacitation.

In undertaking these reforms, policymakers need to proceed with caution. One of the major lessons from experience with policy initiatives in criminal justice over the past twenty years is that nothing is simple. The system is complex and responds to change in ways that are difficult to anticipate. There is much that we do not know about how specific types of offenders will respond to different types of sanctions. Any jurisdiction that decides to implement more selective sentencing policies should therefore proceed gradually, continuously monitoring the impact of its policies on the disposition of cases and the subsequent behavior of offenders. Any less systematic approach will in all likelihood miss the mark.

V

Politics and Governance

14

SEYMOUR MARTIN LIPSET

The American Party System

It is an accepted truism in political science that American political parties are weaker than comparable organizations elsewhere. Currently, they have little say about the nomination of candidates for public office, particularly at the national level. Unlike the situation in most other democratic countries, national legislators here are under little constraint to follow the policies advanced by a president or congressional leader of their party.

Reasons for Party Weakness

The reasons for party weakness are inherent in the division of powers in the constitutional system. The Founding Fathers, who drew up the Constitution, did not anticipate or desire parties, while their experience with autocratic British power had taught them to fear strong executive authority. They deliberately

---

This essay originally appeared as "The American Party System: Concluding Observations" in *Party Coalitions in the 1980s*, edited by Seymour Martin Lipset (1981). References to other papers are to chapters in that book.

designed a government in which political power would be frag-
mented between and within federal and state governments,
among an executive not responsible to parliament, two legislative
houses, and the judiciary, each of which would be motivated to
restrain the others.

In parliamentary countries, the cabinet and prime minister are
responsible to parliament, and the fact that the government falls
or new elections are called when a majority votes against the in-
cumbents encourages party discipline. Members of parliament
almost invariably follow party policy. Candidates for parliament
are usually chosen for their contribution to party activities. The
electorate generally votes for a party, not for the particular individuals running in the constituencies. Cabinet members are
chosen from parliament. Parties have strong national organizations, frequently own newspapers, and are represented to the
media by officially designated spokespersons.

In the United States, on the other hand, party strength in Congress has no bearing on the choice of president, how long he holds
office, or the composition of his cabinet. Members of the latter
rarely come from congressional ranks. Even though the president
and members of Congress are elected independently, the contests
for all representatives and a rotating third of the senators are held
at the same time as that for president. Still, many voters do not
vote by party; they may split their tickets by supporting a Republican for president and a Democrat for the Senate and/or the
House. In the six presidential years from 1956 to 1976, over 30
percent of the House districts were carried by a presidential
nominee of one party and a House candidate of a different party.[1]
As a result, the president, though the official leader of his party,
has no control—and sometimes not much influence—over the
behavior of his party colleagues in Congress. Representatives and
senators are more interested in the particular concerns of their
constituents than in the proposals of their own party's president
or their party leaders in Congress.

The Party System

The fact that the president is chosen in a national election rather
than by parliament plays a special causal role in the nature of the

party system.[2] Since the executive power—the presidency— cannot be divided among parties, and the cabinet is appointed by the head of state and responsible only to him, elections for president have been forced into a two-candidate or two—major party race ever since the first election took place in 1796. In a parliamentary country, voters may support and elect representatives of small parties to parliament; these representatives, in turn, may influence the choice of prime minister or may even have cabinet members in a coalition, multiparty government.

Efforts to form stable third parties in the United States invariably fail because the effective constituency in national elections is basically the entire country.[3] The emphasis on presidential elections has prevented third parties from building up enduring local constituency strength in the way that labor, agrarian, religious, or ethnic based parties have done in parliamentary, single-member, district systems. American third parties thus have gained their greatest strength in municipal—or occasionally, state—elections, and have invariably lost support in subsequent presidential elections. They have also been more successful in congressional races held in nonpresidential election years.

Significant third-party efforts have occurred invariably under conditions in which particular factions or interest groups have found themselves excluded from the coalition with which they are normally involved because of presidential nominations or the adoption of policies that affront their concerns. Thus, in 1924, both major parties nominated conservatives, a development that led to the candidacy of Robert La Follette on the Progressive ticket. In 1948, and again in 1968, the Democratic presidential nominees were anathema to Southern white racists, a fact which produced independent candidacies by Southern Democratic politicians Strom Thurmond and George Wallace. But support for these and other third-party candidacies, such as John Anderson's in 1980, has always been vitiated by those factors that lead people to see a third-party vote as "wasted." Hence, as opinion polls taken during election years have shown, backing for third-party candidates drops off sharply as Election Day approaches. But if a third-party candidate does reasonably well, one or the other of the major parties will make overtures to his supporters and bring them back into the main two-party system by the following election.

Recognizing the near impossibility of creating a new national party has led many American radicals, who would have preferred a party of their own, to operate as factions within one of the major parties. At different times since the late 1910s, socialist or near socialist groups have either controlled or greatly influenced a major party in a number of states. Currently, various socialist organizations—the Social Democrats, USA, led by Bayard Rustin, the Democratic Socialist Organizing Committee chaired by Michael Harrington, and the Campaign for Economic Democracy formed by Tom Hayden—are working within the Democratic party. And at the other end of the political spectrum, Richard Viguerie[4], leader of the New Right movement, notes that conservatives like himself, who would like to "organize a brand new broadly based party, designed to replace the Republican Party," have been forced to recognize that "the two party system . . . is probably too solidly entrenched for any such effort." Hence they, too, consciously accept the fact of coalition politics and seek "to nominate conservative candidates, promote conservative positions and create conservative majorities in both parties."

The United States is at least as heterogeneous in social structure as most other countries with numerous parties, but the diverse American classes, ethnic groups, religions, regions, value groups, which could form the base of separate parties, must coalesce into two very broad coalition parties if they want to influence the outcome of the presidential contest. In effect, the United States has a concealed multiparty system; its many factions take part in *pre-election coalitions*, called parties. In much of Europe, autonomous and relatively homogeneous parties join to form a *post-election coalition* government.[5]

Parties as Coalitions

Given the diversity of membership, American parties have always been loose coalitions of dissimilar elements. The Democratic party, the oldest continuously operating party in the world, included Southern slaveholders and Northern Jacksonian populists and labor-union advocates before the Civil War. Its opponents, then known as "the Whigs," combined within one national party Southern plantation owners, Northern business interests, and middle-class evangelical Protestants, many of the latter strongly abolitionist.

The Republicans, from the Civil War on, tended to represent the dominant cultural and economic groups of the country—largely urban and rural, Northern evangelical, Protestant whites of British and Northern European descent, and industrialists—plus the blacks, who kept voting for the party of Lincoln. Democratic supporters were drawn from highly diverse "out" groups—recent immigrants, nonpietistic Protestant sects, non-Protestant elements, trade unionists, and Southern white Protestants—who, for historic and regional economic and cultural reasons, opposed the Republicans (see chapter 4 by Paul Kleppner).

In the first third of this century, the Republicans included some of the most Left-wing politicians in the country, some near socialists from Midwest radical agrarian areas, *and* spokespeople for big business from Eastern states, plus the impoverished blacks. The Democratic coalition assembled by Franklin Roosevelt in the 1930s incorporated Southern racists, blacks, evangelical whites—who had backed the anti-Catholic and anti-Semitic Ku Klux Klan and favored prohibition of liquor—and most Catholics, Jews, and trade unionists.

It should be obvious, from this listing of the various elements in both electoral coalitions, that they could not have cooperated in the same "party" if there had been any real party discipline—i.e., if in the 1920s North Dakota and other Midwestern Republican radicals who favored government ownership of major industries had to support the program of those primarily concerned with the welfare of business, or if during the 1930s Democratic representatives of black or trade-union districts were obliged to vote for the policies of Southern racists. What brought these groups together was the need to nominate and support a presidential candidate; but the condition for their membership in a national party was total absence of party discipline at the legislative level.

The glue that helped preserve what there was of a national party structure, and that sustained relatively strong local organizations, was patronage. Many federal jobs, such as postmasters, did not come under civil service merit rules and were awarded to loyal members of the president's party, usually on recommendation of local party leaders. State and city or county organizations were

much stronger than the national, in part because of their extensive local patronage, but also because such parties were less
heterogeneous in social composition and thus less factionalized
than the national organization.

The national parties basically have only existed to select a presidential nominee at a national convention every four years. Until
recently, the convention brought together party leaders from all
the states to decide on the party's choice. Given the diversity within each party, nominees—almost invariably—had to be nonideological individuals chosen because they were least likely to an-
tagonize the various elements in the party and electorate, and
because their past record suggested political or administrative
competency.

Changes in the Parties

This system gradually has broken down since the 1930s. As
Everett Ladd points out in chapter 7, the Roosevelt New Deal
helped to realign the base of the parties as class and ideology came
to differentiate the two coalitions more dramatically than before.
Reacting to the Great Depression, the Democratic party took on a
social-democratic cast. It included the growing number of economic Leftists, even most avowed socialists and communists, the
rapidly increasing trade-union movement, many of the previously
Republican Midwestern, agrarian radicals, and the blacks, while it
retained the support of the Southern, largely rural and impoverished, whites.

The Roosevelt coalition advocated a strongly interventionist
welfare and planning state that supported trade unions and higher, guaranteed, farm prices. While the Republicans gained some
support from previously Democratic business people, they did not
make up for the massive party losses, and the GOP became the
minority party in Congress and in presidential elections.

From the New Deal era on, economic and social ideology divided
the two coalitions. The Democrats added social liberalism, particularly support of black civil rights, to their economic liberalism. The
Republicans remained anti-statist, opposed—in principle if not in
practice—to government intervention, whether for economic,
welfare, or social (civil rights) concerns. During the post—World

War II period, white Southerners began to leave their Democratic national home, at times for regional, racist, third parties but, together with other less-privileged social conservatives, more permanently for the Republican ranks. And as noted by Ladd and by Schneider (chapters 7 and 9), the Democrats gained among sectors of the socially liberal, college-educated, and professional population.

The more coherent ideological and interest differences between the two major coalitions logically should have produced more unified and more disciplined parties. Such was not to be, however, because of the decline in patronage and the enlargement of the system of nominating candidates through publicly held party primary elections. Reform elements, including most intellectuals, had long sought to weaken party organizations and leadership, which they labeled scornfully as "machines" and "bosses," by placing government employment under the merit civil service, and by changing the nomination process from one controlled by delegates selected by lower-level party organizations to one in which candidates and/or convention delegates are selected in primary elections, open to participation by any voter who declared or registered him or herself as a party supporter.

Both of these proposed reforms were gradually carried out at the national and local levels. The elimination of patronage reduced the number of nonideological party activists who worked hard before elections to mobilize support for all party nominees and who were uncritically loyal to the leaders of the organizations. The spread of the primaries limited the ability of professional party leaders to choose those who ran for office. Whoever could mobilize money and other forms of support could run in the primaries, regardless of his or her past relations with the party organization or leaders.

The presidential nomination process, however, remained under control of party leaders until the 1960s.[6] But the protest movements of that decade engendered a strong wave of support for the greater democratization of society, which included extending the system of primaries. New Politics reformers in the Democratic party took the lead in changes which by 1980 meant that, for most of the states, Democrats designated their delegates for presidential nomination conventions in primary elections while the Republicans were reluctantly forced to follow suit. Since three-quarters of the delegates in both parties were chosen in primaries or bound by their results, this meant that primary voters chose the nominee.

The breakdown of organization and the extension of popular choice in nominations gave increased influence to better educated, more ideologically committed persons. Such people are more likely to vote in primaries, which tend to be low turnout contests, and more willing to work actively for primary candidates. As a result, Right-wing Republicans and Left-wing Democrats have become influential within their parties to a far greater extent than their numbers in the electorate or among party adherents suggest.

As this process developed, ideology penetrated into party leadership itself. Those who serve on national and state committees increasingly reflect the views of their opinionated activists rather than those of typical party supporters who take a more moderate or centrist position.

The differences between those most active in the parties and party supporters are pointed up in the results of two midyear 1981 surveys—conducted by CBS News and the *Los Angeles Times*—which dealt with the views of those in the leadership of their parties as well as of their rank and file. Some findings of the CBS News polls are presented in table 1.

As is evident from table 1, the national Democratic leaders are much more liberal than those who identify with the party, while among Republicans, party supporters are less conservative than those on the national committee. A similar pattern of variations between the opinions of party activists (members of the state committees) and the rank and file was revealed in polls taken in mid-July among Californians by the *Los Angeles Times*. Richard Bergholz[7] reported for the poll:

Democratic Party activists view themselves as more liberal than rank-and-file Democrats, while Republican activists see themselves as more conservative than the GOP members. . . .

A clear majority—65%—of the Democratic activists said they were liberals, while only 26% of the Democratic rank and file said they were liberal. . . .

On the Republican side, ideological differences showed up, though to a lesser degree. A whopping 81% of the activists . . . said they were conservatives, while 60% of the GOP voters put themselves in that category.

Table 1

Views of Members of the Democratic and Republican National Committees and Party Supporters, 1981

	Democratic		Republican	
	Committee	Rank and File	Committee	Rank and File
Political philosophy				
Liberal	36%	24%	1%	11%
Moderate	51%	42%	31%	33%
Conservative	4%	29%	63%	51%
Military/defense spending				
Increase	22%	48%	89%	60%
Decrease	18%	13%	1%	5%
Keep same level	51%	36%	7%	31%
Equal rights amendment				
Favor	92%	61%	29%	46%
Oppose	4%	29%	58%	44%
Too much government regulation of business				
Agree	35%	59%	98%	72%
Disagree	49%	30%	1%	22%

Source: CBS News Election and Survey Unit (5 June, 12 June 1981).

Most Democratic voters take conservative positions on such issues as voluntary prayers in schools, the death penalty and Proposition 13, the property tax—cutting initiative passed in 1978, whereas the Democratic Party activists take the liberal view.

Most Republican voters line up in support of the equal rights amendment while the party officials are overwhelmingly against it.

Effect on Nominations

New Politics, Left-wing, candidate George McGovern was able to defeat Hubert Humphrey for the Democratic nomination in 1972 by winning in the primaries. The support of most party and trade-union leaders for his opponent Hubert Humphrey was not enough to bring the bulk of the less educated, pro-Humphrey, Democratic electorate to vote in the primaries. In 1976 an unknown Jimmy Carter, who started off actively campaigning for the presidency in 1974, presented himself at the end of the Watergate era as an anti-Washington, anti-Establishment, populist spokesman of the common people and was able to win the nomination against much better known opponents, who had backing from party and trade-union leaders. In 1980, though, an elected incumbent, Carter, in turn, had a difficult contest for renomination against New Politics Senator Edward Kennedy. The president was saved from a humiliating defeat in the primaries by foreign events, the Iranian hostage situation and the Russian invasion of Afghanistan, and by the damage to the Kennedy candidacy that resulted from the reemergence of the Chappaquiddick issue—his role in the death of a woman in an automobile accident.

The Republicans, as the smaller party with only 25 percent of the electorate identifying with them, were influenced even earlier than the Democrats by strong ideologues—in their case, ardent antistatist, *laissez-faire*, conservatives. Barry Goldwater, as leader of the party's rightist faction, captured the GOP nomination in 1964 by beating the candidate of the moderate wing, Nelson Rockefeller, in key primaries. In 1976 Ronald Reagan, identified as a spokesman for the Right wing, came very close to defeating an incumbent, centrist, Republican president—Gerald Ford—in the primaries. And in 1980 he swept through these contests and received the nomination, although many party leaders and outside observers believed that, from an electoral-appeal point of view, a more moderate Republican such as George Bush or Howard Baker would do better in the general election. As events turned out, of course, Reagan went on to win overwhelmingly against Jimmy Carter. This victory, however, does not necessarily prove that Reagan was a strong candidate in his own right, since Carter—according to the opinion polls—was regarded as the least-competent president since polling began in the 1930s and was held responsible by most voters for extremely adverse economic conditions.

The opposition to strong party organization among the more populistically inclined reformers also has affected the operation of Congress. Although, as noted, there has been much less party discipline here than in European parliaments, some party leadership structure and power has existed in the form of the influence over the legislative agenda and process by committee chairpeople. These limited powers were reduced in the mid-1970s by reforms linked to attitudes influenced by the Watergate affair.

The 1980s

The United States enters the 1980s with her national party structure, as reflected in the power and influence of the presidential and congressional party leadership, in weaker condition than in any period since the Civil War. But the situation may be about to change. Given the disastrous conclusions to the last four administrations—Johnson, Nixon, Ford, Carter—and the seeming inability of the executive to cope with the domestic economy and foreign policy, there is an increasing tendency among opinion molders, political scientists, journalists, and politicians, to put some of the responsibility for these outcomes on the political and electoral systems. Many criticize the elements which make it difficult to mobilize the presidency and Congress behind common policy. For the first time in close to three decades, discussions of reforming the system do not refer to proposals to weaken the power of officials and extend that of the electorate. Reformers are looking now for ways to enhance the authority of presidential and congressional leadership, and to revise the nomination process in ways designed to increase the influence of party leaders, e.g., by designating various elected officials and party officers *ex officio* voting delegates to party conventions.

As the "out" party, the Republicans began a process of strengthening party organization and control following their defeat in 1976. As noted by David Broder in chapter 1, the party's national committee under the leadership of its chairman, Bill Brock, undertook an extensive program of recruiting, counseling, and financing legislative and congressional candidates, and of trying to define congressional elections in national partisan rather than in local terms. Following the GOP's gains in the 1980 elections, its representatives in the Senate and the House exhibited more party discipline in support of their president's legislative program in the 1981 session than occurred at any time since the early 1930s.

The Democrats, in turn, responding to the tighter organization of their opponents and their electoral losses, have also shown a disposition to close ranks and to give congressional party leaders more power. Although a number of conservatives, largely Southerners, opposed the party's leadership and supported the Reagan spending-and-taxation program, the Democratic defectors to the bipartisan conservative coalition were, in fact, considerably fewer in number in 1981 than in the congressional sessions of the 1960s and 1970s.[8] As reported by Richard Cattani, the 43 Democrats in the House who voted for the Reagan tax package in July and had previously served in Congress had a strongly conservative voting record. "Their liberal-conservative ratings for 1980, according to the Americans for Democratic Action scores on key votes, averaged 23.9 percent. This was remarkably close to the conservative 21.4 percent of all Republican congressmen in 1980."[9]

The Democratic party is also about to change the procedures of selecting national convention delegates. The 1982 Democratic miniconvention will be held under new rules which give party leaders considerable representation. It is probable that party officials and elected officeholders will have increased influence at the 1984 nominating convention, at the expense of reducing somewhat the number of delegates chosen in primaries. The party's new national chairman, Charles Manatt, has appointed a commission to propose revisions in procedures for choosing delegates to national conventions. At the first meeting of the Commission on Presidential Nominations in August 1981, Donald Fraser, cochairman with George McGovern of the 1970 party organization commission which produced the sharp increase in primaries, set the tone for the 1980s, stating "presidential primaries denigrate a party's responsibility for selecting its own candidate." He proposed that no state party be allowed to choose more than half its delegation through a primary. The 1981 commission was divided between two major factions—labor union representatives and supporters of Walter Mondale who favored cutting back on the primaries, and New Politics backers of Edward Kennedy and minority group members who wanted to preserve the predominance of the primaries.[10]

It is much too early, however, to predict that party organization will be greatly strengthened. The growing concern to do so on the part of many in the political elite is countered by the declining commitment to party and to voting participation by the electorate. The proportion who identify themselves as "independents" rather than as Democrats or Republicans, who do not vote for the same party regularly, who do not vote at all, or who express cynicism about the political process and the role of government, has grown greatly since the mid-1960s. While majorities of those interviewed in opinion polls indicate that they still support government policies designed to protect people against misfortunes flowing from economic or health reverses or to enhance opportunity for the deprived, they have increasingly lost faith in the competency of their leaders and even of the institutions themselves. Hence, they would still prefer to further reduce rather than increase the power of officials.

The traditional American disdain for politicians—the word itself is invidious—and for parties and politics in general, has grown. Although the differences between a libertarian, antistatist, business-linked, socially conservative Republican party and a much more interventionist, statist, trade-union linked, socially permissive Democratic party are great, the proportion of the public who feel that it makes little or no difference who is elected has increased steadily. In any case, these variations in the dominant outlook of both parties, while real, should not be exaggerated. Among the Republicans, the growing number of advocates of supply-side economics emphasize tax reductions, while actually opposing many spending cuts that are favored by *laissez-faire* enthusiasts. The Democrats, on the other hand, have responded to the growing sentiment that government intervention has hampered economic development and encouraged inflation. Their congressional leadership is emphasizing the need to encourage investment to foster growth through reducing taxes on business, liberalizing depreciation allowances, and modifying regulatory policies.

The Future

What may be anticipated, given this background? At most, there will be some minor adjustments in the nominating process to give leaders more influence. But the basic structural features, dictated by the division of powers in the Constitution, will continue to produce weak parties and tensions between Congress and the presidency, even when the same party controls both institutions. American presidents will still find it difficult to commit the country to an effective foreign policy.

The two major parties will continue, more or less as they have been—as Nelson Polsby notes in chapter 8—to function as mechanisms through which highly diverse groups and strata compete to nominate and elect candidates and to influence public policy. Ideologically motivated tendencies and pressure groups, such as those supported by feminists, religious fundamentalists, environmentalists, opponents of abortion, will play a major role in this process. The Democrats will continue to fight among themselves in the "five parties" that Tip O'Neill says they would break into in a parliamentary system—socialists, who include a few congressmen and the heads of some major trade unions, a New Politics Left led by Edward Kennedy, a New Deal center identified with Walter Mondale, a neoconservative (or, as they prefer to call themselves, neoliberal) faction linked to Henry Jackson and Daniel Patrick Moynihan, and on the right the conservative "boll weevils," led by Philip Gramm of Texas, who support Reagan's economic program. The GOP is divided into three tendencies: a small liberal Left which, however, involves a number of senators —Percy, Mathias, Weicker, Cohen, Spector, Packwood, and Heinz—a center supportive of Vice-President Bush and Senate majority leader Baker, and the New Right, led in Congress by Jesse Helms. Ronald Reagan bridges the center and Right, but as the emphasis in policy debate shifts from the economic issues to the social ones, it is probable, as I noted in chapter 2, that the president will be positioned in the center. Roughly 20 percent of the Democratic House members are "boll weevils," while about 10 percent of the Republicans are classified as liberal "gypsy moths."

The direction in which the parties and the country moves from one election to another will continue to depend on larger, often uncontrollable events, the state of the business cycle, international developments, as well as on the competency of the president and other leaders. Democrats and Republicans will govern the United States, but whether they can deal with the major problems of contemporary society effectively, given a government consciously designed by its eighteenth-century founders to be weak, is questionable. But it is the only political system we have, and providence or luck has given us great men, such as Lincoln and Roosevelt, as leaders during periods in which effective leadership was necessary.

15

AARON WILDAVSKY

Toward a New
Budgetary Order

Budgets reflect social orders; what is true of one is soon enough true of the other. Living one way and budgeting another is too contradictory to last. When we experience basic changes in budgeting, or hear that radical changes in budgetary relationships are afoot, we know that society is not what it was or will be. Political cultures are in contention.

To assess the potential for and desirability of budgetary changes in the 1980s, therefore, it is worth considering how this nation used to budget, why these budgetary relationships were transformed, and why Americans are now contemplating reforming their prior reforms. Knowing where we have been will help us

This essay originally appeared as "The Budget as New Social Contract" in *Journal of Contemporary Studies* (Spring 1982). A slightly different version also appeared as the first two chapters in *The Federal Budget: Economics and Politics,* edited by Michael J. Boskin and Aaron Wildavsky (1982).

understand today's choices about where we might go. This historical review is especially necessary because earlier patterns of
budgetary thought and action have been lost to our contemporary
consciousness.

The Original Compact

The winning side of the American Revolution was composed of
three social orders: a weak social hierarchy that wanted to replace
the English king with a native variety better suited to colonial
conditions, emerging market men who wanted to control their
own commerce, and the heirs of a continental republican tradition
that stressed small, egalitarian voluntary associations.[1]

The balanced budget at low levels, except in wartime, was the
crucial compromise that allowed these three social orders to co-
exist. Of course, unlike the signing of the Declaration of Independence, the compromise was not made in a single day, nor was
there a formal declaration. The informal understanding, however,
lasted for a century and a half; it was undone in the 1960s, and
whether our generation can forge a new consensus that will do as
well in our time and last as long as the old is being decided now.

What was this understanding? How was it verified and enforced? And what was in it for everyone concerned?

It is well to remember that the Revolution was fought against
the power of the English king. Even the Federalists, who joined
social hierarchy and market forces to form the first independent
American establishment, had their qualms about how strong the
executives, like the president and the departmental secretaries,
should be. They wanted political unity and economic order, but on
a minimal, not a maximal, basis. Republicans—first the social
order, then the political party, originally known as Anti-
Federalists—knew best what they were against: established
churches, standing armies, and powerful executives. They were
for life on a smaller scale and limitations on status and economic
differences so as to permit people to manage their own affairs.[2]

Left to their own devices, our social hierarchs would have
wanted relatively high revenues and expenditures to support a
stronger and more splendid central government. Since the market
men would have to pay, they preferred a smaller central ap-

paratus, except where spending and taxing provided direct aid. Together this establishment supported what, in American political life, were called "internal improvements"—subsidies for canals, harbors, railroads, and the like.

But the establishment had to contend with the republican believers in small, egalitarian collectives who threatened to withdraw consent to union unless the size and scope of the central government were severely limited. For these egalitarians did not believe that government spending was good for the common man, the small farmer and artisan of their day. Government took from the people (or so they believed) for the establishment. Limiting, not expanding, central government was the byword of republicanism.

Governments that ran deficits might have been acceptable to the hierarchical social order as a necessary accompaniment of domestic grandeur. The "public interest" was their phrase. But continuous deficits were unacceptable to market forces, who feared financial instability, debasement of currency, and inflation. So market men would pay more to balance the budget. It was the egalitarian republicans who insisted on lower levels of taxing and spending. Alone, they might have allowed imbalance—lower revenue than expenditure—since taxes discriminated against the ordinary citizen.

In the compromise that emerged, market men—adherents of competitive individualism—won the opportunity to seek economic growth with government subsidy (i.e., internal improvements) and gained the stability that comes from knowing that spending will be limited by willingness to increase revenues. Egalitarian republicans were able to place limits on the establishment. And the supporters of social hierarchy obtained a larger role for collective concerns, provided they were able to gather sufficient revenue. No order of society got purely what it wanted, but all got assurances that they would not be subject to severe disadvantages.

Thus the doctrine of the balanced budget, a doctrine that became so powerful over time that terrible things were supposed to happen should it be violated with impunity, was far more than an economic theory. The "balance" referred to was not only between revenue and expenditure but between social orders.

Debt: The Great Equation

Thenceforth, the history of American attitudes toward public debt
may be translated into formulas for relating revenues to expenditures that were no less powerful for being simple. The first of
these budgetary great equations[3] was simplicity itself: revenues
minus interest on the public debt equalled allowable national
government spending. The new Constitution provided ample
authority for all sorts of taxes, including direct levies on individuals and internal excise taxes. In the debate over ratification,
however, the proponents of the Constitution frequently insisted
that the bulk of taxes be raised by custom duties and sale of public
lands, with income and excise taxes reserved for emergencies.
Despite Alexander Hamilton's major effort both to exert executive
authority and simultaneously to give the government a sounder financial basis by invoking internal taxes,[4] Jefferson and his republican followers soon reverted to their preferred version in which
tariffs predominated. Given the widespread agreement on balanced budgets and parsimony in government, as well as the desire
to pay off the public debt, the first great equation had appeal.

Life soon provided the circumstances that lawyers say alter
cases. In times of war, the second great equation prevailed:
revenues, this time including internal taxes, equalled ordinary
civilian expenditures minus wartime debt. When surpluses appeared or the attractiveness of internal improvements proved ir-
resistible, or both, a third equation operated: revenues in surplus
minus interest on debt, minus ordinary spending, minus internal
improvements, equalled central government spending. It was only
with the revolution in fiscal thought following the Great Depression of the 1930s that the fourth equation, sometimes called a full
employment surplus, took center stage. The idea was to balance
not the budget but the economy at full employment. The fourth
great equation stipulated that revenues plus a deficit sufficient to
secure full employment equalled spending. The formulation of a
fifth equation is under discussion today.

The Faith in Balance

In the nineteenth century, American presidents did not believe
government spending would further redistribution from the rich

to the poor; to the contrary, "melancholy is the condition of that people," President Polk (1845–1849) wrote, "whose government can be sustained only by a system which periodically transfers large amounts from the labors of the many to the coffers of the few."[5] For these men, as for the citizens they governed, debt was equated with privilege.

Faith in the balanced budget ideal was strengthened by an economic theory that tied wages negatively to debt. As Secretary of the Treasury Robert J. Walker claimed in 1838, "Wages can only be increased in any nation, in the aggregate, by augmenting capital, the fund out of which wages are paid. . . . The destruction or diminution of capital, by destroying or reducing the fund from which labor is paid must reduce wages." This wage-fund argument had the added value of suggesting that the wage earner would be hurt by any effort to go into debt to improve his lot.[6] During the recession of 1837 and 1838, when efforts were made to increase federal spending in order to alleviate suffering, President Van Buren invoked the sagacity of the founding fathers who "wisely judged that the less government interferes with private pursuits the better for the general prosperity."[7] The economy would improve by reducing the deficit, not by building railroads or canals. President Buchanan blamed the financial panic and recession of 1857 and 1858 on "the habit of extravagant expenditures."[8]

Thus, for the federal government, the era before the Civil War remained a time of tiny government. Between 1800 and 1860, as table 1 shows, federal expenditures rose from almost 11 to 63 million dollars in total. More than half were military expenditures. The general category of "civil and miscellaneous" included a substantial amount for the postal deficit, thus covering everything except defense, pensions, Indians, and interest on the debt. Kimmel is correct in his conclusion that "federal expenditures made little or no contribution to the level of living. Only a minor portion of Civil and miscellaneous expenditures were for developmental purposes. . . ."[9]

The Civil War changed all that. The government grew from tiny to small. It promoted the interests of businessmen and farmers, sometimes aiding railroads and other times intervening to regulate them in the interests of farmers. Beginning with the Morrill Act of 1862, which gave huge land grants to states for the purpose of establishing agricultural and mechanical universities, a variety of measures were adopted to aid education. Post—Civil War presidents generally, like Thomas Jefferson before them, regarded education as an exception to whatever strictures they laid upon unnecessary expenditures. And as the nation was settled and the frontier neared its end, the beginnings of a movement to set aside land for conservation purposes appeared. Still, it is not in these modest departures from the strict doctrine of the minimum state that one can find the sources of budgetary conflict or the seeds of future spending.

Deficit and Surplus

The Civil War also marked the first break in the consensus on debt reduction. Balanced budgets, to be sure, remained the norm, but the growth of presidential discretion and the rise of industrial expansion left the role of debt open to argument. Abraham Lincoln (1860—1865) thought that citizens "cannot be much oppressed by a debt which they owe to themselves." His idea, followed by President Rutherford B. Hayes a decade later (1877—1881), was to secure a wider distribution of the debt among citizens. Considering that the debt might be paid over time, Presi-

Table 1
Federal Expenditures
Fiscal Years 1800, 1825, 1850, and 1860
(in millions of dollars)

	1800	1825	1850	1860
Civil and miscellaneous	1.3	2.7	14.9	28.0[a]
War Department	2.6	3.7	9.4	16.4
Navy Department	3.4	3.1	7.9	11.5
Indians	—	0.7	1.6	2.9
Pensions	0.1	1.3	1.9	1.1
Interest	3.4	4.4	3.8	3.2
Total	$10.8	$15.9	$39.5	$63.1[a]

[a]Includes postal deficit of $9.9 million.

Source: Lewis H. Kimmel, *Federal Budget and Fiscal Policy, 1989—1958* (Washington, D.C.: The Brookings Institution, 1959), p. 57. Data from *Annual Report of the Secretary of the Treasury on the State of the Finances for the Fiscal Year Ended June 30, 1934.*

dent Ulysses S. Grant (1869–1877), usually not considered a father of supply-side economics, asserted that the capacity to pay grew with the wealth of the nation. Rather than raising taxes to pay the debt in a shorter time, he would cut taxes to increase wealth and hence provide greater subsequent revenues.[10] During a time of expansion, the desire for internal improvements seemed compatible with fiscal prudence.

Money may or may not be the root of all evil. But the availability of substantial surpluses in the post–Civil War period proved a greater temptation than most private interests and public officials were able to withstand. No one can say whether it was the change in national opinion accompanying the swift pace of the industrial revolution, or whether it was the huge revenues generated by the growing protective tariff or the attendant changes in the process of budgeting that mattered most. Suffice it to say that soon enough even the $3 billion Civil War debt became readily manageable and that higher tariffs still produced substantial surpluses. Repeating the litanies of the presidents of old, Grover Cleveland (1885–1889) voiced the fear that growing surpluses would "tempt extravagance" and, what was worse, that public extravagance "begets extravagance among the people."

Yet between 1870 and 1902 there was no growth in per-capita expenditures in the federal government of the United States. Spending in absolute terms increased approximately 3.3 percent per year, but gross national product, adjusted for inflation, increased by more than 5 percent per year. Thus the federal sector of government was continuously growing smaller in regard to the size of the economy.[11]

Viewing debt as something a people owes itself (to be judged not as an inherent evil, but relative to a country's ability to pay) is not far from the idea that the size of the deficit matters less than the government's (and through it the people's) return on monies expended. Although the presidents from 1898 to 1920 (McKinley, Roosevelt, Taft, and Wilson) all said they were opposed to unbalanced budgets, the number of deficits began to increase at a rapid rate. For this new breed of presidents, efficient organization and "value for money," as the English say today, mattered more than parsimony.[12] The American people, Woodrow Wilson said, "are not jealous of the amount their Government costs if they are

sure that they get what they need and desire for the outlay, that
the money is being spent for objects of which they approve, and
that it is being applied with good business sense and management."[13] Whether the idea was to do what was being done at less
expense, or to do more, was left unclear.

Fiscal prudence, both against the growing debt and for a balanced budget, reasserted itself in the 1920s. World War I had
largely been fought on borrowed money. From 1914–1918, the
government's role in directing economic activity expanded enor-
mously. In response, there was sudden public concern that the
profligate habits of wartime would carry over into peacetime
civilian life. The Victory Liberty Loan Act of 1919 established a
sinking fund to reduce the debt, which was cut a third (from $24 to
$16 billion) by the end of the decade. Wilson's secretary of the
treasury, Carter Glass, pointed out the "grave danger that the extraordinary success of the Treasury in financing the stupendous
war expenditures may lead to a riot of public expenditures after
the war, the consequences of which could only be disastrous." His
successor under President Harding (1921–1923), David F.
Huston, similarly observed that "we have demobilized many
groups, but we have not demobilized those whose gaze is concentrated on the Treasury."[14]

Reform and Expansion

The Budget Act of 1921 was thought by its sponsors to be the
reform to end all reforms. The executive budget, introduced by the
president with the aid of his new Bureau of the Budget, through
which all agency requests had to go, would simultaneously introduce order, expertise, and economy. And for a time there was
more of all of these good things. But not for long. Just as there was
more volatility in the money supply after the creation of the
Federal Reserve Bank than before,[15] spending expanded much
more rapidly after than before 1921. Those of us (present company included) enamored of structural solutions may say that the
Budget Act of 1921 did not change basic political incentives, which
is true enough, but the other truth is that life overwhelmed the expectations of the reforms. There was greater coherence, which
was expected, but also far greater spending, which was not.

Using 1902 as a benchmark, federal spending constituted 2.4 percent of GNP, and this had more than doubled by 1922 to 5.1 percent. Nonfederal spending had also grown but not as quickly, from 4.4 to 7.5 percent of GNP. By 1932 the budget reform of 1921 had been in operation for a decade. During that time, nonfederal spending almost doubled to 14 percent of GNP; federal spending increased by around 40 percent to 7.3 percent. These comparisons may be taken to mean that the rate of increase in federal spending was about the same from 1913 to 1922 (2.4 to 5.1 percent) as from 1922 to 1932 (5.1 to 7.3 percent), and that the reform of 1921 was essentially extraneous to the forces promoting increased spending. Or the figures could be taken to mean that spending would have been still higher in the absence of reform or that, in ways unmeasured by these brute numbers, the quality of spending improved. Between 1902 and 1932, the larger trend was that spending at all levels of government more than tripled from 6.8 to 21.3 percent of GNP.[16] An alternative theory is that the constitutional amendment ratifying the income tax justified the old concern that whatever revenue was raised would be spent.[17] Whatever the explanation, the inauguration of the executive budget ushered out the era of small government in the United States.

When things go well, one tends to credit the doctrines and practices that one has followed; when things go badly, one may still hope to recover by doing more of the same. Though his administration urged a variety of methods to enhance business activity, Herbert Hoover insisted that "we cannot squander ourselves into prosperity." To President Hoover (1928–1932) a balanced budget was the "very keystone of recovery" without which the depression would continue indefinitely. He stressed lowering federal expenditures and, if that failed, raising taxes.[18]

The Democratic opposition firmly shared his opinion that achieving a balanced budget was essential to ending the depression.[19] The new president, Franklin D. Roosevelt (1933–1945), was so concerned about the near $1.6 billion deficit—"a deficit so great that it makes us catch our breath"—that he promised both in his campaign and in his inaugural address to make a balanced budget top priority.

Gradually the federal government's goal of achieving a balanced budget during a depression came under attack. Waddill

Catchings and William Trufant Foster wrote against the idea of a negative state that relied on the private sector to generate income and employment; instead, they advocated maintaining employment through long-range public works. Though new debt would be created, the additional economic activity and increased revenue would make repayment of the debt easier than an ongoing depression. "We must conquer the depression by collective action," Foster insisted in 1932. "This necessarily means the leadership of the federal government—the only agency which represents all of us. . . . We must abandon our policy of defeatism, our worship of the budget, our false economy program. . . . Instead, we must collectively put into use enough currency and credit to restore the commodity price level of 1928."[20]

As conditions worsened, economists and publicists began to talk about "spending" the nation out of the depression. The publishing magnate William Randolph Hearst promoted a "prosperity" bonds issue in the then-unheard-of amount of $5.5 billion. The philosopher John Dewey, president of the People's Lobby, asked for $3.5 billion for public works and relief. However, instead of debt financing that might be inflationary, he proposed that debts be written down and interest rates reduced.[21] Yet there were still those to counter with the traditional belief that continously unbalanced budgets lead to inflation, and that that could only weaken an already depressed economy.[22] Petitions of all kinds, signed by economists of all persuasions, both for and against increased government spending, proliferated.[23]

"Virtuous" Deficits

By the early 1930s, a number of Americans in the Democratic party had begun to seek a rationale for encouraging the government to expand public works and thus increase employment. They found this rationale in the work of John Maynard Keynes and introduced his thought to key figures, including President Roosevelt.[24] Building on ideas advanced in 1931 by his collaborator R. F. Kahn, Keynes argued that it was appropriate, in a deflationary period when vast economic resources went unused, for the government to create deficits as a means of expanding demand. When economic activity was slow, government should step in to speed it up; when the economy overheated, and inflation resulted, government could decrease spending. In short, raising and lowering the deficit became a prime means of economic control. The important point, however, was not the practice of Keynesian doctrine—any student of politics knows that it would be much easier to raise than to lower spending—but that it provided a strong intellectual rationale for doing what many people wanted. At long last politicians could combine spending with virtue.

The triumph of Keynesian doctrine marked both an end to the primacy of the balanced budget and a beginning of variable expenditure as an instrument of economic stabilization. The great budgetary equation had been fundamentally reoriented; the emphasis shifted from matching spending and revenue at the lowest possible level, to manipulation of the difference between them. The Employment Act of 1946 signalled a new equation focusing federal policy on the goal of full employment, with deficits and surpluses apparently left to vary in its wake. Spending and owing, instead of being the great enemies of the economy, had become its greatest friends.

By the mid-to-late 1960s, a new budgetary compromise had been made. Its essence was the unbalanced budget (or, if one prefers, balance at the spending level to achieve full employment, which mostly meant the same thing). Its principle was the change in belief among egalitarians (by then allied with the Democratic party) to the view that government spending was a good thing, especially if done in a redistributive direction. They could help their friends, whom they hoped to recruit, and hurt their enemies at one and the same time by taking from the rich and giving to the poor. So far, so obvious. The less obvious question is what was in it for the establishment? Belief in hierarchy, which is based on the sacrifice of the parts in favor of the whole goes along with a sacrificial ethic. So long as status distinctions are maintained (say, officers coming from the upper class), they should be willing to do their all (say, leading the troops, thus suffering higher casualties). So long, therefore, as labor unions, racial minorities, and poor regions, the relevant disadvantaged interests, accepted the existing social structure, hierarchs were willing to buy them off. The other side of the establishment, corporate and commercial interests, obtained their own *quid pro quo*: while everyone else

Table 2

Amount of and Increase in Per-Capita Personal Income and Individual Income Tax, 1970–1979

Year	Personal income Amount	Increase (percent)	Individual income tax Amount	Increase (percent)
1970	$3,911	—	$441	—
1971	4,149	6.1	416	−5.7
1972	4,513	8.8	453	8.9
1973	5,002	10.8	490	8.2
1974	5,449	8.9	561	14.5
1975	5,879	7.9	573	2.1
1976	6,420	9.2	611	6.6
1977	7,061	10.0	727	19.0
1978	7,856	11.2	828	13.9
1979	8,723	11.0	988	19.3

Source: Dennis S. Ippolito, *Congressional Spending: A Twentieth Century Fund Report* (Ithaca, N.Y., and London: Cornell University Press, 1981), p. 210. Data from *Economic Report of the President, 1980.*

was getting theirs, thus necessitating higher tax rates, they received direct subsidies, such as those for tobacco and ship building, and indirect subsidies, such as loan guarantees and tax preferences. "Socialism for the rich" went hand-in-hand with redistribution to the poor. In case anyone was left out, the "middle masses" received medical and housing subsidies. And, most important, the elderly of whatever class, because they were numerous and organized, achieved a rapid growth in pension and medical payments. The point is that once the mutual restraint of the budget balance had been replaced by the free-for-all of the welfare state, the necessary social accommodations lacked the necessary income (spending increased as a proportion of national product while taxes went up faster than personal income, as figure 1 and table 2 show), which explains why it lasted only a decade.

All this spending depended upon doing what was done without (a) decreasing the standard of living for most Americans, and/or (b) significantly disadvantaging the major participants in the political process. Within ten to fifteen years, however one counts, roughly from 1965 to 1980, both conditions were violated. The social order favoring equality found welfare insufficient and began a direct attack on corporate capitalism. To the social in-

Figure 1

**Federal Budget Outlays as Percentage of
Gross National Product
Fiscal Years 1955–1981**

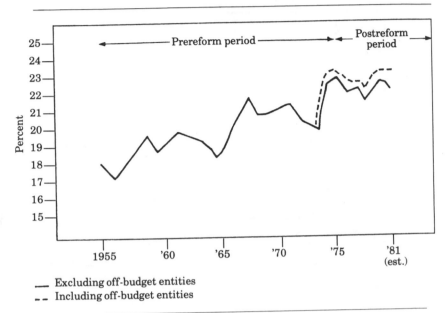

— Excluding off-budget entities
-- Including off-budget entities

Source: Dennis S. Ippolito, *Congressional Spending: A Twentieth Century Fund Report* (Ithaca, N.Y., and London: Cornell University Press, 1981), p. 205. Data from *Budget of the United States Government, Fiscal Year 1978* and *Budget of the United States Government, Fiscal Year 1981.*

surance state and the subsidy state (the old welfare state) was added the regulatory state. Eventually, corporations concluded that subsidy was not worth the cost of regulation. The amalgam of social orders that constituted American culture was coming apart. And this unloosening of the ties that bind was nowhere more evident than in budgeting.

As long as the rate of economic growth exceeded the rate of spending, government could be supported without increasing taxes. The actual decline in growth and the increase in spending, whatever the reasons, meant that this easy exit was closed. The next step (see figure 2) was to decrease defense as a proportion of total spending, from some 49 percent in 1960 to about 23 percent in 1978.[25] This reversal of priorities would work providing that the

Figure 2

Federal Budget Outlays, Fiscal Years 1950–1982

(in constant 1982 dollars)

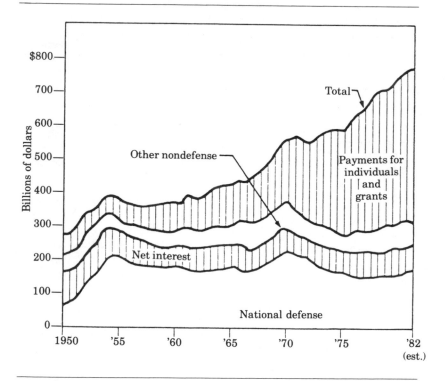

Source: Dennis S. Ippolito, *Congressional Spending: A Twentieth Century Fund Report* (Ithaca, N.Y., and London: Cornell University Press, 1981), p. 27. Data from *United States Budget in Brief, Fiscal Year 1982*.

adherents of hierarchy did not become overly worried about the puncturing of their precious social system by foreign forces. This changed, for any number of reasons from the Soviet arms buildup to the invasion of Afghanistan to pure paranoia, but it changed. At the same time, whether the responsibility lies with oil price increases, declining labor productivity, lack of sufficient savings, overpopulation, deficit spending, or all or none of the above, inflation rose and take-home pay declined.

Quarrel within the Establishment

The budgetary crunch occurred because everyone wanted out. The hierarchical social order wanted to slow down domestic spending, speed up defense expenditure, and, if necessary, raise taxes, though this would be done *sub rosa*—in the manner of hierarchies—by "bracket creep" as people were pushed into higher brackets, by social security increases, and by the excise taxes on oil. Egalitarians wished to expand domestic spending, keep defense down, and either raise taxes or run deficits as preferable to unemployment or income disparity. Competitive individualists wanted to give market mechanisms freer play by cutting both taxes and spending. When one arrays these preferences—raising versus reducing taxes and spending—their incompatibility becomes evident. So does the difficulty the major political parties have in coming to an internal accommodation. The Republican party of today is something like two-thirds market to one-third hierarchy (some would say 55–45). Its internal conflict is between the hierarchs whose overriding consideration is social stability and the market forces that want to expand the private and contract the public sectors. The quarrel of these semirival and semicooperative social orders, the quarrel within the establishment about budget balance, is not at all surprising, for one side cares about size and the other about the composition or balance among expenditures.[26] Because he takes a hierarchical, collectivist view of defense and a free-market, individualist view of domestic policy, President Ronald Reagan encapsulates these conflicts within his own administration.

The Democratic party is divided in a different direction between its hierarchical and egalitarian wings. Once the restraint of budget balance was removed, they came together in support of the welfare state. With the hierarchical elements returning to support of higher defense and lower domestic spending in an effort to reestablish a social and financial equilibrium, the Democratic coalition is in danger of splitting.

The thesis of this analysis is that narrowly focused conflict over budgeting is best understood as part and parcel of a broad-gauged concern over the role of government in society. The rule that budget balance was desirable in peacetime (and that wartime debt was to be paid off in the next generation) enabled market, hierarchical, and egalitarian social orders to live with one another within the same political framework. The alternative rule, the unbalanced budget of the welfare state, created cohesion while it lasted but by 1980 had run its course. The question Americans must answer is whether any new rule will help create (or express) a social compact that the adherents of the various American social orders will find desirable or at least satisfactory. From this social perspective, the odd vocabulary (budget reconciliation means budget conflict, and loan guarantees for some mean lack of loans for others) and the arcane technical terms, which leave people wondering why there is so much fuss over the relative importance of the first versus the second congressional budget resolutions, should make much more sense.

One sign of the times is the proliferation of constitutional amendments designed, in the view of their sponsors, to remedy what James Madison referred to as the "discovered faults" in our basic political arrangements. Regardless of the remedy proposed, the terms of discourse—*defects* in the existing political process, *biases* in political arrangements, structural *impediments* to spending limits—suggest a renegotiation of long-standing arrangements. Let us begin looking at the implications of current choices by inquiring into possible pro- or antispending tendencies in the existing federal budgetary process. Then we can examine constitutional versus statutory approaches to improving budgeting either by making it more neutral or by giving it a different bias.

A Biased Budgetary Process?

Is the congressional budgetary process as it now exists neutral in regard to claims for higher or lower spending? The Budget Act of 1974 expressed Congress's desire to enhance its own power of the purse by giving it the ability to visibly relate revenue and expenditure. Since the broad coalition supporting the act was made up both of high and low spenders, however, the new process was not designed to favor either side.[27] On the one hand, the mere existence of budget committees raised another possible impediment to higher spending; on the other hand, the need for these committees to maintain collegial relations with the tax and spending committees, as well as to remain subject to the will of Congress, meant that they had to subordinate themselves to the rampant desires for higher spending. The evidence from Allen Schick's *Congress and Money* is conclusive:

> In almost a hundred interviews with Members of Congress and staffers, no one expressed the view that the allocations in budget resolution had been knowingly set below legislative expectations. "We got all that we needed," one committee staff director exulted. The chief clerk of an Appropriations subcommittee complained, however, that the target figure in the resolution was too high: "We were faced with pressure to spend up to the full budget allocation. It's almost as if the Budget Committee bent over backwards to give Appropriations all that it wanted and then some."[28]

In considering the related question of mandatory spending, required by law and not subject to the annual appropriations process, Schick makes a powerful plea to consider this a conscious choice:

> "Uncontrollability" is not an accident or an inadvertence of the legislative process but a willful decision by Congress to favor nonbudgetary values over budgetary control.[29]

Since budgeting, like history, is a matter of selectivity, Congress makes its most important choices by choosing what not to consider. Uncontrollability is a form of control. If much domestic spending is mandated and indexed and most defense spending is not, is that a bias in budgeting or just democracy at work?

Just as consumers find it more difficult to organize than producers, so spending interests are advantaged because their concern is concentrated while taxpayers' are diffused. A billion-dollar program has a greater effect on recipients than on taxpayers who contribute only a few hundred cents apiece. Are those advantages and disadvantages built into political life, a natural process like photosynthesis, or are they helped along by voting on items rather than on totals? Is budgeting by addition of items rather than subtraction under ceilings the only natural way?

Reducing the total size of the budget requires not only eternal *vigilance* but *information* on where to cut and *coordination* among programs so that increases in some do not balance out decreases in others. Increasing spending is easy, requires little information (any area will do), and even less coordination. Without a spending limit, no spending agency has an incentive to cut its budget because the contribution to the total is small and uncertain.[30] Is that natural, as Mother Nature intended, or unnatural, a bias that explains why government grows?

The difference between an out-and-out balanced budget and an expenditure limitation constitutional amendment is this: balance can take place at any level of spending, provided it is matched by revenues, whereas limits are designed to secure a specific (always lower) size of government. The balance people may wish to raise taxes; the limits people always want to lower spending. Thus the two pro-amendment sides would differ in the way in which they would answer a critical question: would they prefer a $600 billion budget with a $100 billion deficit, or a $900 billion budget with no deficit? Is it the size of government or the balance between taxing and spending that matters?

Size vs. Balance

The crucial character of the difference between size and balance also emerges from Congress's consideration of reforming the budget process it reformed in 1974. Political life is speeding up. The seemingly obscure debates over the relative importance of the first and second budget resolutions are in fact over whether, by statute or rule, Congress will impose on itself spending ceilings.

Nowadays budgeteers speak in strange tongues—e.g., "first solution" and "second resolution" (the first setting a ceiling for total outlays, the second fixing allocations for specific categories). What would happen if the last became the first? That depends. The Budget Reform Act of 1974 did not decree lower spending, nor did it alter political incentives one whit. What the act did do was change calculations so that Congress could work its will, whatever that was, more effectively. The purpose of the second resolution, as was clear from discussion at the time, was to legitimize budgeting by addition by formalizing the usual congressional tendency to lump together its item-by-item decisions and call this a budget, much as presidents do when the document has to be sent to the printer. Making the first resolution binding might signify a desire to introduce budgeting by subtraction (or "resource allocation," as the old-fashioned phrase had it), through which agencies and programs compete under a fixed total. It might but it might not.

Figure 3

**Entitlement and Other Uncontrollable Spending
as Percentage of Federal Budget, Fiscal Years 1967–1980**

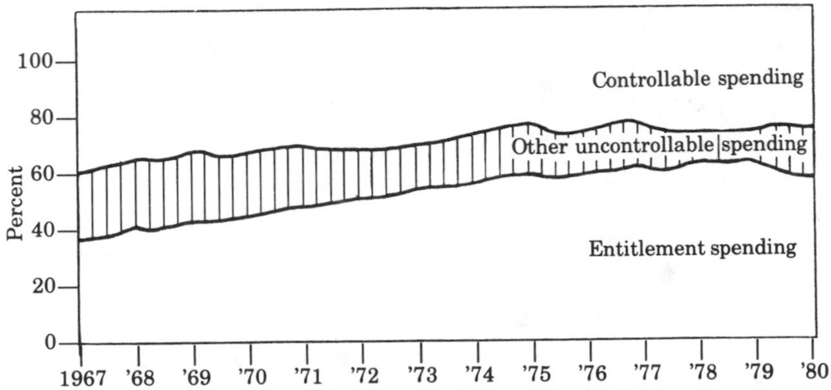

aSpending required by contracts made in past years, borrowing authority, guaranteed loans, and other obligations.

Source: Dennis S. Ippolito, *Congressional Spending: A Twentieth Century Fund Report* (Ithaca, N.Y., and London: Cornell University Press, 1981), p. 214. Data from *Congressional Quarterly Weekly Report,* January 19, 1980.

Those who wish to make the first resolution binding argue that the Budget Reform Act of 1974, setting up House and Senate Budget Committees and establishing the Congressional Budget Office, does not work well enough. There remains a lack of control over entitlements (see figure 3); the size of the budget has increased more afterwards than before; and delays in passing the budget have, if anything, proved worse.[31] The hope is that by setting a ceiling and requiring competition among programs, Congress would become financially responsible. But would it?

An easy way out would be for Congress to set the ceiling so high that no increase in one place implied a decrease in another. The result of trying to make the first resolution all-important would be to make it trivial.

If the ceiling set by the first resolution is to be meaningful, it must be at or below the level where the budget is today. If the resolution is to be helpful, it must be consistent over a period of years, for otherwise the size of programs would vary in fits and starts, leaving everyone worse off. Willy-nilly, therefore, supporters of an effective first resolution must be interested in a semipermanent rule for setting ceilings. Tying spending to national product, the rule that the size of government should not increase faster than the growth of the economy may not be the best rule, but it is hard to see how there could be a significant departure from it that would still leave a significant ceiling.

A major difficulty with a spending limit, whether constitutional or statutory (or by cabinet agreement, as in Canada), is that it does not include a commitment to a balanced budget, which, as it turns out, has most of the popular political support. In order to overcome this drawback, a substantial number of senators reached agreement on Senate Joint Resolution 58. Though it is called a balanced budget amendment, its title actually inverts its priorities. S.J. Res. 58 requires, insists upon, enforces expenditure limitation related to economic growth. Indexing for tax brackets is also mandated. But budget balance, though expected, is only suggested. According to the calculations of those who support a spending limit, it would lead to balanced budgets most of the time without demanding balance when the economy was in recession or increasing the size of government by raising taxes. Nevertheless, the advocates of market methods—and hence smaller government—prefer spending limits, and the adherents of hierarchy—and hence social stability—prefer budget balance.

Two main budgetary alternatives face us. (1) Budgetary balance on a higher level. America will imitate European social democracies. (2) Spending limits with budget balance at a lower level. The conclusion and the questions, both about budgets and social relations, are the same: the conclusion is that there will be balance; the questions are at what level? How will we get there? Who will pay? And what will that tell us about the American way of life?

16

ROBERT M. ENTMAN

The Imperial Media

President Reagan was elected after a lengthy campaign which dominated the domestic news and stimulated widespread expectations that his presence in the White House would really mark a fresh start for the nation. The media will be quick to focus on how well his performance matches his promises. In recent years—particularly since the Vietnam war—presidents and the media have seemed to be adversaries. For presidents, the question has not been *whether* the media would obstruct their leadership, but *when* and *how*. And journalists have suspected presidents of manipulating them and even of lying in order to further political objectives. At best, relations have been cool; at worst, hostile.

The media clearly have a responsibility to report what they find and to criticize effectively the institutions of government. It is right for reporters to be alive to the hazards of manipulation. On the other hand, from the president's point of view, they should not be allowed to reduce his capacity for firm leadership.

This essay originally appeared in *Politics and the Oval Office: Towards Presidential Governance*, edited by Arnold J. Meltsner (1981).

This chapter will outline some of the ways in which the media can and do obstruct the president.* They include confusing the president's responsiveness to their demands with sensitivity to the public interest; inhibiting private negotiation between the president and other national leaders, particularly those in Congress; complicating executive management by magnifying conflict within the cabinet; and imposing conflicting standards of behavior which mean that, whatever he does, he cannot escape unfavorable judgment.

But the president is far from helpless. If he understands the limitations of his office, he can circumvent some of these problems and turn others into opportunities. He can use his "honeymoon"— the first few months in office—to reduce the unrealistic expectations which soon lead to frustration. He can negotiate with Congress in private. He can staff and manage his press office with discretion and care. And he and his staff can use the media selectively and with precision.

Presidents Can Manipulate But Not Dictate the News

The president's resources for managing media relations are well known.[1] They include monopolizing and selectively releasing information; controlling the forum and timing of contact with the press; secrecy;[2] co-optation of reporters and editors through personal friendship; televised news conferences orchestrated to convey favorable impressions;[3] and applying licit and illicit pressure through government agencies such as the Federal Communications Commission. In general, these resources give the president an unmatched capacity to get the news he wants into the press. But keeping news out is another matter. Politicians and others with power—as well as journalists themselves—contribute significantly to the composite depiction of a chief executive.

Media practices thrust the president into the news. Presidential management of the media is often compatible with journalists' needs. In choosing and defining political news stories, journalists look for a powerful cast of characters, for conflict or

*James David Barber and Francie Seymour offered helpful comments on an earlier draft of this paper. I am grateful to them.

controversy between its members, and for potential personal impact on audiences. The precluding definition of news allows a president to make news virtually whenever he wants to do so. Over the past two decades attention to the president has increased; 25 percent of all domestic national news now concerns presidents or presidential candidates.[4]

Among the processes that journalists use to construct political news stories are: *personalization*, the neglect of historical or structural explanations by concentrating on individuals whose deliberate choices cause events; *source standardization*, the use of the same group of informants on the beat; *dramatization*, the depiction of interactions of news personalities so as to generate audience interest, pity, fear, catharsis, where possible; and *surrogate representation*, the enforcement of government responsiveness to the public by pressing politicians to explain candidly their actions, motivations, and plans. Because these practices are almost universal, different media (and even the same ones) tend to repeat similar stories, themes, questions, and answers. These practices often help presidents. Personalization, for example, permits them to claim credit for just about anything the government does well; the duplication of content enables them to reach the entire electorate with the same basic message.[5]

The tone of the news—set by journalist incentives and elite opinions. Hindered by the president's control over much newsworthy information and constrained by conventional definitions of news, reporters and their editors nonetheless have considerable autonomy, especially in seeking out news that can be narrated as drama unfolding. In stories like these, their interests and his often diverge. Drama lies in stories of presidential involvement in domestic conflict and in history-making ventures, usually overseas. Drama is magnified when the outcomes are either highly uncertain or likely to mark a major change from previous patterns, or both. Reporters and editors face personal incentives— having little to do with ideological bias—to emphasize any drama they can find. Good for journalists' prestige but often bad for that of the president, dramatic stories which center on domestic conflict tend to convey the impression that the chief executive is incompetent, rigid, or cynical.

Aside from the president and his administration, the normal sources of national political news are Washington elites. When these congressmen, bureaucrats, and other powerful individuals generally agree with the president, journalists have few sources for concocting dramatic narratives. Such reports emerge mainly when some elites decide to publicize their criticisms of the president.

Clashes among Washington newsmakers over presidential policy and purpose stimulate news. The more conflict, the more the media will fill with criticisms of the president. These undermine the president's preferred image as a competent consensus-builder. They publicize alternative views of policy problems and suggest solutions the president opposes. The conflict feeds on itself: the more discord, the more dramatic the story possibilities. Coverage which is damaging to the president further emboldens his opponents, as shown by the presidencies of Lyndon Johnson, Richard Nixon, and Jimmy Carter.[6]

The contest between press and president is normally played out somewhere between the basking of the early John Kennedy and the thrashing of Richard Nixon. Within these bounds a president's skill at media relations can make news a little brighter. Maladroit media management does the reverse. But more important for the tone of the coverage may be the level of elite support the president enjoys and the treatment that news organizations and employees, acting out of their own habits and interests, affords presidential activities.

Four Media Impacts on Presidential Leadership

Journalists have taken a more aggressively critical stance toward the presidency since the perceived betrayals of Vietnam and Watergate. One facet of the practice of surrogate representation, the critical perspective assumes purely political motives behind presidential ideas and actions and then tries to confirm that theory by doggedly pursuing presidents and their aides until they admit its accuracy. Confined largely to the major national media, the technique seeks to enforce a moral and responsive *process* of presidential leadership. It casts a president less as a leader with special legitimacy than as a politician—one with a special calling and high responsibility, but a politician nonetheless.

The country has benefited from this approach, to a point. But the advantage of process-oriented reporting recedes if it prevents presidents from reaching their policy objectives; democracy requires effective policy as well as pristine process. This section explores four potentially damaging consequences of the media's skeptical mood.

Confusing press interests with the public interest. The press tends to judge a president's responsiveness to the public on the basis of his cooperativeness with reporters. They demand that he reveal and fully explain all his major decisions. This expectation is as unrealistic as it is self-serving. Unrealistic, because all presidents will—and to some degree should—make decisions they neither disclose in detail nor justify to the press. Self-serving, because the emphasis on full disclosure seems to be rooted more in the media's production practices than in a well-grounded theory of journalism's proper political role.

Open White House news sources make for cheaper production— fewer reporters and less hard work are required to ferret out information. James Deakin of the *St. Louis Post-Dispatch* defines the mission of White House news hunters: "We are ... making a consistent attempt underneath all the bombast and fury of the press conference and the briefing, to find out why the president did what he did in the past."[7]

The other major goal of the White House news corps is to find out what the president plans to do in the future. Yet a politician cannot explain past actions or future plans without trying to fit news reports to his political needs, to the expectations of his elite audiences. So the president and his staff are among the less-helpful sources on the president's plans. Better answers could be found by digging about Washington, probing the innards of the bureaucracy, plowing through congressional hearings and reports. To ask a president or press secretary why the president did something offers the appearance of critical reporting without its reality.

Consider televised press conferences. In most of them we learn mainly how the president parries, rephrases, and ignores tough queries. A president who has significant information to release will rarely do so involuntarily in response to a reporter's question; he will choose his own time and place. The event becomes a ritual

of predictable thrust and parry. Reporters give a show of un-
daunted inquisitiveness; presidents, of ersatz candor.

Why a president does something should be less newsworthy
than *what* he does. The "why" we largely know in advance: partly
to help the country, partly to advance his policy goals, partly to
protect his political future; post-Watergate reporters highlight
only the latter. Citizens and voters need also (perhaps mainly) to
know the "what"—what effects presidential policies will have on
inflation and economic growth, on their children's education and
health, and on national security.[8] But again, providing such information would require a more diligent, tedious brand of reporting
along with a diminution of the drive to unmask the selfish political
goals behind every presidential action.

Present practices often compel the president and his staff to
reveal information they do not want to divulge. While on occasion
this is beneficial to the public, press officers sometimes answer
prematurely, incorrectly, or unwisely. They are upbraided if they
backpedal, abandon, or repudiate the earlier position and excori-
ated if they refuse to respond at all. Yet this "news" may be
hollow. Ron Nessen has described an egregious example. As the
Vietnam war drew to its sorry finale in 1975, White House reporters continually hectored him with questions about when the
United States would evacuate Saigon.[9] But the Ford administration could hardly have revealed the answer—even if it knew—
without jeopardizing the safety of those still in Saigon. More important, even if the answer had been forced out of the White
House, knowing it would not have strengthened the citizen's voice
in government in any meaningful way.

**Dissolving the distinction between public office and pri-
vate leadership.** Leadership has both public and private dimensions. One of a president's major tasks is to inspire the public. But
publicity alone does not propel policies through the bureaucracy
and Congress and into action. Leadership also entails private communication—in person, over the telephone, by letter—with
power brokers and decision-makers. Presidents and their staff
deploy technical arguments, emotional appeals, veiled threats.
deft flattery, adroit bluffs, tantalizing hints—the whole repertoire
of persuasive tools—*in private*. Publicity vitiates these tools.

Media coverage of the tactics, their rationales, and different actors' reactions add an extra dimension of strategic complexity into a president's already Byzantine political calculus.

A president once could manipulate tacit knowledge or nagging suspicions to his advantage. A member of Congress might say to himself, "I know he's flattering me but I like it" or "He sounds as if he might really carry out his (wholly implicit) threat," and then conclude "I'd better go along." Now, quite frequently, the president's underlying strategy is publicized. The press tells those on the receiving end what the president is trying to do to them, how, and why.

Consider Jimmy Carter's early run-ins with House Speaker "Tip" O'Neill. Carter failed to appoint one of O'Neill's cronies to a top administrative post. The personal offense given and taken was detailed in the press, as was Carter's calculated attempt to regain O'Neill's affection. Similar developments occurred in Carter's relationship with AFL–CIO president George Meany. Granted the Georgian's apparent ineptitude in such matters, it is doubtful that wide media coverage of his strained relationships and awkward attempts at reconciliation efforts made things easier.

This phenomenon corrodes presidential leadership in a number of ways. First, it increases the tactical intelligence of those he is trying to persuade. Without publicity, a president's manipulative maneuvers might not be recognized as such by his less-insightful adversaries and allies; when his tricks are exposed and dissected in the news, even the most obtuse lobbyist or senator can fend better. Second, once a president's technique for handling a particular task of persuasion is publicized, other actors are forewarned and hence forearmed. Third, the publicity changes the decision calculations of those the president attempts to lead. Public knowledge that a president is trying to soothe or strong-arm an individual may compel the latter to spurn the president's offer; it ill-behooves most politicians to appear to respond to presidential pressure or flattery. Fourth, such publicity may embarrass a president, generating pressure to avoid perfectly legitimate tactics of political life and reducing his list of options. It may also make his own responses to the political acts of others more problematic; he of all politicians must avoid appearing too willing to compromise with interests which are merely powerful or cunning. Finally, these persuasive tactics are quintessentially those of party maintenance: to the list of formidable centrifugal forces operating on party organizations and politics must be added the journalistic foible of publicizing a president's private leadership activities.

Complicating executive management. Beyond the direct focus of the chief executive himself, the White House staff, cabinet officers, and departments sometimes tumble into the media net. They are all politicized, loyal to the president, and thus part of his story. The media's attraction to presidential subordinates can pose management problems because of three strong media impacts — on the agendas of executive officials and agencies, on the relationships between those individuals and offices and the president, and on the president's control over information.

First, public attention is drawn only sporadically to most federal offices. When the Federal Aviation Administration, the Environmental Protection Agency, or the White House Counsel's office make major news, it is generally because reporters scent controversy over, say, a plane crash, a hazardous waste spill, or an ethically questionable legal maneuver on behalf of the president. These offices are hypersensitive to such publicity because they make the papers relatively infrequently. One bad story comprises a substantial portion of an entire year's coverage. Those involved tend to believe that the stories harm the agency's public image and reduce its clout with the president and Congress, so they scurry frantically to redress publicized misfeasance, clearing their normal and long-range agendas to focus on the object of attention. Not surprisingly, the bureaux anticipate and fear negative media reactions. They may become overly cautious and rigid in applying their rules to stave off future onslaughts.

Second, publicizing personality feuds and policy debates within the administration complicates the president's task of coordinating his top officials. Stories about whose influence is ascending, whose plummeting, who is at whose throat or in whose pocket, can only exacerbate jealousies and tensions. Recall Rogers and Kissinger, Vance and Brzezinski. Highly publicized internecine quarrels make the president look like a poor manager, even if they are not his fault. Such reportage discourages frank and open dialogue between a president's advisors as it poisons the relationships among them.

Third, news can turn reputation into reality: a press imputation of clout can actually bestow influence.[10] So, innocently enough, cabinet officers and White House staffers cultivate reporters. But then they may leak information that undermines a president's proposals or credibility. The media's craving for conflict within the administration provides a tempting opportunity. The threat of disobedience gives the president an incentive to limit access to the most important information to a very small group of trusted personal aides. This practice in turn overloads him with decisions and with public expectations.

Reinforcing double binds. Americans expect a great deal of their president. Above all, they want leadership; survey respondents indicating the country needs strong leadership increased from 49 percent in 1976 to 63 percent in 1979.[11] But citizens are ambivalent; they have traditionally disapproved of many of the traits exhibited by strong leaders. Post-Watergate journalists have made this element of tradition into a creed. By subjecting presidents to a daily buffeting of charges and countercharges of failure to fulfil the contradictory high standards of presidential office, news reports reinforce a number of double binds that tie the hands of leadership. For news of presidential defaults is unavoidable and unremitting; by satisfying one standard, a president frequently violates another.

The man on the white horse versus the man in the White House. A president usually begins his term after a long election campaign during which media practices have encouraged him to indulge in oversimplified attacks on opponents, to promise to solve policy problems while simultaneously remaining fuzzy and uncontroversial, and to avoid too many expressions of doubt, hesitation, and realism about the intractability of problems. Dominating the domestic news of election years, the very magnitude of campaign coverage implies that the selection of a new president can really make a difference. After the election, the press brims over with paeans to the overworked transition staff as it culls applications for posts in the new administration and selects only the brightest and the best. The composite picture is of a fresh beginning glistening with promise.

Then reality moves into the White House. Contradictory promises that slipped by in the hurly-burly of the campaign lose their
luster. News reports call attention to the incompatibilities among
proposals. Attacks on predecessors and opponents return to haunt
the new incumbent as he realizes the complexity of the problems
he faces or acknowledges them for the first time. Fuzziness is no
longer an option, for a president's legislative proposals have to be
specific: they force him to take a stand. Contumely and controversy inevitably follow and with them, negative reporting.
Supporters who relied upon the fulfillment of campaign slogans
and symbols, or who read into them a message of future commitment, become disillusioned. Opponents see their charges
confirmed.

If a president does propose a bold initiative to fulfil a campaign
pledge, he often faces energetic opposition. The media are drawn
to policy shoot-outs. Their eagerness to focus on his critics may implicitly impel him to avoid proposing innovative policies. The
cautious president takes refuge in incrementalism—only to be
assaulted all too often by accusations of failure to provide the
courageous, visionary leadership the country's predicaments
demand.

The media do not cause the cycle of boom and bust in public expectations; but their campaign coverage encourages the boom,
their Washington coverage, the letdown. The new president needs
to recognize the change in the logic of media relations that occurs
when the campaign becomes incumbency. President Carter never
did.

Machiavelli versus St. Francis. Journalists require the president
to observe the norms of two distinct levels of discourse. On the
first, which might be called personal discourse, journalists demand the same kind of decency and candor that people depend on
for rational communication in everyday life. On the second level,
that of political discourse, journalists recognize the significance of
language for controlling the behavior of others, that is, for leadership. Yet reporters cry "Foul!" when a president responds to them
as they expect him to respond to all other political actors—with
strategic artifice and a calculated choice of data and words.

Consider another example from James Deakin. He has expressed deep resentment at the Nixon administration's misleading statements during the India-Pakistan War of 1971, calling them "an affront to the intelligence of reasonable people".[12] Judged by norms of personal discourse, the administration's words *were* deceitful and offensive. But on the political level it would have been an affront to intelligence for the administration to subvert its own delicate policy initiative by announcing its strategy openly. And journalists would have pounced on any such careless and unstrategic revelation, as they later did when a different administration's United Nations ambassador (Andrew Young) spoke too freely. This problem confronts presidents in domestic policymaking as well.

A profile in courage versus a head in the sand. One set of journalistic standards calls for the president to do what is best for the country, not what is popular. In this view, he should not pander to public opinion; he should point the populace in the right direction; where it is unmovable, he should plow ahead and damn the political consequences. Yet a president who takes this tack often gets into trouble. Attacks on his stewardship proliferate as his reported isolation from public opinion grows. It is alleged that a president who neglects the evidence of surveys and other public expressions misuses his great office, misreads its traditions and purposes.

John F. Kennedy's book, *Profiles in Courage*, revealed the continuing American ambivalence on this issue. But none of Kennedy's profiles were subject to the continual and contrary public jostling of these two incompatible standards which suffuses recent media reporting.

Again it should be emphasized that the press alone does not create these three warring expectations. It does, however, repeatedly thrust them into public consciousness—and thus into the calculations of the elites—by its intimate and insistent coverage of the presidency. In that way press reports frequently diminish a president's potential to transcend the double binds that tradition imposes.

Leading Congress by Seeking Public Support: Onward or Downward?

Under the circumstances just depicted, presidential leadership has become increasingly problematic. More than ever, a president's ability to lead comes down to his capacity to persuade.[13] Supportive public opinion may be a significant component of a president's stock of persuasive resources. Yet the double binds reinforced by the media have magnified the difficulty of meeting the public's expectations and retaining its approval.

There is a growing body of research on presidential popularity based on the Gallup Poll question, "Do you approve or disapprove of the way [the incumbent] is handling his job as president?" But there is little understanding of its impact on presidential power or its roots in media coverage. What follows, then, is one observer's speculative version of the relationship between the press, public support, and presidential success in Congress.

Why the Congress decides. A president is only one of the forces acting on a Congress member. The most recent comprehensive studies have found that the president has little direct and distinct impact on most roll call votes.[14] This should not be surprising: Congress members cultivate independent local power bases which minimize their dependency on the president.[15] As Congress has enhanced its ability to initiate and analyze proposals in recent years, even the president's power to dominate the congressional agenda has suffered.

The key to presidential success is probably in convincing legislative leaders, committee heads, and interest groups to support the president's policies. These three, along with members' constituents and their own personal beliefs, determine most decisions. If a president's position coincides with the dominant slant of these forces, legislators will go along. If not, under conditions of weak party organization, presidents have relatively little to offer individual members to induce them to buck the tide.

Enter public support. A president who has high public approval can argue that voting with him against the wishes of interest group moguls or legislative leaders will win accolades for the solons back home. Such claims may sway some members.[16] Public support might also enhance a president's ability to obtain the cooperation of committee, party, and interest group chieftains.

If there are any advantages to individual members in voting with a president against the push of other Washington power brokers, however, they must disintegrate when the president is perceived as unpopular. Then, going along with the president exposes members and leaders to guilt by association, as some Democrats discovered in the 1980 election.

Media impact: more harm than good? Congressmen, along with the rest of the citizenry, receive a major part of their information about presidential popularity through the media. It comes not only from direct reporting of the Gallup Poll results but from the tone and content of editorials, columns, and news stories. Although research evidence is scant, it appears that lower Gallup ratings may stimulate less-positive portrayals of the president. When presidents seem to be in declining favor, the practice of surrogate representation may lead reporters to probe more sharply. Low approval rating and negative media coverage feed each other, heightening the perception that the president is floundering, deepening the drumbeat of decline—dissolving one of his few persuasive resources, the notion that public opinion is on his side.

Some scholars have unearthed a relationship between media content and approval rating. They find that when news of presidents' actions is good or better than what came before, presidential popularity tends to increase.[17] But other research indicates that economic conditions, national calamities, and partisan feelings have the major impacts on the approval rating. Growth in real income and employment is especially helpful; decline, harmful.[18] Prosperity may contribute more to a president's support than can media notices, however glowing. If so, and if the above analysis of Congress is accurate, it may be that negative coverage can sap the president's leadership strength more decisively than positive news can fortify it.

The argument would go as follows. The economic situation, and the presence or absence of such disastrous domestic or foreign entanglements as Vietnam or Watergate, establish a baseline of approval. If events go well and the economy perks along, elite support will tend to be high and press coverage will tend to be favorable without a great deal of presidential machination. Approval ratings will rise—or not deteriorate unduly. If the economy remains volatile, if the international situation continues to be tense, the news will obtrude in two ways. The press will cover the economic dilemmas or the unresolved world tensions; because of popular expectations of the presidency, this news implicitly indicts the incumbent. And the press will report the elite controversy that generally envelops such problems. Lower approval ratings follow and help to produce more unfavorable coverage. A downward spiral ensues, compounding the president's difficulty in garnering elite support for the solutions the public expects.

What Is to Be Done? Reduce and Shift Media Focus

Although this paper focuses on the negative impacts on leadership, all is not lost. Particularly if he enjoys an ideologically sympathetic majority in Congress, the president still possesses the potential to fashion favorable media images, to garner public and elite support, and to get things done. And the positive contributions of good media relations should not be gainsaid. But neither should this potential obscure the obvious and veiled costs of the media's unyielding concentration on the White House. On balance, a chief executive would probably profit from engineering a reduction in the media's inordinate obsession with him. Then he should work to reshape the character of the coverage remaining.

1. Reduce reliance on media events.

Do not make a fetish of getting on television. One of the noteworthy changes in reporting since Vietnam and Watergate is that journalists now depict politicians' overt attempts to create media events just so. With a president involved, the media do cover the events—the Rose Garden ceremony, Carter's putatively nonpolitical hegira through the hinterlands, the minor announcement cloaked as major pronouncement. But if, as they transmit the events, reporters convey the political strategy behind them, they vitiate both.

Presidents have helped erect barriers to their own leadership by overemphasizing media events, which frequently only reinforce the cynicism of journalists and citizens alike.

Use the honeymoon to dampen, not raise, expectations. All new presidents enjoy a glowing press. Washington waits, journalistic deference prevails, as the pomp of inauguration and drama of peaceful transfer of power unfold.[19] Coming directly after the legitimizing hoopla of an election, this coverage tends to raise approval levels—and expectations—to their highest points, whence they can only tumble. Although media-induced exhilaration encourages otherwise, the honeymoon is precisely the best time for new administrations to inject caution and realism into public (and journalistic) consciousness. If offered only after the inevitable failures come, such caveats appear as apologia rather than as prudence.

2. Reduce publicized conflicts with Congress.

Handle the media's tendency to amplify conflict with Congress by negotiating in private. A president should not automatically assume that taking to the airwaves to publicize his position against that of a recalcitrant Congress will help. There is no assurance that the public will be swayed by his speech[20] or that an independent Congress would necessarily respond even if the public were moved. Moreover, televised appearances can inject precisely the element of open discord that draws attention to a president's congressional adversaries, elevating them to page one (and Walter Cronkite) rather than page thirty-six (*sans* TV). When Congress attacks publicly, presidents should not automatically respond in kind. It is astonishing how quickly the media lose interest when there is only one voice clamoring instead of two— especially when that one is *not* the president's. Consider the nearly instant disappearance from page one of the Iranian hostages (post–rescue mission) and Billygate (post–press conference) when President Carter stopped his constant public commenting. The lack of publicity might allow other, more effective, means of persuasion to operate.

Encourage party revival. For too long presidents have neglected their party organizations to build up personal followings through the media. This may make sense in primary and even fall election campaigns, but once in office the party organization, especially in

Congress, should be his most valuable friend. Indirectly pressur-
ing congressional party leaders through the media's putatively
favorable impact on public opinion is less likely to work than is pa-
tient cultivation of organizational bonds.

3. Attempt to change news practices.

Reduce reporters' expectations. Tame White House—beat reporting by decreasing reporters' expectations of full access to officials,
by directly asserting that the demands of leadership require a
modicum of confidentiality. Take advantage of the country's growing preference for strong leadership to legitimize this approach.
And repeat frequently that bargaining and mutual adjustment
are the essence of democratic politics, not its antithesis.

*Shift reporters' attention from politics and plans to facts and
figures.* While discouraging discussions of the president's political
motivations and strategies, staffers should be open and accom-
modating with the technical policy analysis that undergirds decisions. This tactic should defuse complaints about total inac-
cessibility. It could reduce the total volume of reporting, since dry
data are often defined as unnewsworthy. To the extent data are
covered, Americans would obtain more of that elusive information
about the "what" of presidential policy. Such information, better
than the current skeptical but banal stress on the "why," would
enforce democratic accountability by telling citizens more clearly
just "what" government is doing to and for them.

*Discourage personal mingling between press officers, other White
House staff, and journalists.* While something surely is gained by
social interaction, and it probably cannot be reduced very much,
the president should realize that the advantages of personal
friendships dissolve when the news gets juicy—as Ron Ziegler,
Ron Nessen, and Jody Powell found. Co-optation works both ways.
Reporters may get more out of presidential staff (for instance,
through "off-the-record" backgrounders that can be used to frame
on-the-record questions, or through alcohol- or fatigue-induced
slips) than vice versa.

Beware the pitfalls of cabinet government. In the current environment of intense media attention, cabinet government could saddle the president with more responsibility for media relations without enhanced power to control them. The media might hold presidents accountable both for the decisions cabinet departments make and for the bad news they generate. Nixon, Ford, and Carter all promised a larger role for cabinets, yet their moves in that direction were stymied in part by media pressures. For the buck not only stops at the Oval Office; it inexorably *goes* there, no matter where it originated. The president will be asked to explain and justify the newsworthy controversies a cabinet member arouses, as suggested by the storms over Earl Butz's bad jokes and Joseph Califano's antismoking campaign. More autonomy for cabinet officers may make sense, but it might be wise to limit their authority to the less-newsworthy (which are not always less-important) matters.

4. Staff the press office and use the media with selectivity and precision.

Employ a press staff that understands how the national media cover incumbent presidents. This means selecting journalists or others who know well the operations of the Washington press corps. Those whose experience is limited to running advertising campaigns or state and local press offices should generally be avoided.

Keep the press staff (except the secretary) in the dark about the politics of White House decision-making. If press officers are not privy to the president's political strategies and future plans but are well briefed on policy substance, they can honestly fend off reporters' gossipy "why" inquisitions and steer the focus to the "what."

For pushing policy proposals, the media are most helpful early or late in the decision cycle. In the beginning, before there are set views, presidential talks can weave a favorable aura around a proposal. Later, near decision time, undecided members of Congress can occasionally be swayed by the swell of media attention a president kindles. But note the boomerang threat: if voting with the president means voting against home-district sentiment, publicity and visibility may be the last thing potential allies need.

Use the different media for the purposes they can best accomplish. For example, television is best for ephemeral rousing of mass sentiment through symbolism. It is not the medium for rational persuasion. Jimmy Carter's energy and inflation speeches provide a paradigm to avoid. The *New York Times, Washington Post,* and *Wall Street Journal* are the papers of record for the powers that be. These are the best places for agenda setting and reasoning with elites. These papers also guide the news judgments of the networks. *Time* and *Newsweek* are read by the better-educated and politically interested public. News magazines can shape the issues their audience ponders and some of the standards their readers use to evaluate presidents and policy.

Pumping up approval ratings through the media is feasible mainly in connection with foreign policy initiatives and crises. The approval question probably taps a combination of what the public thinks the main job of the president is and how well he is doing it. When a chief executive is immersed in a major diplomatic quest (Begin and Sadat at Camp David, Nixon in China) or a threat to national sovereignty (the *Mayaguez,* Iranian hostage seizure), elites generally support him and drama suffuses the story. The president receives reams of positive coverage that focus overwhelming public attention on one aspect of his job: handling the foreign affair. Approval ratings usually spurt upward. But elite support, media favor, and public approval may fade as second guesses supplant the cheers. More important, the approval increase is linked to the initiative or threat. As these become old news, perceptions of the president's "job" revert to other (usually domestic) matters on which he is less likely to enjoy an elite consensus and beneficent press. But this story contains a useful lesson: to the extent that he can, a president should encourage circumscribed perceptions of what his proper "job" should be. That way, when asked if they approve of the way the president is handling it, more people are likely to respond affirmatively.

All the above tactics could fizzle or backfire. As Watergate showed, the media have considerable autonomy; if antagonized, they can strike back in many ways. The president must mix new techniques with traditional ones. Others will appear in time. Their success would immeasurably enhance his leadership. In the final analysis, his own style—his ability to command respect because of the way he understands his own political power stakes—may prove to be his most valuable asset.

NOTES

2. Armen A. Alchian: "Energy Policy: An Introduction to Confusion"

1. That so many distinguished economists, acknowledged as having served as advisers or as early members of the staff, would have so little effect on the final Report suggests refusal to have paid attention to them. They were reported to be Kenneth Boulding, Hendrik Houthakker, William Iulo, Walter Mead, Marc Roberts—a really excellent group of economists (plus, apparently, aid from the Brookings Institution). Economists of that calibre simply would not make the errors in the Report. Somebody else must have been responsible. It is professionally gratifying to a fellow economist that none are listed as members of the staff responsible for the final Report.

2. More enlightening is *Energy Self-sufficiency,* by the M.I.T. Energy Laboratory Policy Study Group (Washington, D.C.: American Enterprise Institute for Public Policy Research).

3. Worthy of attention are F. Baxter, *People or Penguins: The Case for Optimal Pollution* (New York: Columbia University Press, 1974) and E. W. Erickson and L. Waverman, *The Energy Question* (Toronto: University of Toronto Press, 1974), especially vol. 1, parts 2 and 3.

3. Michael J. Boskin: "Taxation and Government"

1. See Michael J. Boskin, "Social Security: The Alternatives Before Us," in *The Crisis in Social Security* (San Francisco: Institute for Contemporary Studies, 1977).

2. See Michael J. Boskin and Martin Feldstein, "The Charitable Deduction and Contributions by Low- and Middle-Income Families: Evidence from the National Survey of Philanthropy," *Review of Economics and Statistics* (August 1978); Michael J. Boskin, "Estate Taxation and Charitable Bequests," *Journal of Public Economics* (1976); Martin Feldstein, "Tax Incentives for Charitable Contributions," *National Tax Journal* (1976).

4. William R. Havender: "Government Regulation: Assessing and Controlling Risks."

1. *San Francisco Chronicle,* 17 August 1981.

2. R. Doll and R. Peto, "The Causes of Cancer: Quantitative Estimates of Avoidable Risks of Cancer in the United States Today," *Journal of the National Cancer Institute* 66 (1981): sec. 4.1 and app. D.

3. World Health Organization, Technical Report Series 276, *Prevention of Cancer* (Geneva, Switzerland, 1964).

4. Doll and Peto, p. 1205.

5. These agents are by no means to be equated with "chemicals" or "pollutants," a common misinterpretation. Instead, the estimate refers to the *total* sources of environmental differences, which are in the main related to cultural and personal practices. Whether or not one smokes, chews betel nut, chooses to reside in sunny climes at high altitudes, eats fibrous or fatty or pickled foods or moldy peanuts or corn, drinks alcoholic beverages such as Calvados, is sexually promiscuous or abstemious, or bears one's first child at an early or late age, are all factors that have been shown to be correlative with—and in some cases, causal to—particular cancers. Only a small fraction of all cancer in the United States is presently thought to be attributable to workplace chemicals or to general environmental pollution with man-made chemicals, namely, 4 percent and 2 percent respectively. See Doll and Peto, pp. 1245, 1251 and table 20.

6. Doll and Peto, tables 11, 19.

7. There are many theoretical reasons for thinking inflection points or thresholds must frequently exist. For one, the human organism has evolved in a sea of naturally occurring carcinogens, so it is likely to have developed defenses for coping with these in normal circumstances. In fact, we have direct evidence of such a defense in skin pigmentation, the level of which determines sensitivity to ultraviolet (i.e., sunlight) induced skin cancers. Another defense is DNA repair, which can be accomplished by many identified enzyme systems. One genetically caused defect in DNA repair—namely, xeroderma pigmentosum—leads to greatly elevated proneness to sunlight induced skin cancer. Other enzymatic systems are known to be in the liver where they are constantly at work cleansing the blood of toxic materials. Any of these systems can be saturated or overloaded by sufficiently high doses, and there is little reason to expect that cancer effects seen only in animals whose normal defense mechanisms have been overloaded by high doses must necessarily be predictive, either qualitatively or proportionately, of the results to be seen at doses which allow these systems to function normally. In addition, some enzyme systems are known that not only metabolically *activate* carcinogenic substances but whose level is inducible by those same substances. For these, the dose response must be nonlinear, curving upwards at high doses. Finally, many apparent carcinogens may be acting by means of "promotion" rather than by "initiation"—that is, by enhancing the effects of true carcinogens. Practically nothing is known about the dose response of promotion; there is not the slightest theoretical reason to think that its dose response must in general be linear.

8. Only one such "megamouse" test has been carried out. In brief, the chemical used (2-acetyl amino fluorene) induced tumors in only two organs, the liver and the bladder. For liver tumors, the incidence at the lowest dose (which was only five times less than the highest dose) was excellently predictable from the incidence seen at the higher doses by a linear model; but for the bladder tumors there was a clear inflection point, and the low-dose risk would have been overpredicted manyfold by linear extrapolation from the higher doses (see N. A. Littlefield, J. H. Farmer, D. W. Gaylor, and W. G. Sheldon, "Effect of Dose and Time in a Long-Term, Low-Dose Carcinogensis Study, *Journal of Environmental Pathology and Toxicology* 3 (1980): pp. 23, 27). Nature is not yielding her secrets easily!

9. Office of Technology Assessment (U.S. Congress), *Cancer Testing Technology and Saccharin* (Washington, D.C.: U.S. Govt. Printing Office, 1977): p. 88.

10. For saccharin, see W. R. Havender, "Ruminations on a Rat: Saccharin and Human Risk," *Regulation* (March/April 1979): pp. 17–24, R. N. Hoover and P. H. Strasser, "Artificial Sweeteners and Human Bladder Cancer," *The Lancet* (19 April 1980): pp. 837–40, E. Wynder and S. D. Stellman, "Artifical Sweetener Use and Bladder Cancer: A Case Control Study," *Science* 207 (1980): pp. 1214–16, A. S. Morrison and J. E. Buring, "Artificial Sweeteners and Cancer of the Lower Urinary Tract," *The New England Journal of Medicine* 302 (1980): pp. 537–41; for hair dyes, see J. Clemmesen, "Epidemiological Studies into the Possible Carcinogenicity of Hairdyes," *Mutation Research* 87 (1981): pp. 65–79; for DDT, see E. R. Laws, A.

Curley, and F. J. Biros, "Men with Intensive Occupational Exposure to DDT," *Archives of Environmental Health* 15 (1967): pp. 766–75, World Health Organization, "The Place of DDT in Operations Against Malaria and Other Vector-Borne Diseases," *Official Records of the World Health Organization,* no. 90 (Geneva, Switzerland, 1971), Council on Occupational Health, "Evaluation of the Present Status of DDT with Respect to Man," *Journal of American Medical Association* 212 (1970): pp. 1055–56.

11. For sugar, see Hoffman LaRoche Co., "Tumorigenicity and Carcinogenicity Study with Xylitol in Long-Term Dietary Administration to Mice," study no. HLR 25/77774, 30 January 1978, prepared by Huntingdon Research Centre, Huntingdon, Cambridgeshire, England (available from the U.S. Food and Drug Administration, Rockville, MD); for pepper, see J. M. Concon, D. S. Newburg, and T. W. Swerczek, "Black Pepper *(Piper Nigrum):* Evidence of Carcinogenicity," *Nutrition and Cancer* 1 (1979): pp. 22–26; for eggs, see D. Nelson, P. B. Szanto, R. Wilheim, and A. C. Ivy, "Hepatic Tumors in Rats Following the Prolonged Ingestion of Milk and Egg Yolk," *Cancer Research* 14 (1954): pp. 441–45; for Vitamin D, see G. H. Gass and W. T. Alaben, "Preliminary Report on the Carcinogenic Dose Response Curve to Oral Vitamin D_2," *IRCS Medical Science* 5 (1977): p. 477.

12. In fact, in the famous saccharin rat studies, males but not females developed tumors. Thus, even within a single species under uniform test conditions, males failed to predict the outcome for females (Office of Technology Assessment, pp. 50–60). This weakens the basis for predicting a significant cancer risk to humans, particularly women, from these results.

13. B. N. Ames, N. K. Hooper, C. B. Sawyer, L. S. Gold, and W. R. Havender, "Carcinogenic Potency: The Data Base." In preparation.

14. J. McCann and B. N. Ames, "Detection of Carcinogens as Mutagens in the *Salmonella* Microsome Test: Assay of 300 Chemicals: Discussion," *Proceedings of the National Academy of Sciences* (U.S.) 73 (1976): pp. 950–54.

15. M. Hollstein, J. McCann, F. A. Angelosanto, and W. W. Nichols, "Short-Term Tests for Carcinogens and Mutagens," *Mutation Research* 65 (1979): pp. 289–356.

16. Paul J. Quirk, "Food and Drug Administration," in James Q. Wilson, ed., *The Politics of Regulation* (New York: Basic Books, 1980), pp. 226–32.

17. Personal communication from John Mendeloff in 1981.

18. Steven Kelman, "Occupational and Health Administration," in James Q. Wilson, ed., *The Politics of Regulation* (New York: Basic Books, 1980), pp. 244–46.

19. Ibid., p. 246.

20. Quirk, p. 207.

21. For a general discussion of the "knowledge" problem, see F. A. Hayek, "The Use of Knowledge in Society," *The American Economic Review* 35, (1945), and Thomas Sowell, *Knowledge and Decisions* (New York: Basic Books, 1980).

22. *Federal Register* (22 January 1980): pp. 5001–296; *Regulation* (March/April 1980): pp. 4–7.

23. Jeffrey R. Smith, "Aspartame Approved Despite Risks," *Science* 213 (1981): pp. 986–87.

24. J. D. Graham and J. W. Vaupel, "Value of a Life: What Difference Does It Make?" *Risk Analysis* 1 (1981): pp. 89–95.

25. Carl Djerassi, *The Politics of Contraception* (New York: Norton, 1979): pp. 63–65, 194.

26. W. M. Wardell and L. Lasagna, *Regulation and Drug Development* (Washington, D.C.: American Enterprise Institute, 1975).

27. S. Peltzman, *Regulation of Pharmaceutical Innovation* (Washington, D.C.: American Enterprise Institute, 1974).

28. J. E. Lee, "How to Fight Air Pollution," *Newsweek,* 14 September 1981, p. 19.

29. Lester B. Lave, "Conflicting Objectives in Regulating the Automobile," *Science* 212 (1981): p. 897.

30. This is another instance of maximin thinking—taking the worst possible case in the population (fetuses and young children) as the basis for regulating everyone else.

31. Quirk, p. 206.

32. A. L. Nichols and R. Zeckhauser, "Government Comes to the Workplace: An Assessment of OSHA," *The Public Interest* (Fall 1977): p. 61.

33. Charles A. Lave, "The Costs of Going 44," *Newsweek,* 23 October 1978, p. 37.

34. Doll and Peto, pp. 1240–41, app. F.

35. G. B. Kolata, "Love Canal: False Alarm Caused by Botched Study," *Science* 280 (1980): pp. 1239–42.

36. P. J. Hilts, "The Day Bacon Was Declared Poison," *The Washington Post Magazine,* 26 April 1981, pp. 18ff.

37. Hoover and Strasser, pp. 837–40; Wynder and Stellman, pp. 1214–16; Morrison and Buring, pp. 537–41.

38. M. K. Hayes, *The Health Effects of Herbicide 2,4,5,-T* (New York: American Council of Science and Health, 1981): pp. 75–77, 92–93.

39. R. H. Furman, discussion in F. Coulson, ed., *Regulatory Aspects of Carcinogenesis and Food Additives: The Delaney Clause* (New York: Academic Press, 1979): p. 141.

40. E. Zeusse, "Love Canal: The Truth Seeps Out," *Reason* (February 1981): pp. 16–33.

41. *Newsweek,* 14 September 1981, p. 14.

42. *Newsweek,* 24 August 1981, p. 72.

43. S. Taylor, "Trial Lawyers See Greater Role in Product Safety," *New York Times,* 30 July 1981.

44. Eugene Bardach and Robert A. Kagan, *Going by the Book: The Problem of Regulatory Unreasonableness* (Philadelphia, PA: Temple University Press, 1982).

5.   Wilson E. Schmidt: "The Role of Private Capital in Developing the Third World"

1. Nathaniel Leff, "Rates of Return to Capital, Savings, and Investment in Developing Countries," *Kyklos* (December 1975).

2. D. Lecraw, "Direct Investment by Firms from Less-Developed Countries," *Oxford Economic Papers* (November 1977).

3. Center on Transnational Corporations, *National Legislation and Regulations Relating to Transnational Corporations* (New York: United Nations, 1978), p. 10.

6.   Elmo R. Zumwalt, Jr.: "Heritage of Weakness: An Assessment of the 1970s"

1. The most recent official estimates are from Donald F. Burton, testimony as Chief, Military-Economic Analysis Center, Office of Strategic Research, National Foreign Assessment Center, before the Subcommittee on General Procurement, Committee on Armed Forces, U.S. Senate (1 November 1979).

2. The SALT II treaty permits the USSR to maintain the numerical advantage in strategic launchers through 1985 by the artifice of not counting the 375 strategic Backfire bombers the USSR will have.

3. See Paul H. Nitze, testimony before the Armed Services Committee, U.S. House of Representatives (15 November 1979).

4. For one such set of calculations, see Paul H. Nitze, statement to Committee on Armed Services, U.S. Senate (9 October 1979).

5. Ibid.

6. Ibid.

7. John M. Collins, *American and Soviet Military Trends* (Washington, D.C.: Center for Strategic and International Studies, 1978).

8. Dr. Brown's statement is cited in an article by John E. Lacouture, "Seapower in the Indian Ocean: A Requirement for Western Security," *U.S. Naval Institute Proceedings* (August 1979).

9. Recent reports are that Dr. Brown is advocating that the United States, beginning in 1985 and completing in 1989, build a five-ship forward deployed capability to land a marine brigade of equipment and thirty days' supplies.

10. Raymond Aron, "From American Imperialism to Soviet Hegemonism," *The Washington Quarterly* (Summer 1979).

11. *Los Angeles Times*, 9 April 1978, p. 1.

12. Memorandum of conversation dated 3 July 1977.

13. This statement is quoted in Banning Garrett, "China Policy and the Strategic Triangle," in Kenneth A. Oye, Donald Rothchild, Robert J. Lieber, eds., *Eagle Entangled: U.S. Foreign Policy in a Complex World* (New York: Longman, 1979).

14. For a pathbreaking analysis of these activities, see Bradford Dismukes and James McConnell, eds., *Soviet Naval Diplomacy* (New York and Oxford: Pergamon Press, 1979).

15. *New York Times*, 20 March 1979, p. A8.

16. During three weeks in South Africa in February 1977, the author asked a score of black leaders, individually, what the children were doing. A number reported that children were in the black front-line countries, Algeria, or the USSR, receiving Marxist military training.

17. In a leadership succession crisis, the winner typically is the Praesidium member who allies himself with the military establishment against the advocates of increased emphasis on soft goods. See Elmo R. Zumwalt, "The Problems of Succession in the USSR," doctoral thesis, National War College, 1962.

18. Quotations from Burton.

7. Wendell John Coats, Jr.: "The Ideology of Arms Control"

1. "Deterring war is the only sure way to deter use of nuclear weapons." Bernard Brodie, *War and Politics* (N.Y.: Macmillan, 1973), p. 404.

2. "Military strategy can no longer be thought of . . . as the science of military victory." Thomas Schelling, *Arms and Influence* (New Haven, Conn.: Yale University Press, 1966), p. 34. "Thus far the chief purpose must be to avert them. It can have almost no other useful purpose." Bernard Brodie in 1946, proudly reaffirmed in *War and Politics,* p. 377.

3. See, in general, the books, articles, and speeches of, *inter alia,* Bernard Brodie, Thomas Schelling, Robert McNamara, Cyrus Vance, and McGeorge Bundy.

4. "The freeze proposal articulates grave reservations many people have about Ronald Reagan. It will be in his continuing political interest to allay these fears and sound like a peace president, whatever his own instincts and preferences." Michael Barone. "The Political Fallout," *The Washington Post,* April 27, 1982, p. 19.

5. This development is apparent in the differences between the 1962 and 1976 versions of U.S. Army tactical operations doctrine as stated in FM 100–5. Although the new manual pays lip service to the idea of victory, the exposition, unlike that of the 1962 version, is not directed and integrated by that idea but around the problems of targeting with new, fast accurate weapons.

6. Those "military sociologists" interested in accounting for problems in retension of serious officers and noncommissioned officers might address this fundamental dilemma rather than simply concentrating on its effects.

7. The first volume of Henry Kissinger's memoirs provides an interesting account of this process during the Vietnam war.

8. See the article "Nuclear Weapons and the Atlantic Alliance" by McGeorge Bundy, George Kennan, Robert McNamara, and Gerard Smith in *Foreign Affairs,* Spring 1982, pp. 761–2.

9. The U.S. Air Force has had to deal with its own version of this problem—the requirement in the logic of arms control to target enemy cities with nuclear weapons rather than to target enemy missiles.

10. For a classic exposition of this view, see Thomas Schelling, op. cit.

9.   Robert A. Goldwin: "Common Sense vs. 'The Common Heritage'"

1. " . . . the creation of the International Seabed Authority by the consensus of practically the entire world community (in which the consent of the U.S. must be counted, because it was given at the Conference *and will, I am sure, be given again*). . . ." (Emphasis added.) Elisabeth Mann Borgese, "The Law of the Sea," *Scientific American* (March 1983): 42–49.

2. "Does President Reagan know what he is doing in preparing a final decision not to sign the law of the sea treaty?" *The Washington Post* editorial, 9 July 1982.

3. "The guardians of pure conservative ideology may have won a battle when the United States stood alone at the Law of the Sea Conference, but the United States may lose a very important war." Leigh Ratiner, "The Law of the Sea: A Crossroads for American Foreign Policy," *Foreign Affairs* 60 (Summer 1982): 1020. Ratiner's essay, revised, appears in this volume as "The Costs of American Rigidity."

4. "If President Reagan understood the realistic prospects . . . he would have had second thoughts about the pursuit of principle over pragmatism." Ratiner, p. 1018. Discourse on this subject has rarely been dispassionate and often descends to vituperative name-calling. A comparatively mild example appeared as a column in *The New York Times* by one Clifton E. Curtis, identified as an attorney with the Center for Law and Social Policy; in it Curtis characterized the Reagan administration as "jingoistic ideologues" suffering from "ideological paranoia," who "should be deep-sixed." The title of his column is the imperious command "Sign the Sea Law Treaty," *The New York Times,* 21 February 1983, p. A17. Mr. Curtis is professionally concerned with control of ocean pollution but he seems less concerned about the consequences of polluting rational discourse.

5. Statement by the President, 9 July 1982, The White House, Office of the Press Secretary (Santa Barbara, Calif.).

6. For a full discussion of "the common heritage of mankind" as an ideological doctrine and the theoretical errors it has led to in the Law of the Sea Treaty negotiations, see my article "Locke and the Law of the Sea," *Commentary* (June 1981): 46–50.

7. I, unfortunately, was not one of them, relying as I did on what others were saying about the factual matters. See my references to "resources worth billions of dollars" and how the world "suffers from a shortage of these metals," ibid.

8. "Manganese Nodule Mining: Background Information," submitted to Special Standing Committee of the House of Commons on the Deep Sea Mining (Temporary Provisions) Bill by Consolidated Gold Fields Limited, Rio Tinto-Zinc Corporation Limited, and BP Petroleum Development Limited, May 1981. Other members of the Kennecott Consortium are Kennecott Corporation (USA), Mitsubishi Corporation (Japan), and Noranda Mines Limited (Canada).

9. Reported in *Financial Times* (London), 6 October 1982, p. 26.

10. "Minesweeping," *The Economist* (London), 11 December 1982, p. 60.

11. Hobart Rowen, "The Ceramic Example," *The Washington Post,* 17 February 1983, p. A19.

12. "Manganese Nodule Mining: Background Information."

13. "Declining commodity prices made the resource-exporting developing countries wary of a new source of competition for their native ones. Against the opposition of the North (with the exception of Canada) these countries became more interested in limiting production from the seabed than in managing it." Borgese, p. 47.

14. C. R. Tinsley, "The Financing of Deep-Sea Mining," unpublished paper for a conference on U.S. Interests in the Law of the Sea, American Enterprise Institute, October 1981.

15. "There exists no politician in India daring enough to attempt to explain to the masses that cows can be eaten." Indira Gandhi, talking to Oriana Fallaci, quoted in *The Quotable Woman, 1800–1981,* ed. Elaine Partnow; from a book review by Edmund Fuller, *The Wall Street Journal,* 28 March 1983, p. 22.

16. Borgese, p. 47.

10. Patrick Glynn: "The Moral Case for the Arms Buildup"

1. Robert Scheer, *With Enough Shovels: Reagan, Bush, and Nuclear War* (New York: Random House, 1982), p. 3.

2. "The Pastoral Letter of the U.S. Bishops on War and Peace: The Challenge of Peace: God's Promise and Our Response," reprinted in *Origins* 13, no. 1, May 19, 1983, p. 23.

3. Alain C. Enthoven and Wayne K. Wayne, *How Much Is Enough? Shaping the Defense Program 1961–69,* quoted in Lawrence Freedman, *The Evolution of Nuclear Strategy* (New York: St. Martin's Press, 1983), p. 246.

4. Bernard Brodie, *Strategy in the Missile Age* (Princeton, N.J.: Princeton University Press, 1965), p. 9.

5. Thomas W. Wolfe, *The SALT Experience* (Cambridge, Mass.: Ballinger, 1979), pp. 136–37.

6. Freedman, p. 378.

7. Leon Wieseltier, "Nuclear War, Nuclear Peace," *The New Republic,* January 10 & 17, 1983, pp. 7–38.

8. Quoted in Freedman, p. 257.

9. Gen. Maj. A. S. Milovidov, ed., *The Philosophical Heritage of V. I. Lenin and the Problems of Contemporary War (A Soviet View),* quoted in Joseph D. Douglass, Jr., and Amoretta M. Hoeber, *Soviet Strategy for Nuclear War,* forward by Eugene V. Rostow (Stanford, Calif.: Hoover Institution Press, 1979), p. 10.

10. Ibid., p. 16.

11. Col. M. P. Skirdo, "Leadership in Modern War," *Selected Soviet Military Writings 1970–75,* tr. U.S. Air Force (Washington, D.C.: U.S. Government Printing Office, n.d.), pp. 151–52.

12. Freedman, p. 258.

13. Ibid., p. 248.

14. "The Real Paul Warnke," *The New Republic,* March 26, 1977, p. 23.

15. Jerome H. Kahan, "Arms Interaction and Arms Control," reprinted from Jerome H. Kahan, *Security in the Nuclear Age: Developing U.S. Strategic Arms Policy* (1975), in John F. Reichart and Steven R. Sturm, eds., *American Defense Policy,* 5th ed. (Baltimore and London: The Johns Hopkins University Press, 1982), p. 396.

16. Seymour Weiss, ". . . But Let's Not Overlook the Hurdles," *The Wall Street Journal,* April 8, 1983, p. 20: "Euphemistically described as the Moscow system, the Soviet ABM defense provides protection to a substantial portion of the western USSR, containing about 75 percent of Soviet population and industry and a substantial portion of Soviet military capabilities."

17. Henry Kissinger, *Years of Upheaval* (Boston and Toronto: Little, Brown, 1982), p. 261.

18. "Soviet ABM Breakout," *The Wall Street Journal,* August 16, 1983, p. 32; cf. Rowland Evans and Robert Novak, "A 'Smoking Gun' in Siberia," *Washington Post,* August 17, 1983.

19. For a fuller description of the apolitical character of assured destruction thinking, see Wendell John Coats, Jr., "The Ideology of Arms Control," *Journal of Contemporary Studies* 5, no. 3 (Summer 1982): 5–15.

20. Richard Smoke, "The Evolution of American Defense Policy," in Reichart and Sturm, eds., p. 121. Reprinted, with revisions, from "National Security Affairs," in *Handbook of Political Science,* vol. 8, *International Politics,* ed. Fred I. Greenstein and Nelson W. Polsby (Reading, Mass.: Addison-Wesley, 1975).

21. Peter W. Rodman, "The Missiles of October: Twenty Years Later," *Commentary,* October 1982, pp. 39–45.

22. Wolfe, pp. 332–33, n79.

23. Ibid., pp. 136–37.

24. *Report of the President's Commission on Strategic Forces* (Washington, D.C.: U.S. Government Printing Office, 1983), pp. 7ff.

25. Elmo R. Zumwalt, Jr., "Heritage of Weakness," in W. Scott Thompson, ed., *National Security in the 1980s: From Weakness to Strength* (San Francisco: Institute for Contemporary Studies, 1980), p. 24; cf. Harold Brown, *Thinking about National Security: Defense and Foreign Policy in a Dangerous World* (Boulder, Colo.: Westview Press, 1983), pp. 66–67.

26. See Gerard Smith, *Doubletalk: The Story of the First Strategic Arms Limitation Talks* (Garden City, N.Y.: Doubleday, 1980), pp. 323–61.

27. U.S. Department of Defense, *Soviet Military Power,* 2nd. ed. (Washington, D.C.: U.S. Government Printing Office, 1983), pp. 6, 7, 78, 80.

28. See U.S. Department of Defense, *Soviet Military Power* (Washington, D.C.: U.S. Government Printing Office, 1981), pp. 9–13; idem, *Soviet Military Power,* 2nd. ed. (Washington, D.C.: U.S. Government Printing Office, 1983), pp. 73–74; Caspar W. Weinberger, Secretary of Defense, *Annual Report to Congress, Fiscal Year 1983* (Washington, D.C.: U.S. Government Printing Office, 1983), pp. I-5, I-20, II-26–29; International Institute for Strategic Studies, *The Military Balance, 1982–83* (London: International Institute for Strategic Studies, 1982), pp. 12–13.

29. McGeorge Bundy, "The Bishops and the Bomb," *The New York Review of Books,* June 16, 1983, p. 8.

30. Ibid., p. 4.

31. For an elaboration of the relevance of this distinction to the concept of deterrence, see Brent Scowcroft's chapter in this volume.

32. Theodore Draper, "How Not to Think about Nuclear War," *The New York Review of Books,* July 15, 1982, p. 42.

33. "The Pastoral Letter," p. 13.

34. See Richard Grenier, "The Horror, the Horror" (rev. of Anton Antonov-Ovseyenko, *The Time of Stalin: Portrait of a Tyranny), The New Republic,* May 26, 1982, pp. 27–32.

35. *Report to the Congress on Forced Labor in the USSR,* U.S. Department of State, February 9, 1983; quoted in Arnold Beichman and Mikhail S. Bernstam, *Andropov: New Challenge to the West,* introduction by Robert Conquest (New York: Stein and Day, 1983), pp. 184–85, 239–40n. See also David Satter, "The System of Forced Labor in Russia," *The Wall Street Journal,* June 25, 1982, p. 26; cf. Beichman and Bernstam. On the number of political victims in psychiatric hospitals, see Sidney Bloch and Peter Reddaway, *Psychiatric Terror: How Soviet Psychiatry Is Used to Suppress Dissent* (New York: Basic Books, 1977), pp. 258–63; cf. "Psychiatric Abuse in the USSR: Statistical Survey, July 1982," *Freedom Appeals,* September/October 1983, p. 42.

36. See Michael Barry, "Afghanistan—Another Cambodia?" *Commentary,* August 1982, pp. 29–37; Rosanne Klass, "Soviet Terror in Afghanistan," *Freedom at Issue,* March–April 1983, pp. 3–5.

13. Peter W. Greenwood: "Controlling the Crime Rate through Imprisonment"

1. Lee Sechrest, Susan O. White, and Elizabeth D. Brown, eds., *The Rehabilitation of Criminal Offenders: Problems and Prospects* (Washington, D.C.: National Academy of Sciences, 1979).

2. Daniel Glaser, "Disillusion with Rehabilitation: Theoretical and Empirical Questions," in *The Future of Childhood and Juvenile Justice,* ed. LeMar Empey (Charlottesville, Va.: University Press of Virginia, 1979).

3. Franklin Zimring and G. Hawkins, *Deterrence: The Legal Threat in Crime Control* (Chicago: University of Chicago Press, 1973).

4. Alfred Blumstein, Jacqueline Cohen, and Daniel Nagin, eds., *Deterrence and Incapacitation: Estimating the Effects of Criminal Sanctions on Crime Rates* (Washington, D.C.: National Academy of Sciences, 1978).

5. C. R. Shaw and H. D. McKay, *Juvenile Delinquency and Urban Areas* (Chicago: University of Chicago Press, 1942); Sheldon Glueck and Eleanor Glueck, *Unraveling Juvenile Delinquency* (New York: The Commonwealth Fund, 1950).

6. E. H. Sutherland, *The Professional Thief* (Chicago: University of Chicago Press, 1937).

7. M. Wolfgang, R. M. Figlio, and T. Sellin, *Delinquency in a Birth Cohort* (Chicago: University of Chicago Press, 1972).

8. Lyle W. Shannon, "A Longitudinal Study of Delinquency and Crime," in *Quantitative Studies in Criminology,* ed. Charles Wellford (Beverly Hills, Calif.: Sage, 1978); David P. Farrington, "Longitudinal Research on Crime and Delinquency," in *Crime and Justice: An Annual Review of Research,* vol. 1, ed. Norval Morris and Michael Tonry (Chicago: University of Chicago Press, 1979).

9. Joan Petersilia and Peter W. Greenwood with Marvin Lavin, *Criminal Careers of Habitual Felons,* The Rand Corporation, R–2144–DOJ, August 1977.

10. Mark A. Peterson and Harriet B. Braiker, with Suzanne M. Polich, *Who Commits Crimes: A Survey of Prison Inmates* (Cambridge, Mass.: Oelgeschlager, Gunn, and Hain, 1981).

11. Mark A. Peterson, et al., *Survey of Prison and Jail Inmates: Background and Method,* The Rand Corporation, N–1635–NIJ, August 1982.

12. Michael Hindelang, Travis Hirschi, and Joseph G. Weis, *Measuring Delinquency,* vol. 23, Sage Library of Social Research (Beverly Hills, Calif.: Sage, 1981).

13. Stevens Clarke, "Getting 'Em Out of Circulation: Does Incarceration of Juvenile Offenders Reduce Crime?" *Journal of Criminal Law and Criminology,* vol. 65, no. 4 (1974): 528–35; J. Marsh and M. Singer, *Soft Statistics and Hard Questions,* Discussion Paper HI–1712–DP (Croton-on-Hudson, N.Y.: Hudson Institute, 1972); M. A. Greene, "The Incapacitation Effect of Imprisonment Policy on Crime" (Ph.D. diss., Carnegie-Mellon University, 1977); David Greenberg, "The Incapacitation Effect of Imprisonment: Some Estimates," *Law and Society Review,* vol. 9, no. 4 (1975): 541–80; B. Avi-Itzhak and R. Shinnar, "Quantitative Models in Crime Control," *Journal of Criminal Justice,* vol. 1, no. 3 (1973); S. Shinnar and R. Shinnar, "The Effects of the Criminal Justice System on the Control of Crime: A Quantitative Approach," *Law and Society Review* 9 (1975).

14. Jacqueline Cohen, "The Incapacitative Effect of Imprisonment: A Critical Review of the Literature," in *Deterrence and Incapacitation: Estimating the Effects of Criminal Sanctions on Crime Rates,* Assembly of Behavioral and Social Sciences (Washington, D.C.: National Academy of Sciences, 1978).

15. Shinnar and Shinnar.

16. Clarke; Greenberg.

17. Shinnar and Shinnar.

18. Cohen.

19. Peterson and Braiker.

20. Alfred Blumstein and Jacqueline Cohen, "Estimation of Individual Crime Rates from Arrest Records," *Journal of Criminal Law and Criminology,* vol. 70, no. 4 (1979): 561.

21. John Monahan, Stanley L. Brodsky, and Saleem A. Shah, *Predicting Violent Behavior: An Assessment of Clinical Techniques* (Beverly Hills, Calif.: Sage, 1982).

22. Peter B. Hoffman and Sheldon Adelberg, "The Salient Factor Score: A Nontechnical Overview," *Federal Probation* 44 (March 1980): 44–52; Michael Gottfredson and Don Gottfredson, *Decisionmaking in Criminal Justice: Toward the Rational Exercise of Discretion* (New York: Ballinger, 1980).

23. Peterson, et al.

24. Peter W. Greenwood with Allan Abrahamse, *Selective Incapacitation,* The Rand Corporation, R–2815–NIJ, August 1982.

25. Ibid.

26. Andrew von Hirsch, *Doing Justice* (New York: Hill and Wang, 1976).

27. Michael Sherman and Gordon Hawkins, *Imprisonment in America* (Chicago: University of Chicago Press, 1981).

28. Longitudinal arrest histories can give the rate at which offenders are arrested for any specific crime (u). Their offense rate is then just

$$\lambda = \frac{u}{\text{probability of arrest}}$$

(Blumstein and Cohen).

29. Of course, to be used as predictor variables, the arrest histories would have to be combined with another file containing the individual characteristics.

14. Seymour Martin Lipset: "The American Party System."

1. John F. Bibby, Thomas E. Mann, Norman J. Ornstein, *Vital Statistics on Congress* (Washington, D.C.: American Enterprise Institute for Public Policy Research, 1980): p. 19.

2. E. E. Schattschneider, *Party Government* (New York: Rinehart and Winston, 1942).

3. Seymour Martin Lipset, "Why No Socialism in the United States?" in Seweryn Bialer and Sophia Sluzar, eds., *Sources of Contemporary Radicalism* (Boulder, CO: Westview Press, 1977): pp. 126–30.

4. Richard A. Viguerie, *The New Right: We're Ready to Lead* (Falls Church, VA: The Viguerie Company, 1981): pp. 87–88.

5. Seymour Martin Lipset, *The First New Nation: The United States in Historical and Comparative Perspective* (New York: W. W. Norton and Company, 1979): pp. 286–317.

6. Byron E. Shafer, "Anti-Party Politics," *The Public Interest* (Spring 1981): pp. 96–100.

7. Richard Bergholz, "The Times Poll. Voters and Party Leaders Far Apart on the Issues," *Los Angeles Times,* 2 August 1981, pp. 1, 18.

8. Bibby, Mann, Ornstein, pp. 104–6.

9. Richard J. Cattani, "Analyzing President's Tax Triumph," *Christian Science Monitor,* 3 August 1981, p. 3.

10. David S. Broder, "Demos Again Wrestling with Delegate Reforms," *San Francisco Chronicle,* 22 August 1981, p. 8.

15. Aaron Wildavsky: "Toward a New Budgetary Order"

1. J. G. Pocock, *The Political Works of James Harrington* (Cambridge, Mass.: Cambridge University Press, 1977).

2. Herbert J. Storing, *The Complete Anti-Federalist, Volume I: What the Anti-Federalists*

Were For (Chicago: The University of Chicago Press, 1981); and William A. Schambra, "A Beginning from Old Principles," typescript, American Enterprise Institute, 1981.

3. See Samuel P. Huntington, *Common Defense: Strategic Programs in National Politics* (N.Y.: Columbia University Press, 1961); and Patrick Crecine, "Defense Budgeting: Constraints and Organizational Adaptation," Discussion Paper #6 (Ann Arbor: University of Michigan Press, 1961), for contemporary versions during the administrations of Harry S Truman and Dwight D. Eisenhower.

4. Dall W. Forsythe, *Taxation and Political Change in the Young Nation, 1781–1833* (N.Y.: Columbia University Press, 1977), p. 38.

5. Lewis H. Kimmel, *Federal Budget and Fiscal Policy, 1789–1958* (Washington, D.C.: The Brookings Institution, 1959), p. 23.

6. Ibid., pp. 24–25.

7. Ibid., pp. 25–26.

8. Ibid., p. 26.

9. Ibid., p. 57.

10. Ibid., pp. 65–69.

11. Thomas Borcherding, "A Hundred Years of Public Spending, 1870–1970," in Thomas Borcherding, ed., *Budgets and Bureaucrats: The Sources of Government Growth* (Durham, N.C.: Duke University Press, 1977), p. 21.

12. Lewis H. Kimmel, op. cit., pp. 84–85.

13. Ibid., pp. 87–88.

14. Ibid., p. 88.

15. Milton Friedman and Anna Jacobson Schwartz, *A Monetary History of the United States, 1867–1960* (Princeton, N.J.: Princeton University Press, 1963), pp. 9–10.

16. Thomas Borcherding, op. cit., p. 26.

17. William J. Shultz and M. R. Caine, *Financial Development of the United States* (N.Y.: Prentice-Hall, 1937), pp. 518–19.

18. Lewis H. Kimmel, op. cit., p. 160; and Joseph Dorfman, *The Economic Mind in American Civilization, 1918–1933* (N.Y.: Viking Press, 1959), pp. 610–16.

19. Lewis H. Kimmel, op. cit., p. 148.

20. Ibid., p. 155.

21. Joseph Dorfman, op. cit., pp. 617, 637.

22. Lewis H. Kimmel, op. cit., pp. 157, 222–23.

23. Joseph Dorfman, op. cit., pp. 659–75.

24. For Felix Frankfurter's efforts in this direction, see H. N. Hirsch, *The Enigma of Felix Frankfurter* (N.Y.: Basic Books, 1981), p. 113.

25. Dennis S. Ippolito, *Congressional Spending: A Twentieth Century Fund Report* (Ithaca, N.Y., and London: Cornell University Press, 1981), p. 179.

26. See Aaron Wildavsky, "The Party of Government, the Party of Opposition, and the Party of Balance: An American View of the Consequences of the 1980 Election," in Austin Ranney, ed., *The American Elections of 1980* (Washington, D.C.: The American Enterprise Institute, 1981), pp. 329–50. A shorter version, "The Three-Party System—1980 and After," can be found in *The Public Interest* 64 (Summer 1981): 47–57.

27. Aaron Wildavsky, "The Annual Expenditure Increment," Working Papers on House Committee Organization and Operation (#96-321), Select Committee on Committees, Ninety-Third Congress (Washington, D.C.: U.S. Government Printing Office, 1973). A revised version, "The Annual Expenditure Increment—Or How Congress Can Regain Control of the Budget," can be found in *The Public Interest* 33 (Fall 1973): 84–108.

28. Allen Schick, *Congress and Money* (Washington, D.C.: The Urban Institute, 1980), p. 313.

29. Ibid., p. 571.

30. See Aaron Wildavsky, *How to Limit Government Spending* (Los Angeles and Berkeley, Ca.: University of California Press, 1980).

31. See Louis Fisher, "In Dubious Battle? Congress and the Budget," *The Brookings Bulletin 17 (Spring 1981): 6*–10.

16   Robert M. Entman: "The Imperial Media"

1. David L. Paletz and Robert M. Entman, *Media Power Politics* (New York: Free Press, 1981), pp. 57-59; Timothy Crouse, *The Boys on the Bus* (New York: Random House, 1973), pp. 227-56; Michael B. Grossman and Francis E. Rourke, "The Media and the Presidency: An Exchange Analysis," *Political Science Quarterly* 91 (1976): pp. 455-70.

2. Grossman and Rourke, p. 459.

3. Paletz and Entman, pp. 60-61.

4. The figures vary from year to year. See Herbert J. Gans, *Deciding What's News* (New York: Pantheon, 1979): pp. 9-10; see also Martha J. Kumar and Michael B. Grossman (with Leslie Lichter-Mason), "Images of the White House in the Media." Paper delivered at the annual meeting of the American Political Science Association, Washington, D.C., 28-30 August 1980, pp. 5-7, 10-11; and Alan P. Balutis, "Congress, the President, and the Press," *Journalism Quarterly* 53 (1976): p. 511.

5. Cf. Paletz and Entman, pp. 16-22; Kumar and Grossman, pp. 5-7, 10-11.

6. Paletz and Entman, pp. 65-78, on Nixon and Carter.

7. Quoted in Hoyt Purvis, ed., *The Presidency and the Press* (Austin TX: Lyndon B. Johnson School of Public Affairs, University of Texas, 1976): p. 49.

8. Cf. James David Barber, "Not the *New York Times,*" *Washington Monthly* 11 (September 1979): p. 21.

9. Purvis, pp. 45-46.

10. See "Candid Reflections of a Businessman in Washington," *Fortune* (29 January 1979): pp. 36-49.

11. Stephen J. Wayne, "Expectations of the President." Paper delivered at the annual meeting of the American Political Science Association, Washington, D.C., 28-30 August 1980, pp. 5, 9.

12. Purvis, p. 48.

13. Richard E. Neustadt, *Presidential Power: The Politics of Leadership from FDR to Carter* (New York: John Wiley, 1980); cf. Peter W. Sperlich, "Bargaining and Overload: An Essay on *Presidential Power*" in Aaron Wildavsky, ed., *Perspectives on the Presidency* (Boston: Little Brown, 1975): pp. 406-30.

14. See the findings of John W. Kingdon, *Congressman's Voting Decisions* (New York: Harper & Row, 1973): pp. 169-91; and Aage R. Clausen, *How Congressmen Decide: A Policy Focus* (New York: St. Martin's Press, 1973): pp. 192-212, who finds presidential impact only on issues of international involvement; cf. Eric L. Davis, "Legislative Reform and the Decline of Presidential Influence on Capitol Hill," *British Journal of Political Science* 9 (1979): pp. 465-79; Neustadt, pp. 212-16.

15. Cf. David R. Mayhew, *Congress, the Electoral Connection* (New Haven, CT: Yale University Press, 1974).

16. For evidence of weak correlations between approval ratings and success, see George C. Edwards III, *Implementing Public Policy* (Washington, D.C.: Congressional Quarterly Press, 1980): pp. 101-13.

17. Richard Brody and Benjamin I. Page, "The Impact of Events on Presidential Popularity: The Johnson and Nixon Administrations," in Aaron Wildavsky, ed., *Perspectives on the Presidency* (Boston: Little, Brown, 1975): pp. 136-47; Timothy R. Haight and Richard Brody, "The

Mass Media and Presidential Popularity, Presidential Broadcasting and News in the Nixon Administration," *Communications Research* 4 (1977): pp. 41-59.

18. Douglas A. Hibbs, Jr., Douglas R. Rivers, Nicholas Vasilatos, "On the Demand for Economic Outcomes: Macroeconomic Performance and Mass Political Support in the United States, Great Britain, and Germany." Paper delivered at the annual meeting of the American Political Science Association, Washington, D.C., 28-30 August, 1980, p. 29; cf, Samuel Kernell, "Explaining Presidential Popularity," *American Political Science Review* 72 (June 1978): pp. 506-72.

19. Kumar and Grossman, p. 12; cf. Roger Morris, "Carter's Cabinet: The Who's Who Treatment," *Columbia Journalism Review* 14 (Sept./Oct. 1975): pp. 49-52.

20. For example, recall the failures of President Ford's WIN, Carter's energy talks; cf. John E. Mueller, *Wars, Presidents and Public Opinion* (New York: John Wiley, 1973); Lee Sigelman, "Rallying to the President's Support: A Reappraisal of the Evidence," *Polity* 11 (1979): pp. 542-61.

CONTRIBUTORS

ARMEN A. ALCHIAN is professor of economics at the University of California, Los Angeles.

MICHAEL J. BOSKIN is professor of economics, chairman of the Center for Economic Policy Research, and senior fellow (by courtesy) at the Hoover Institution, Stanford University. An authority on taxation and public finance, he edited the ICS 1977 publication, *The Crisis in Social Security,* the 1980 publication, *The Economy in the 1980s,* and, with Aaron Wildavsky, the 1982 study, *The Federal Budget: Economics and Politics.*

A. LAWRENCE CHICKERING is executive editor of the Institute for Contemporary Studies. He is currently writing a book on the decline of authority and its impact on contemporary politics.

WENDELL JOHN COATS, JR., is visiting assistant professor of political science at Kenyon College.

ROBERT CONQUEST is senior research fellow at the Hoover Institution, Stanford University. His many books on Soviet matters include *The Great Terror, Power and Policy in the USSR,* and *V. I. Lenin.*

ROBERT M. ENTMAN is assistant professor of public policy studies and political science at Duke University. His writings include co-authorship of *Media Power Politics,* and articles in the *Journal of Communications, Journal of Politics,* and elsewhere. Currently on leave as manager of the information technology policy program at the National Telecommunications and Information Administration, he is writing a book entitled *News Diversity and American Democracy.*

PATRICK GLYNN is co-editor of the *Journal of Contemporary Studies.* His articles have appeared in numerous magazines, including *The New Republic, Commentary,* and *The Public Interest.*

ROBERT A. GOLDWIN is resident scholar and director of constitutional studies at the American Enterprise Institute, adjunct lecturer at the John F. Kennedy School of Government, Harvard University, and intermittent policy consultant to the undersecretary of defense. His recent articles include "Rights versus Duties: No Contest," in *Ethics in Hard Times* and "Locke and the Law of the Sea," in *Commentary.*

PETER W. GREENWOOD is senior researcher for The Rand Corporation. His special area of expertise is criminal justice policy. He has served on the faculties of the California Institute of Technology, The Rand Graduate Institute, and the Claremont Graduate School. His works include *Prosecution of Adult Felony Defendants, Selective Incapacitation,* and *Youth Crime and Juvenile Justice in California.*

WILLIAM R. HAVENDER is currently a private consultant on environmental carcinogens and has been a research biochemist at the University of California, Berkeley. He is a member of the Board of Scientific Advisors of the American Council of Science and Health, and a contributing editor to *Regulation* magazine. His articles have appeared in *Regulation, The American Spectator, The Wall Street Journal,* and elsewhere. He is a contributor to the forthcoming book, *Arthur Jensen: Consensus and Controversy.*

SEYMOUR MARTIN LIPSET is Caroline S. G. Munro Professor of Political Science and professor of sociology at Stanford University. He is also a senior fellow at the Hoover Institution at the same university. He is co-editor of *Public Opinion* magazine. He is the past president of the American Political Science Association, the president-elect of the Sociological Research Association and of the World Association for Public Opinion Research, and vice-president of the International Political Science Association. Among his many books are *Political Man: The Social Bases of Politics,* and, with William Schneider, *The Confidence Gap: Business, Labor and Politics in the Public Mind.*

MICHAEL NOVAK is resident scholar in religion and public policy at the American Enterprise Institute in Washington, D.C., and in 1983 was named to the George Frederick Jewett Chair in Public Policy Research there. His twice weekly column, "Illusions and Realities," is syndicated nationally and his articles have appeared in *The New Republic, Commentary, Harpers, The Atlantic,* and elsewhere.

WILSON E. SCHMIDT was professor of economics and director for international programs in the Center for the Study of Public Choice at Virginia Polytechnic Institute and State University prior to his death in June 1981. Formerly a consultant to government agencies on policy questions of international finance and economic development, his writings appeared in several books and scholarly journals.

THOMAS SOWELL is a senior fellow at the Hoover Institution, Stanford University. A former project director at the Urban Institute, he is the author of a number of books and articles on race issues, including *Ethnic America, The Economics and Politics of Race: An International Perspective,* and *Civil Rights: Rhetoric or Reality?*

AARON WILDAVSKY is professor of political science and public policy at the University of California, Berkeley, and was dean of the university's Graduate School of Public Policy from 1969 to 1977. He is the author of *How to Limit Government Spending, The Nursing Father: Moses as a Political Leader,* and, with Carolyn Webber, *A History of Taxation and Expenditure in the Western World* (forthcoming). He also co-edited, with Michael J. Boskin, the 1982 ICS volume *The Federal Budget: Economics and Politics,* and edited the 1983 ICS study *Beyond Containment: Alternative American Policies Toward the Soviet Union.*

ELMO R. ZUMWALT, JR., Admiral, U.S. Navy (ret.) was chief of naval operations from 1970 to 1974. He had previously organized and directed the navy's System Analysis Division and served as deputy scientific officer to the Center for Naval Analyses. He is the author of *On Watch* and of numerous articles and commentaries published worldwide. He is currently serving as Chairman/CEO of American Medical Buildings, Inc., as president of Admiral Zumwalt & Associates, Inc., and as a public governor of the American Stock Exchange.

Publications List 1975–1984
Institute for Contemporary Studies
785 Market St., Suite 750, San Francisco, CA 94103

AMERICAN FEDERALISM: A NEW PARTNERSHIP FOR THE REPUBLIC
Edited by Robert B. Hawkins, Jr.
$7.95. 281 pages. Publication date: July 1982
ISBN 0–917616–50–2
Contributors: Lamar Alexander, Benjamin L. Cardin, Albert J. Davis, Eugene
Eidenberg, Daniel J. Elazar, Alan F. Holmer, A. E. Dick Howard, Michael S.
Joyce, Paul Laxalt, John McClaughry, W. S. Moore, E. S. Savas, William A.
Schambra, Stephen L. Schechter, Wm. Craig Stubblebine, David B. Swoap,
Murray L. Weidenbaum, F. Clifton White, Aaron Wildavsky, Richard S.
Williamson

BEYOND CONTAINMENT: ALTERNATIVE AMERICAN POLICIES TOWARD
THE SOVIET UNION
Edited by Aaron Wildavsky
$8.95 (paper). ISBN 0–917616–60–X
$21.95 (cloth). ISBN 0–917616–61–8
264 pages. Publication date: October 1983
Contributors: Ernst B. Haas, James L. Payne, Paul Seabury, Max Singer, Robert
W. Tucker, Aaron Wildavsky, Charles Wolf, Jr.

BUREAUCRATS AND BRAINPOWER: GOVERNMENT REGULATION OF
UNIVERSITIES
$6.95. 170 pages. Publication date: June 1979
ISBN 0–917616–35–9
Contributors: Nathan Glazer, Robert S. Hatfield, Richard W. Lyman, Paul
Seabury, Robert L. Sproull, Miro M. Todorovich, Caspar W. Weinberger

THE CALIFORNIA COASTAL PLAN: A CRITIQUE
Publication date: March 1976
Out-of-print

CRIME AND PUBLIC POLICY
Edited by James Q. Wilson
$8.95. 334 pages. Publication date: June 1983
ISBN 0–917616–51–0
Contributors: Alfred Blumstein, Jan M. Chaiken, Marcia R. Chaiken, Brian Forst,
Richard B. Freeman, Daniel Glaser, Peter W. Greenwood, Richard J.
Herrnstein, Travis Hirschi, Mark H. Moore, Charles A. Murray, Steven R.
Schlesinger, Lawrence W. Sherman, Jackson Toby, James Q. Wilson

THE CRISIS IN SOCIAL SECURITY: PROBLEMS AND PROSPECTS
Edited by Michael J. Boskin
Publication date: April 1977
Out-of-print

DEFENDING AMERICAN: TOWARD A NEW ROLE IN THE POST-DETENTE
WORLD
Publication date: April 1977
Out-of-print

THE ECONOMY IN THE 1980s: A PROGRAM FOR GROWTH AND STABILITY
Edited by Michael J. Boskin
$7.95 (paper). ISBN 0−917616−39−1
$17.95 (cloth). ISBN 0−87855−399−1
462 pages. Publication date: June 1980
Contributors: Michael J. Boskin, George F. Break, John T. Cuddington, Patricia
Drury, Alain Enthoven, Laurence J. Kotlikoff, Ronald I. McKinnon, John H.
Pencavel, Henry S. Rowen, John L. Scadding, John B. Shoven, James L.
Sweeney, David J. Teece

EMERGING COALITIONS IN AMERICAN POLITICS
Edited by Seymour Martin Lipset
Publication date: June 1978
Out-of-print

THE FAIRMONT PAPERS: BLACK ALTERNATIVES CONFERENCE
Publication date: March 1981
Out-of-print

THE FEDERAL BUDGET: ECONOMICS AND POLITICS
Edited by Michael J. Boskin and Aaron Wildavsky
$8.95. 411 pages. Publication date: July 1982
ISBN 0−917616−48−0
Contributors: James W. Abellera, Marcy E. Avrin, Michael J. Boskin, George F.
Break, Alain C. Enthoven, Robert W. Hartman, Herschel Kanter, Melvyn B.
Krauss, Roger P. Labrie, Arnold J. Meltsner, Rudolph G. Penner, Alvin
Rabushka, Robert D. Reischauer, Laurence S. Seidman, Aaron Wildavsky

FEDERAL TAX REFORM: MYTHS AND REALITIES
Edited by Michael J. Boskin
Publication date: September 1978
Out-of-print

GOVERNMENT CREDIT ALLOCATION: WHERE DO WE GO FROM HERE?
$4.95. 208 Pages. Publication date: November 1975
ISBN 0−917616−02−2
Contributors: George Benston, Karl Brunner, Dwight M. Jaffe, Omotunde
Johnson, Edward J. Kane, Thomas Mayer, Allan H. Meltzer

THE INDUSTRIAL POLICY DEBATE
Edited by Chalmers Johnson
$8.95 (paper). ISBN 0−917616−64−2
$21.95 (cloth). ISBN 0−917616−65−0
275 pages. Publication date: May 1984
Contributors: Michael J. Athey, Bruce Bartlett, Eugene Bardach, Yolanda
Henderson, Walter E. Hoadley, Chalmers Johnson, Melvyn Krauss, Regis
McKenna, Robert S. Ozaki, Paul Seabury, Murray L. Weidenbaum, Aaron
Wildavsky

LAW OF THE SEA: U.S. POLICY DILEMMA
Edited by Bernard H. Oxman, with David D. Caron and Charles L. O. Buderi
$7.95 (paper). ISBN 0−917616−53−7
$21.95 (cloth). ISBN 0−917616−59−6
184 pages. Publication date: July 1983
Contributors: Lance N. Antrim, Frank S. Brokaw, W. Scott Burke, David D. Caron,
Lewis I. Cohen, Robert A. Goldwin, Joseph S. Nye, Jr., Bernard H. Oxman,
Arvid Pardo, Leigh S. Ratiner, James K. Sebenius

NATIONAL SECURITY IN THE 1980s: FROM WEAKNESS TO STRENGTH
Edited by W. Scott Thompson
$9.95 (paper). ISBN 0−917616−59−6
$19.95 (cloth). ISBN 0−87855−412−2
524 pages. Publication date: May 1980
Contributors: Kenneth L. Adelman, Richard R. Burt, Miles M. Costick, Robert F.
Ellsworth, Fred Charles Ikle, Geoffrey T. H. Kemp, Edward N. Luttwak,
Charles Burton Marshall, Paul H. Nitze, Sam Nunn, Henry S. Rowen,
Leonard Sullivan, Jr., W. Scott Thompson, William R. Van Cleave, Francis
J. West, Jr., Albert Wohlstetter, Elmo R. Zumwalt, Jr.

NEW DIRECTIONS IN PUBLIC HEALTH CARE: A PRESCRIPTION FOR THE
1980s
Edited by Cotton M. Lindsay
$6.95 (paper). ISBN 0−917616−37−5
$16.95 (cloth). ISBN 0−87855−394−0
290 pages. Publication date: February 1980 (revised edition)
Contributors: Alain Enthoven, W. Phillip Gramm, Leon R. Kass, Keith B. Leffler,
Cotton M. Lindsay, Jack A. Meyer, Charles E. Phelps, Thomas C. Schelling,
Harry Schwartz, Arthur Seldon, David A. Stockman, Lewis Thomas

NO LAND IS AN ISLAND: INDIVIDUAL RIGHTS AND GOVERNMENT
CONTROL OF LAND USE
Publication date: November 1975
Out-of-print

NO TIME TO CONFUSE: A Critique of the Ford Foundation's Energy Policy
Project: *A Time to Choose America's Energy Future*
Publication date: February 1975
Out-of-print

NUCLEAR ARMS: ETHICS, STRATEGY, POLITICS
 Edited by R. James Woolsey
 $8.95 (paper). ISBN 0−917616−55−3
 $22.95 (cloth). ISBN 0−917616−56−1
 289 pages. Publication date: February 1984
Contributors: Richard Burt, Newt Gingrich, Patrick Glynn, Colin S. Gray, Charles
 Krauthammer, Robert Kupperman, Amory B. Lovins, L. Hunter Lovins,
 John Madison, Hans Mark, Sam Nunn, William J. Perry, Michael Quinlan,
 Brent Scowcroft, Walter B. Slocombe, R. James Woolsey

ONCE IS ENOUGH: THE TAXATION OF CORPORATE EQUITY INCOME
 Charles E. McClure, Jr.
 Publication date: May 1977
 Out-of-print

OPTIONS FOR U.S. ENERGY POLICY
 Publication date: September 1977
 Out-of-print

PARENTS, TEACHERS, AND CHILDREN: PROSPECTS FOR CHOICE IN
 AMERICAN EDUCATION
 $5.95. 336 pages. Publication date: June 1977
 ISBN 0−917616−18−9
Contributors: James S. Coleman, John E. Coons, William H. Cornog, Denis P.
 Doyle, E. Babette Edwards, Nathan Glazer, Andrew M. Greeley, R. Kent
 Greenawalt, Marvin Lazerson, William C. McCready, Michael Novak, John
 P. O'Dwyer, Robert Singleton, Thomas Sowell, Stephen D. Sugarman,
 Richard E. Wagner

PARTY COALITIONS IN THE 1980s
 Edited by Seymour Martin Lipset
 $8.95 (paper). ISBN 0−917616−43−X
 $19.95 (cloth). ISBN 0−917616−45−6
 480 pages. Publication date: November 1981
Contributors: John B. Anderson, David S. Broder, Walter Dean Burnham, Patrick
 Caddell, Jerome M. Clubb, E. J. Dionne, Jr., Alan M. Fisher, Michael
 Harrington, S. I. Hayakawa, Richard Jensen, Paul Kleppner, Everett Carll
 Ladd, Seymour Martin Lipset, Arthur D. Miller, Howard Phillips, Norman
 Podhoretz, Nelson W. Polsby, Richard M. Scammon, William Schneider,
 Martin P. Wattenberg, Richard B. Wirthlin

POLITICS AND THE OVAL OFFICE: TOWARDS PRESIDENTIAL
 GOVERNANCE
 Edited by Arnold J. Meltsner
 $7.95 (paper). ISBN 0−917616−40−5
 $18.95 (cloth). ISBN 0−87855−428−9
 332 pages. Publication date: February 1981
Contributors: Richard K. Betts, Jack Citrin, Eric L. Davis, Robert M. Entman,
 Robert E. Hall, Hugh Heclo, Everett Carll Ladd, Arnold J. Meltsner, Charles
 Peters, Robert S. Pindyck, Francis E. Rourke, Martin M. Shapiro, Peter L.
 Szanton

THE POLITICS OF PLANNING: A REVIEW AND CRITIQUE OF CENTRALIZED
ECONOMIC PLANNING
Edited by A. Lawrence Chickering
Publication date: March 1976
Out-of-print

PUBLIC EMPLOYEE UNIONS: A STUDY OF THE CRISIS IN PUBLIC SECTOR
LABOR RELATIONS
Edited by A. Lawrence Chickering
Publication date: June 1976
Out-of-print

READINGS IN PUBLIC POLICY
Edited by A. Lawrence Chickering
$9.95. 338 pages. Publication date: September 1984
ISBN 0−917616−66−9
Contributors: Armen A. Alchian, Michael J. Boskin, A. Lawrence Chickering,
Wendell John Coats, Jr., Robert Conquest, Robert M. Entman, Patrick
Glynn, Robert A. Goldwin, Peter W. Greenwood, William R. Havender,
Seymour Martin Lipset, Michael Novak, Wilson E. Schmidt, Thomas Sowell,
Aaron Wildavsky, Elmo R. Zumwalt, Jr.

REAGANOMICS: A MIDTERM REPORT
Edited by Wm. Craig Stubblebine and Thomas D. Willett
$14.95 (cloth). 232 pages. Publication date: March 1983
ISBN 0−917616−54−5
Contributors: Henry J. Aaron, David Berson, Michael J. Boskin, William H.
Branson, Jacob Dreyer, Ross D. Eckert, Susan Feigenbaum, Arthur B.
Laffer, J. Harold McClure, Thomas G. Moore, Peggy B. Musgrave, Richard
A. Musgrave, William A. Niskanen, Wallace E. Oates, Attiat F. Ott, Richard
W. Rahn, Alice Rivlin, Beryl W. Sprinkel, Wm. Craig Stubblebine, Robert
Tollison, Thomas D. Willett

REGULATING BUSINESS: THE SEARCH FOR AN OPTIMUM
Edited by Donald P. Jacobs
$6.95. 261 pages. Publication date: April 1978
ISBN 0−917616−27−8
Contributors: Chris Argyris, A. Lawrence Chickering, Penny Hollander Feldman,
Richard H. Holton, Donald P. Jacobs, Alfred E. Kahn, Paul W. MacAvoy,
Almarin Phillips, V. Kerry Smith, Paul H. Weaver, Richard J. Zeckhauser

SOCIAL REGULATION: STRATEGIES FOR REFORM
Edited by Eugene Bardach and Robert A. Kagan
$8.95 (paper). ISBN 0−917616−46−4
$19.95 (cloth). ISBN 0−917616−47−2
420 pages. Publication date: March 1982
Contributors: Lawrence S. Bacow, Eugene Bardach, Paul Danaceau, George C.
Eads, Joseph Ferreira, Jr., Thomas P. Grumbly, William R. Havender,
Robert A. Kagan, Michael H. Levin, Michael O'Hare, Stuart M. Pape,
Timothy J. Sullivan

338

TARIFFS, QUOTAS, AND TRADE: THE POLITICS OF PROTECTIONISM
$7.95. 332 pages. Publication date: February 1979
ISBN 0-917616-34-0
Contributors: Walter Adams, Ryan C. Amacher, Sven W. Arndt, Malcolm D. Bale,
John T. Cuddington, Alan V. Deardorff, Joel B. Dirlam, Roger D. Hansen, H.
Robert Heller, D. Gale Johnson, Robert O. Keohane, Michael W. Keran,
Rachel McCulloch, Ronald I. McKinnon, Gordon W. Smith, Robert M. Stern,
Richard James Sweeney, Robert D. Tollison, Thomas D. Willett

THE THIRD WORLD: PREMISES OF U.S. POLICY
Edited by W. Scott Thompson
$8.95 (paper) ISBN 0-917616-57-X
$22.95 (cloth). ISBN 0-917616-58-8
319 pages. Publication date: May 1983 (revised edition)
Contributors: Kenneth L. Adelman, Dennis Austin, Peter T. Bauer, Max Beloff,
Richard E. Bissell, S. E. Finer, Allan E. Goodman, Robert E. Harkavy,
Nathaniel H. Leff, Daniel Pipes, Marc F. Plattner, Wilson E. Schmidt, Tony
Smith, Basil S. Yamey

UNION CONTROL OF PENSION FUNDS
George J. Borjas
$2.00. 41 pages. Publication date: July 1979
ISBN 0-917616-36-7

WATER BANKING: HOW TO STOP WASTING AGRICULTURAL WATER
Sotirios Angelides and Eugene Bardach
$2.00. 56 pages. Publication date: January 1978
ISBN 0-917616-26-X

WHAT'S NEWS: THE MEDIA IN AMERICAN SOCIETY
Edited by Elie Abel
$7.95 (paper). ISBN 0-917616-41-3
$18.95 (cloth). ISBN 0-87855-448-3
296 pages. Publication date: June 1981
Contributors: Elie Abel, Robert L. Bartley, George Comstock, Edward Jay Epstein,
William A. Henry III, John L. Hulteng, Theodore Peterson, Ithiel de Sola
Pool, William E. Porter, Michael Jay Robinson, James N. Rosse, Benno C.
Schmidt, Jr.

THE WORLD CRISIS IN SOCIAL SECURITY
Edited by Jean-Jacques Rosa
$9.95. 245 pages. Publication date: May 1982
ISBN 0-917616-44-8
Contributors: Onorato Castellino, A. Lawrence Chickering, Richard Hemming,
Martin C. Janssen, Karl Heinz Juttemeier, John A. Kay, Heinz H. Muller,
Hans-Georg Petersen, Jean-Jacques Rosa, Sherwin Rosen, Ingemar Stahl,
Noriyuki Takayama

JOURNAL OF CONTEMPORARY STUDIES
A quarterly journal of public policy.
$15./one year, $25./two years, $4./single issue
ISSN 0272-7595